Andson Cowie, William C. Cowie

English-Sulu-Malay Vocabulary

with useful sentences, tables

Andson Cowie, William C. Cowie

English-Sulu-Malay Vocabulary
with useful sentences, tables

ISBN/EAN: 9783337287955

Printed in Europe, USA, Canada, Australia, Japan

Cover: Foto ©Andreas Hilbeck / pixelio.de

More available books at **www.hansebooks.com**

ENGLISH-SULU-MALAY
VOCABULARY.

WITH

USEFUL SENTENCES, TABLES, &c.

BY

ANDSON COWIE,

EDITED BY

WM. CLARK COWIE.

———

GRAMMATICAL INTRODUCTION

BY

THE EDITOR.

— — —

LONDON:

Printed for the Editor by THEO. MAY, 138 Tanner's Hill, S.E.

COPIES CAN BE OBTAINED AT THE OFFICES OF

THE BRITISH NORTH BORNEO COMPANY,

15 Leadenhall Street, E.C. and at Sandakan.

—

1893.

PREFACE.

——◆——

The whole of the Sūlū portion of this work is original. It is the result of the labour of my late brother Andson, who devoted much time to the study of several native dialects during the thirteen years he resided in the Island of Sūlū and various parts of Malaya. That he attained an unusual proficiency in the Sūlū and Malay languages is well known, and his voluminous notes in my possession are evidence of the careful investigation which he bestowed upon the Sūlū before placing it against its English and Malay equivalents. All the inaccuracies and literary imperfections to be met with in these pages are attributable to my shortcomings; however, as I did not undertake the editing of this volume from choice, but from a sense of duty, I trust to the indulgence of critics and those for whose benefit it is intended. The idiomatic Phrases and Sentences have been constructed to employ nearly every Sūlū word in the vocabulary.

50097 5

PREFACE.

The Author's object in adding Malay, to what he originally designed as a Sūlū work only, was to accelerate the further fusion of two dialects which have so much affinity and which will make the language of North Borneo the English of the farther East.

I have to acknowledge my indebtedness to Marsden's Dictionary of the Malay Language, and to Maxwell's Manual of the Malay Language for material and information which have aided me in constructing the Malay part of the Introduction. From a small Sūlū vocabulary,* by my esteemed friend Mr. Thomas Henry Haynes, I have adopted a few nautical terms.

W. C. COWIE.

Hurst Villa, Brockley,

London, S.E.

September 19th, 1893.

NOTE.—Mr. Andson Cowie died in Arbroath, Scotland, February 29th, 1888, at the early age of thirty-two.

* The vocabulary referred to was edited by the Hon'ble W. E. Maxwell, C.M.G., and printed by the Straits Branch of the Asiatic Society for circulation amongst its members.

CONTENTS.

CONTENTS.

INTRODUCTION.

The Sūlū language is formed chiefly from Bisaya and Malay. Its similarity to both, in grammatical construction, is very marked, yet the distinction colloquially is most remarkable. It is spoken by all the natives of the Sūlū and Tawi-Tawi archipelagoes, and by a very considerable portion of the inhabitants of Magindano, Palawan, Balabac, Basilan, North Borneo, Darvel Bay and the adjacent Islands, extending southward as far as Cape Kanyongan, including the State of Balongan. These places, at one time, were all tributory to the Chief termed the Sultan of Sūlū. They have been described by Burbridge, in his *Gardens of the Sun*, as " Beauty spots of the Eastern Seas, . . . " blessed with the heat and glory of eternal summer ; " warmed by perpetual sunshine, deluged by copious " rains, and thrilled by electricity ; . . . enormous " conservatories of rare birds and curious animals ; " where man is the Adam of a modern Eden, primi- " tive in habits, and numerically insignificant."

The Sūlū nobility all write with a certain amount of facility. Like the Malays, they have adopted the Arabic character with certain modifications. They, however, always employ *bāris* or signs to assist them

A

in distinguishing their vowels, whereas the Malays generally leave them out.

The Sūlū people are a bold, fearless race, and, up to a very recent date, were most notorious pirates. In their lovely isles they lived comparatively contented until their ancient enemies the Spaniards gained a footing amongst them. Now all is changed! Spanish rule is hateful to them and many are leaving the Sūlū archipelago for British North Borneo. In time they should make valuable subjects to the Chartered Company, but, whilst taming, they will require very careful treatment.

The primary object of this work is to assist the Europeans of North Borneo in acquiring a knowledge of Sūlū to enable them to converse with the Sūlūs in their own dialect rather than through the medium of Malay, which, although understood by many, is still a foreign language to them.

The advantage to those already conversant with Malay in having the Malay equivalent of each Sūlū word in juxtaposition is obvious.

The system of orthography adopted is similar to that employed by Marsden in his Dictionary of the Malay language.

INSTRUCTIONS FOR PRONUNCIATION.

Vowels to be Pronounced :—

ā as a in jar, father; e. g., sāh, wrong; mās, old.

a like the above but shorter.

ē as e in prey; e. g., pēla, how much or how many; mamēla, to fell.

e as e in let; e. g., *dien*, from; *shega*, begone.

ī as i in fatigue, marine; e. g., *bī*, to buy; *püg-bī*, to sell.

i as i in big, bid, bit; e. g., *tūbig*, water; *lūbid*, rope.

ō as o in go; e. g., *agōng*, a gong; *ma-tōg*, to sleep.

o like the above but shorter.

ū as u in blue; e.g., *bāgū*, new; *būtang*.

u like the above but shorter.

ü as u in but, pug, mug; e. g., *püg-daiau-i* to mend or repair; *mäg-dīhil*, to give.

ŭ as u in gude (Scotch), süden (German), sûr (French); e. g., *tŭd*, excessive; *hŭlah*, place of abode; *būkŭn* it is not; *hŭ*, yes. It has no equivalent in English.

DIPTHONGS.

ai as the vowels in lie; e. g., *pai*, paddy, *lantai*, floor; *sobai*, essential.

au as the ow in now, to bow; e.g., *kābau*, buffalo; *sābau*, sauce; *adlau*, day.

oi similar to oy in annoy; e. g., *baboi*, pig; *baloi*, a mat; *pāgoi*, to run away.

ei as the ie in die or ye in dye; e. g., pandei (M.), clever; pakei (M.), to dress.

CONSONANTS.

The consonants *b, ch, g, h, j, k, l, m, n, ng, p, r, s, sh, t, v, w*, are, with the following exceptions, to be pronounced as they are in English:—

ch always to be pronounced like ch in chain,

church; e. g., *chūchūk* a key; *chakap*, ready. The hard sound of ch as in character is represented by k, as—*kalachucho*, cartridge.

f There is no sound equivalent to f in Sūlū, and in all words borrowed from Malay the f has been changed into p; e. g., "fikir" into *pĭkil*, to think; "fakir" into *pakĭl*, a medicant; "faidah" into *pāidah*, advantage.

g should always be pronounced like g in gap; e. g., *hĭgad*, border; *dagtong*, bamboo for carrying water; *āgad*, to follow.

The sound of g as in sage is represented by *j* as *mŭg-jāga*, to watch or be awake; *panji*, flag.

h like the k in Malay is almost mute when it is the final letter of a word but otherwise it is always strongly aspirated.

k should be pronounced like k in kick, stick; it is never mute, as it is in Malay, when the final letter of a word; e. g., *pĕlak*, silver, dollars or money; *ālak*, arrack; *sāālak*, to shout; *mamalŭk*, to pay respect; *bak*, to find.

ng whether at the beginning or end of a word has the same sound as ng in sting; e. g., *mangi*, wicked; *ingān*, name; *pāg-ingān-an*, to style; *bangun*, to rise.

s to be pronounced like s in see; e. g., *bāsī*, iron; *bugas*, rice; *dugbūs*, appearance.

v is used only once in the Sūlū, namely, in the word *asīrī*, small.

In the Malay, v is not used.

OF GRAMMAR.

The grammar of the Sūlū language is very similar to that of the Malay.*

I. NOUNS.

Nouns, both in Malay and Sūlū, undergo no change to indicate number, gender, or case.

NUMBER.

Number, when not sufficiently clear in the context, is denoted " By the use of separate words expressive of plurality and singularity "—as, *ma-taud*, many; *mănga*, some;—or by specific numerals. It is also sometimes expressed by the duplication of the noun; e. g., *bātu*, stone; *bātu-bātu*, stones.

The particle *ma* as prefixed to adjectives, in the Sūlū, signifies intensity of their power. In some instances when it precedes certain nouns it denotes plurality; e. g., *in kūda*, the horse; *in ma kūra*, the horses.

GENDER.

Differences in the sexes are, with two or three exceptions, denoted by the following words expressive of the sex :—

SULU.	MALAY.
Usog, male	Lāki-lāki, male
Babai, female	Perampūan, female

The above should always be applied to persons, but may be applied to animals.

The following should be applied to animals only:-

Mandangan, male   Jantan, male

* All the examples not in italics are Malay.

Omagak, female   Betīna, female

The exceptions are mostly titles, as—

Junjong-an, Sultan.

Pangī-an, Sultana.

Dayang, Lady.

Tñan,* Sir or Mr.

CASES OF NOUNS.

Both in Sūlū and Malay the modifications of the sense, as in English, are expressed by prepositions :-

ENGLISH.	SULU.	MALAY.
To	*pa*	ka, kapada, semā
For	*kan*	akan
With	*īban*	dengan
At	*ha*	di
From	*dien-ha*	deri-pada
By	*dien-pa*	ūlih

EXAMPLES.

Pa bāi, to a house.

Dien ha bāi, from a house.

Ha bāi, at a house.

Ha guah bāi, out of a house.

Ha tās bāi, on top of a house.

Ha sùm bāi, beneath a house.

Kan Allah taāla, unto God.

Iban tābang sin† nabī, with the help of the prophet.

Where the noun is the subject of an action, a preposition is not generally required ; e. g.—

Sōh-a in kāyu, light the fire.

---

* In the Malay, "Tuan" under certain conditions can be applied to women. † *Sin* = of the.

Tigbak kāhōi, cut the wood.

Ma-mēla kāhōi, fell the tree.

Lesag agōng, beat the gong.

The possessive or gentive case, in the Sūlū, is expressed as follows :—

1. By placing the possessive adjunct *kan* **before** the noun, as—

   Kan bāi, of the house.

   Kan Sūltan, the Sultan's.

   Kan kapal, of the ship.

   Kan palentah, of the government.

2. By inserting the word *sin* (of the) between the subject of possession and the possessor, the noun denoting the possessor always to be placed last ; as—

   Sāia sin sūga, brightness of the sun.

   Ka-atās-an sin bād, the height of the hills.

3. Simply by position, the noun, which signifies the possessor, to come immediately **after** the subject of possession ; * as—

   Ata lanang, good belonging to the Chinese.

   Kūra Dātoh, the Datoh's horse.

The genitive or possessive case, in the Malay, is expressed in two forms :—

1. By employing the possessive adjunct "pūnya" after the noun, as—

   Sultan pūnya, the Sultan's.

   Rūmah pūnya, of the house.

   Parentah pūnya, belonging to the government

   Kapal pūnya, of the ship.

* In the Sulu this method is less frequently employed.

XVI.   INTRODUCTION.

2. By position, " the word denoting the subject of possession always **preceding** that which denotes the possessor ; " as—

> Chāya māta hāri, brightness of the sun.
>
> Ka-tinggī-an būkit, height of the hills.

The use of the Malay "pūnya" should be employed only when absolutely necessary. For instance, it is more idiomatic to say "kūda Sultan" than "Sultan pūnya kūda" (the Sultan's horse).

" The only changes, to which the form of nouns is subject, are those which they undergo as derivatives." **This applies to both dialects.**

Derivative nouns or substantives are formed from primitive words by prefixing or affixing certain particles; and frequently both prefix and suffix are employed in constructing a derivative noun.

They are formed :—

1. From nouns by prefixing *ka* and *an* to the radical ; and also by affixing *an* only, as—

Ka-raja-an, royalty	Rāja, King
Ka-datōh-an, royal	*Dātoh*, Prince
O-an, pillow	*O*, head
Dūrū-an, wet-nurse	*Dūrāh*, breast

2. From adjectives by prefixing *ka* and affixing *an* ; and also by affixing *an* only, as—

Ka-rendāh-an, lowness	Rendah, low
Ka-matī-an, death	Māti, dead
Manīs-an, sweetmeats	Mānis, sweet
Ka-sīpŭg-an, nakedness	*Sīpŭg*, ashamed
Ka-taur-an, multitude	*Taud*, many

Săh-an, penalty   *Săh*, wrong

3. (i.) From verbs by prefixing *ka* and affixing *an* to the radicals, as—

Ka-larī-an, flight   Lārī, to run

Ka-nantī-an, expectation   Nanti, to wait

Ka-pagoi-an, flight   *Pāgoi*, to run

Ka-tagad-an, expectation   *Tagad*, to wait

(ii.) From verbs by prefixing *pa* (M. "pe") and affixing *an*, as—

Pe-kirim-an, a messenger   Kīrim, to send

Pe-karja-an, performance   Karja, to work

Pa-tōg-an, sleeping-place   *Tōg*, to sleep

Pa-maigōh-an, a bath   *Maigoh*, to bathe

(iii.) From verbs by prefixing *pŭg* (M. "per" or "pel") and affixing *an*, as—

Pel-ajār-an, a school   Ajar to learn

Per-mandī-an, a bath   Mandī, to bathe

Pŭg-hīnāng-an, work   *Hīnang*, to work

Pŭg-bayad-an, payment   *Bāyad*, to pay

(iv.) From verbs by prefixing *pen*, *pem*, and *peng*. which are all adopted from the Malay, as—

Pen-chūrī, a thief   Chūrī, to steal

Pem-bāyar, payment   Bāyer, to pay

Pen-akau, a thief   *Takau*, to steal

Pem-būnoh, a murderer   *Būnoh*, to kill

Also—

Peng-gālī, a spade   Gālī, to dig

Peng-liāt-an, sight   Līat, to see

Pang-īta-han, sight   *Kītā*, to see

(v.) From verbs by the repetition or duplication

of the initial syllable, as—

Sa-sāpu, a broom   *Sāpu*, to sweep

Si-sīpah, wicker ball   *Sīpak*, to kick

II. ADJECTIVES.

Adjectives, both in Sūlū and Malay, have no case-forms, no gender-forms, and no number-forms. The changes they undergo in the formation of abstract nouns have already been noticed. In simple construction they generally follow their Substantive; as—

Hārī rāya, a festival day.

Kūda pūtih, a white horse.

Kapal ma-tās, a lofty ship.

Tāu mangi, a bad person.

Mangi ka-sudāh-an,* a bad end.

" But, when a quality is predicated of a noun, or in other words, when in the corresponding English phrase the verb substantive intervenes, the qualitive is made to precede the noun, although the verb is not necessarily expressed," as—

Kechil rūmah sāya, my house is small.

Bāik ōrang ītu, that man is good.

Asīvī in bāi sin patek, my house is small.

Maraiau tāu ien, that man is good.

Ma-pūtih in kūra sin lāja, the horse of the King is white.

Adjectives may be formed from substantives by prefixing the particles *nūg* (Sūlū) and " ber " (Malay) as—

* There are many such exceptions in the Sulu.

Nãg-bul-bul, feathered   *Bul-bul*, feathers
Ber-budī, wise   Budī, wisdom

COMPARISON OF ADJECTIVES.

The comparative degree is formed by means of the words *lebih* (more) and *dien* or *dien-ha*** (M. "deri" or "deripada") or by either of them separately.

EXAMPLES.

Lebih pānas deri dahūlu, hotter than formerly.
Lebih mānis deri-pada gūla, sweeter than sugar.
Bāik īni deri ītu, this is better than that.
Ini-lah sūchi deri-pada lāin, this is cleaner than the
 other.
Lebih pāso dien tagnah, hotter than formerly.
Maimoh dien-ha sūkal, sweeter than sugar.
Maraiau dī dien dūn, better here than there.
Lebih mahonet īni dien-ha ietu, this is more difficult
 than that.

The superlative degree, in the Sūlū, is formed by placing the words *tūd* (most) or *pakaraiau* (very, excessively) **after** the positive. In the Malay, it is formed (1) **by prefixing** the intensive particle "ter;" (2) by an adverb to which that particle can be prefixed ; (3) by either placing the word "s'kāli" (entirely) or "amat" (exceedingly) **after** the adjective.

EXAMPLES.

Ter-bersār, very great.
Ter-lebih tūah, extremely old.
Pūtih s'kāli, perfectly white.

* Dien or dien-ha = deri or deri-pada = than, from.

Besàr amat, exceedingly big.

Amū īni in maraiau tūd, this is certainly the best.

In gabok tūd, the worst.

Maraiau pakaraiau, very good.

Maraiau tūd, the best.

Ma-tambok pakaraiau, excessively fat.

	Positive.	Comparative.	Superlative.
(English)	Hot	hotter	hottest
(Sūlū)	*Pāso*	*lebih pāso*	*ma-pāso tūd*
(Malay)	Pānas	lebih pānas	pānas s'kāli

The *ma* prefixed to adjectives, in the Sūlū, seems to be a contraction of the Sanscrit word mahā (great), introduced through the Malay. It tends to intensify the power of those words with which it is employed.

The duplication of adjectives increases their qualifying power.

III. NUMERALS.

The numerals in both dialects are very simple.

The cardinal numbers are:—

ENGLISH.	SULU.	MALAY.
One	*īsa*	sātu
Two	*dūa*	dūa
Three	*tō*	tīga
Four	*ōpat*	ampat
Five	*līma*	līma
Six	*ūnom*	anam
Seven	*pēto*	tūjuh
Eight	*walū*	dilāpan
Nine	*sīam*	simbīlan
Ten	*hangpoh*	sa'pūloh

The term which represents ten, in the Sūlū, is partly
Bisāya and partly Malay; *hang* one, and *poh* is a
contraction of "pūloh" (ten).

From eleven to nineteen inclusive the numerals, in
the Malay, are formed by adding blas to the cardinals.

It will be observed that they are formed in the
Sūlū, by a different arrangement :—

Eleven	*hangpoh-tŭg-īsa*	sa-blas
Twelve	,, ,, -*dūa*	dūa-blas
Thirteen	,, ,, -*tō*	tīga-blas
Fourteen	,, ,, -*ōpat*	ampat-blas
Fifteen	,, ,, -*līma*	līma-blas
Sixteen	,, ,, -*ûnom*	anam-blas
Seventeen	,, ,, -*pĭto*	tūguh-blas
Eighteen	,, ,, -*walū*	dilāpan-blas
Nineteen	,, ,, -*sīam*	simbīlan-blas
Twenty	*kauhan or kāñhan*	dūa-pūloh

Tŭg or *tuga*   plus; possessing, having, owning,
as—

Hangpoh tŭg īsa.	Ten plus one.
Kauhan tŭg dūa.	Twenty plus two.
Ang rātus tŭg ûnom	One hundred and six.
Ai-aun in tāu tŭga bā-rong in sampak-nia tŭga balāwan.	There is a man who hath a barong whose ferrule is of gold.
Hi sīo in tŭg kūda ha kūda īni ?	Who is the owner of this horse ?
Bakas kāmi maka run-gag aun tāu tŭga ekog.	We have heard that there are men with (having) tails.

In the Malay, the decimal numbers, from ten up to ninety inclusive, are formed by placing the digits **before** the term which represents ten. In the Sūlū, they are formed by prefixing *ka* and affixing *an* to the cardinals :—

Twenty	*kaūhan* *	dūa-pūloh
Thirty	*katlūan* *	tīga ,,
Forty	*ka-opat-an*	ampat pūloh
Fifty	*ka-im-an* *	līma ,,
Sixty	*ka-ânom-an*	anam ,,
Seventy	*ka-peto-an*	tūjuh ,,
Eighty	*ka-walu-an*	dilāpan ,,
Ninety	*ka-siam-an*	simbilan ,,
One hundred	*ang-gātus* or *rātus*	sa-rātus

The intermediate numbers, in the Sūlū, from ten upwards, are formed by inserting the word *tüg* between the decimals and the units. In the Malay, they are formed by adding the units to the decimals; as—

Twenty-one	*kauhan tüg īsa*	dūa-pūloh-sātu
Thirty-two	*katluan tüg dūa*	tīga-pūloh dūa
Forty-three	*kaūpatan tüg tū*	ampat-pūloh tīga
Fifty-four	*kaiman tüg ōpat*	līma-pūloh ampat
Sixty-five	*kaûnoman tüg līma*	anam-pūloh līma
Seventy-six	*kapētoan tüg ânom*	tūguh-pūloh anam
Eighty-seven	*kawālūan tüg pēto*	dilāpan-pūloh-tūguh
Ninety-eight	*kasīaman tüg wālū*	simbīlan-pūloh-dilāpan

Above a hundred, the numbers, of whatever

* Originally *ka-dua-an*, *ka-tulo-an*, *ka-lima-an*.

denomination, proceed with equal regularity:—

100	*ang-gātus* or *ang-rātus*	sa-rātus
101	*ang-rātus-tŭg-īsa*	sa-rātus sātu
120	,, ,, *-tŭg-kāñhan*	sa'rātus dūa pūloh
200	*dūa ang-rātus*	dūa rātus
300	*tō ang-rātus*	tīga rātus
400	*ōpat ang-rātus*	ampat rātus
500	*līma ang-rātus*	līma rātus
1000	*ang-ību*	sa-rību
1100	*ang-ību tŭg ang-rātus*	sa-sību sa'rātus
10,000	*sa-laksa*	sa-laksa
20,000	*dūa-laksa*	dūa-laksa
100,000	*hangpoh-laksa*	sa-pūloh-laksa
1,000,000	*ang-rātus-laksa*	sa-rātus-laksa

ORDINALS.

In both dialects, with one exception, ordinals are formed by prefixing *ka* to the numerals as follows :—

First	*ka-īsa*	pertāma
Second	*ka-dūa*	ka-dūa
Third	*ka-tō*	ka-tīga
Fourth	*ka-ōpat*	ka-ampat
Fifth	*ka-līma*	ka-līma
Tenth	*ka-hangpoh*	ka-sa-pūloh
Twelfth	*ka-hangpoh-tŭg-dūa*	ka-dūa-blas
Twentieth	*ka-kauhan*	ka-dūa-pūloh
Hundredth	*ka-ang-rātus*	ka-sa-rātus
Thousandth	*ka-ang-ību*	ka-sa-rību

The words *in* (S.), "yang" (M.) placed before ordinals, etc., are used in the sense of the English definite article; as—"yang pertāma," the first; *in*

ka-dña, the second.

FRACTIONAL NUMBERS.

A quarter	*ang-ūtūd*	sa'sūkū
A half	*ang sīpak*	sa'tengah
Three-quarters	*tō ang ūtūd*	tīga per-ampat
Two-and-a-half	*ka-tō ang sīpak*	tengah tīga

IV. PRONOUNS.

The pronouns of the First Person are :—

ENGLISH.	SULU.	MALAY.
(Singular) I, me	*aku, ku, patek*	aku, ku, sāya
(Plural) We, us	*kāmi, kīta*	kāmi, kīta

"Kāmi" and "kīta," in Borneo, are frequently employed in a singular sense, therefore, the necessity sometimes arises of accentuating the plural. This is done, in the Malay, by adding the word "ōrang" (people) to "kāmi" or "kīta." In the Sūlū it is done by the use of separate words expressive of plurality or by specific numerals but not by the word *tau*, which, in other respects, is the equivalent of the Malay word "ōrang."

Aku is employed both by superiors and inferiors in Sūlū. In the Malay, it is generally employed by superiors in addressing their inferiors or servants.

"Hamba" (your slave, or, your servant), in the Malay, is frequently used in place of the pronouns of the First Person.

Pronouns of the Second Person :—

ENGLISH.	SULU.	MALAY.
(Singular) You, thou	*ēkau, kau, nio,*	angkau, kau
(Plural) Ye	*kāmu*	kāmu

Tuan and "inchi" are effectively employed as pronouns of the Second Person. The former is most commonly applied to Europeans and those natives who have made a pilgrimage to Mecca, whilst the latter can be applied to any untitled native who holds a position above his fellow-men.

Pronouns of the Third Person :—

ENGLISH.	SULU.	MALAY.
(Singular) He, she, it	*sia, nia*	dia, iya
(Plural) They	*nila, sila**	dia ōrang

POSSESSIVE PRONOUNS.

In the Sūlū personal pronouns are made to assume the possessive form by prefixing *kan, ka,* or *kai.* In the Malay the word " pūnya is added."

SINGULAR.

My, mine	*ka-aku, kan-pātek*	sāya pūnya
Thy, thine	*kan-nio, ka-nio*	angkau pūnya
His, hers, its	*kan-sia, kan-nia*	dia pūnya

PLURAL.

Ours	*kan-namu, ka-namu*	kīta pūnya
Yours ·	*kai-mu*	kāmu pūnya
Theirs	*ka-nila, kan-sila*	dia ōrang pūnya

Personals also signify possession when they follow the word denoting the object possessed. As—*pedang ku*, my sword ; *līma ku*, my hand ; *asāwa sin tūan*, your wife ; *sīmud nia*, his or her mouth ; *bāi ku*, my house ; *kūra mu*, your horse ; *bāi kan-nia*, his or her house.

Nila and *sila* are also frequently employed in a singular sense.

DEMONSTRATIVE OR DEFINITE PRONOUNS.

"This class may include not only demonstratives proper, but also the definite articles, together with relatives and interrogatives, which, in these as in other languages, are for the most part the same words employed in a different sense. They are enumerated as follows":—

SULU	MALAY.	
In	yang *	... that which, those, who, the.
Ien †	itu	... that, those, the.
Ini	īni	... this, these.
Uno	apa	... what, which.
Hi-sĩo, sĩo	si-āpa	... who, whom, which.
Ha-dien	māna	... who, whom, which, what.
Baran	dĩrī	... self.

In the Malay, when the personal precedes the reflective pronoun this is changed by prefixing "sin;" as—

> Dia sin-dīrī, he himself.
>
> Angkau sin-dīrī, you yourself.
>
> Hamba sin-dīrī, I myself.

The demonstrative (adjective) pronouns generally follow the word to which they belong; as—

> *Tau ien*, that man or those men.
>
> *Bāi ini*, this house.
>
> Orang itu, that man or those men.
>
> Rūmah īni, this house.

* "Nen" is another form of yang.

† *Itu* and *iaun* are other forms of *ien*.

V.—VERBS.

" The verb, in the same manner as the noun, may be distinguished into primitive and derivative.

The primitive verb is, in its original signification, either transitive, as "—

SULU.	MALAY.	
Sagau	tangkap	... to catch.
Lōbak	pūkul	... to strike.

Or intransitive, as—

Panau	jālan	... to walk.
Tōg	tīdor	... to sleep.

" The derivative verb is either the primitive determined to a transitive or intransitive sense by the application of particles, or it is a verb constituted by means of those particles from other parts of speech, as nouns, adjectives and adverbs."

The following inseparable particles are signs of the verbs which express action :—

SULU.	MALAY.
ma	me
mam	mem
man	men
mang	meng

The above are varieties of the same particle modified to suit the initial letter of the primitive word.

The other Sūlū inseparable particles prefixed to verbs are :— *Pa, mug* and *nug.*

The transitive suffixes are :—

SULU.	MALAY.
Han, ha, an, a, i	kan, ī.

The following examples of the application of those particles will give some idea of the formation of derivative verbs :—

SULU	MALAY.	
Ma-kangi	me-rōsak	... to spoil.
Mam-būnoh	mem-būnoh	... to kill.
Nag-tambal	meng-ūtup	... to shut.
Mäg-oïrah	men-jāmu	... to treat.
Mang-ampān	meng-ampūn	... to pardon.
Lawag-a	men-chari	... to search.
Nag-bōhī	meng-īdūp-ī	... to bring to life.
Mäg-hiñkit	meng-īkat	... to bind.
Nag-hōbus	meng-ābis	... to finish.
Ma-larak-an	mem-benasā-kan	... to destroy.
Mam-bāyad	mem-bāyer	... to pay.
Pa patai-an	me-matī-kan	... to put to death.
Tagar-an	me-nantī-kan	... to expect.
Hēlā-i	me-hēla	... to pull.
Jumlah-a	jumlah-ī	... to reckon.

Primitive words beginning with t, s, p, or k either drop or change the initial letter when being modified or determined into transitive verbs by the application of the particle *man* ("men"), or any of its modifications, as—

SULU.

Primitive.	Derivative.	
Tābang	*man-ābang*	... to assist.
Sampai	*man-ampai*	... to cause to arrive
Pēla	*mam-ēla*	... to fell.
Kīta	*mang-īta*	... to see.

MALAY.

Primitive.	Derivative.	
Tōlong	men-ōlong	... to assist.
Sampei	men-iampei	... to cause to arrive
Pālū	mem-ālū	... to strike.
Kāta	meng-āta	... to acquaint.

The transitive suffixes may be employed either independently or in conjunction with a prefix to enforce the transitive sense of the verb.

EXAMPLES.

Lārut-i pādang, to unsheath a sword.

Eg-a in kūda, let loose the horse.

Nüg-kangi-han banūa, to ruin a country.

Lepas-kan kūda, let loose the horse.

Meng-unūs-kan pedang, to unsheath a sword.

Meng-ārū-ī kabūn, to renew a plantation.

When reciprocity of action is required to be expressed the verb is repeated in both its forms, as—

Tābang-man-ābang, to give mutual assistance.

Tangkis-man-angkis, to parry each other's thrusts.

In the Malay " the particles or modified particle 'ber,' 'bel,' 'be,' denoting the intransitive sense, are prefixed to the verb or word verbally employed without any annexed particle ; " as—

MALAY.

Bel-ajar, to learn.

Ber-dīri, to stand up.

Ber-sūarak, to shout.

Ber-prang, to go to war.

Be-lārī, to run away.

Ber-ānyut, to float or drift away.

Ber-dīam, to keep silence.

Ber-sinyūm, to smile.

The Sūlū equivalents of these particles are " *mŭg* " and " *nŭg*," * as—

SULU.

Mŭg-ānad, to learn.

Mŭg-tindog, to stand up.

Mŭg-būnoh, to go to war.

Mŭg-pāgoi, to run away.

Nŭg-anud, to drift or float away.

Nŭg-dumahong, to keep silence.

Nŭg-humaiam, to smile.

Mŭg and *nŭg* coalesce with any of the letters of the alphabet.

TENSES.

The tenses, where not implied or expressed by " some particular attribution of time," are formed by the aid of the auxiliaries (see paradigms, page xxxvi) and not by any alteration in the form of the verb itself.

The **Present** implied : " hamba līat," *aku kīta,* I see ; " māta hārī nāik," *māta sŭgu domag,* the sun rises.

The **Present** expressed with precision : " dia ada mākan s'kārang īni," *sia ka-maun sin-īni-īni,* he or she is eating now ; " pāgi īni prau ber-lāyar," *na lāyag in sakaian mahainat īni,* this morning the vessel sails.

* *Mug* and *nug* are also prefixed to transitive verbs.

The **Past** is expressed by the words "telah" (past), and "sūdah" (done), in the Malay; and *bakas* (past) and *hōbus* (done), in the Sūlū.

The **Future**, when not expresssed by some word or phrase to indicate futurity of time, is expressed in the Malay by the auxiliaries "māū," "handak," "būlih," and "nanti;" and in the Sūlū by "*mau bayah*," "*pūg-pa*," and "*gana-gana*."

The **Passive Participle** in the Malay is denoted by the prefixed inseparable particle "ter," the Sūlū equivalent of which is *nug* or *nug-ka*. The particle *na* also denotes the passive participle in the Sūlū.

MALAY.	SULU.	
Ter-pūkul	*nug-lōbak*	... struck.
Ter-tūlis	*nug-ka-sūlat*	... written.
Ter-pīlih	*nug-ka-pihpih*	... chosen.

Participle Present.—Present continuity of action is often expressed by the words "lagi," "sambil," *isab, maien,* &c., as—

Lāgi dātang	*rātang na īsab*	... coming.
Lāgi tīdor	*matōg na īsab*	... sleeping.

NUMBER and PERSON.

These distinctions do not apply to the Sūlū and Malay verbs.

MOODS.

"The moods of the verb may be ranked as follows, viz., the imperative, indicative or assertive, conditional and infinitive or indefinite, which admit, for the most part, of being expressed in the present,

the past and the future tenses or times."

Imperative.—To convey a command the simplest form of the verb is used, as —

MALAY.	SULU.	ENGLISH.
Brī	*dihil*	give.
Mākan	*ka-maun*	eat.
Dūduk	*lingkād*	sit down.

But, to emphasize an order or command the annexed transitive particles are frequently added to the verb. The particles or expletives "lah," *tah* or *bah* are also employed to emphasize a command.

EXAMPLES.

MALAY.	SULU.	
Lepas-kan anjing	*eg-i in crok*	... let loose the dog.
Pūlang-kan gadei	*mūi sēnda*	... return the pledge.
Marī lah	*dī na bah*	... come here.
Bangun lah	*bangun tah*	... waken, arise.

When the pronoun of the second person accompanies the imperative, it should follow the verb; as—

MALAY.	SULU.	
Lārī kūmu	*dagan na bah kau*	... run thou.
Jālan kām'ōrang	*panau na kāmu*	... march ye.

Indicative.—"The indicative or assertive mood partakes of the simple quality of the imperative, particularly in the first and second persons of the present tense," as—

MALAY.	SULU.	
Aku māū	*mau bayah na aku*	... I choose.

Hamba jālan *panau na aku** ... I walk.

Sāya minta *miki aku* ... I ask.

Angkau kāta *long mu* ... you say.

"But it sometimes assumes both prefixed and annexed transitive and intransitive particles," as—

Hamba ber-kerim sūrat īni, I send this letter.

Sāya me-nanti tītah tūan, I wait your orders.

Pa-ra aku in sulat ini, I send this letter.

Mūg-tugar-i aku ha titah sin tūan, I wait your orders.

And, in the third person it admits with greater ease the application of those particles; as—

Dia ber-jālan dahūlu, he walks first.

Dia mem-bāsoh tāngan nia, he washes his hands.

Anjing mem-būru rūsa, the dog pursues the deer.

Orang ītu sūdah mem-bāyar ūtang nia, that man has paid his debts.

Sia nūg-panau ha una, he walks first.

Sia nūg-tīmur-a in līma nia, he washes hands.

Irok mūg-panhut āsa, the dog pursues the deer.

Tāu iaun bakas nūg-bāyad in ūtang nia, that man has paid his debts.

"In the interrogative form of the indicative the personal is usually made to follow the verb," as—

Apa kāta kāmu, what sayest thou?

Brāpa kōrang kāmu, how many do you want?

Ka-māna pergi kam'ōrang, whither are you going?

Uno long mu, what sayest thou?

Pela in na kōlang kāmu, how many do you want?

Pakaien na kāmu, whither are you going?

In those examples the verb in the Sulu precedes the subject.

But they also say :—

Meng-āpa kāmu lāri, why do you run ?

Di-māna angkau dāpat ītu, where did you get that ?

Maitu kau pagoi, why do you run ?

Hadien kau nug-bāk ha ien, where did you get that ?

"In the assertive form the agent or nominative usually precedes the verb," as—

Tūkang men-eggā rūmah, workmen build a house.

Orang mem-ikul bāban, men carry burthens.

Ujan jātoh ka-dālam lāūt, rain falls into the sea.

Kāpal ber-lāyer ka tīmor, the ship sails to the eastward.

Tūkang nug-bangun bāi, workmen build a house.

Tāu na ra bābahan, men carry burthens.

Ulan na holog palūm dagat, rain falls into the sea.

Kapal nūg-lāyag pa tīmol, the ship sails to eastward.

Conditional or Potential.—"The rules which govern the assertive apply equally to the conditional or potential form, the word which precedes it in construction, and causes the verb to express a conditional or potential, instead of an assertive or positive sense, not affecting the application of the transitive or intransitive particles;" as—

MALAY.	ENGLISH.
Jeka tūan dātang.	If you come.
Kālau rāja me-lārang.	If the king forbids.
Dāpat kāmi ber-untong.	Provided we are successful.
Sopāya jāngan hamba kena rūgī.	That I may not incur a loss.

Agar sopāya anak nia men-jādi alim.	In order that his children may become learned.

SULU.	ENGLISH.
Bang tūan maka rātang.	If you come.
Bang maka lāng in lāja.	If the king should forbid.
Bang kāmi nŭg-untong	Provided we are successful.
Saguah aian aku nŭg-lūgī	That I may not incur a loss.
Agas anak nya men-jāri alim	In order that his children may become learned.

"'The **Passive Voice** is denoted by the particle ' di ' (in the Malay), preceding the verb. The place of the substantives which express the agent and subject respectively will be understood from the following examples : "—

SULU.	ENGLISH.
Kia lōbak-an sin tāu ha pātek.	I was beaten by men.
Kia lōbak-an sin pātek ha tāu.	The men were beaten by me.
Kia sunog-an sin bāi ha kāyu.	The house was consumed by fire.
Kia pohong-an sin tāu ha kāyu.	The fire was extinguished by men.
Kia tiakau-an sin tāu in kūra.	The horse was stolen by men.
Kia tiakau-an in kūda sin tāu.	The mens' horse was stolen.

MALAY.		ENGLISH.
Hamba di pŭkul ōrang.		I was beaten by men.
Orang di pŭkul hamba.		The men were beaten by me.
Rŭmah di mākan āpi.		The house was consumed by fire.
Api di padam-kan ōrang.		The fire was extinguished by men.

AUXILIARIES.

The auxiliary verbs and adverbs are :—

MALAY.	SULU.	
Ada	*aun*	is, was, are, were.
Sŭdah, telah	*bakas*	... was, did, has been.
Māŭ	*bayah*	... will, shall, would, must.
Jādi	*jādī*	... is, was, become, became.
Handak	*mau bayah*	will, shall, etc.

PARADIGMS.

Tīdor, *tōg*, sleep.

Sāya tīdor	*tōg na aku*	... I sleep.
Ber-tīdor	*ma-tōg*	...asleep, sleeping.
Sāya sŭdah tīdor	*bakas aku ma-tōg*	... I have slept.
Biar dia tīdor	*bīa na sia ma-tōg*	... let him sleep.
Tīdor lah	*pa-tōg-i*	... go to sleep.
Mem-per-tīdōr-kan	*mŭg-pŭg-tōg-an*	... to cause to sleep.
Per-tidōr-an	*pŭg-tōg-an*	... that which belongs to sleep.
Ka-tidōr-an	*ka-tōg-an*	... the act of sleeping.
Ter-tīdor	*nŭg-tōg*	... gone to sleep.

MALAY.	SULU.	
	Lārī, *magoi*, run.	
Sāya lārī	*magoi na aku*	... I run, or was running.
Lārī-lah dia	*magoi na sia*	... he ran, etc.
Ber-lārī	*mŭg-magoi*	... run, running.
Ber-lārī-lārī	*mŭg-magoi-magoi*	... running about incessantly.
Sāya sūdah lārī	*bakas na aku magoi*	... I have or had run.
Sāya mău lārī	*mau bayah aku magoi*	... I want to run.
Lārī lah	*magoi tah*	... run thou.
Biar lah dia lārī	*bial na sia magoi*	... let him run.
Handak lah di lārī nia.	*pug-ka-pagoi-an nila*	... it must be run by him, or he will run it.
Me-lārī-kan	*pa-pagoi-an*	... to carry off (transitive).
Be-lārī-an	*pug-pagoi-an*	... a running, a course.
Be-lārī-lārī-an	*mug-pagoi-pagoi-an*	... incessant running.
Ka-lārī-an	*ka-pagoi-an*	... flight; act of running.
Ka-lārī-an	*pug-pagoi-an*	... flight.
Ter-lārī	*nŭg-pagoi*	... run, run away.
Bāwa lārī	*da-han matoh* *	... to carry off, run off with.

* Pagoi is implied though not expressed.

MALAY.	SULU.	
	Ada, aun, be.	
Ada	*aun*	... I am or was.
Ber-ada	*ma-aun*	... have (poss.), has or had.
Meng-ada		... to cause to be, to make.
Sūdah ada	*bakas na aun*	... have got, have been.
Māū ada	*mau bayah maun*	... must be.
Ka-ada-an	*ka-aun-an*	... state, existence.
	Bawa, da, bring.	
Sāya bāwa	*da ku*	... I bring, or was bringing.
Mem-bāwa	*mag-da*	... bring, to bring.
Sūdah bāwa	*bakas na da*	... has brought.
Māū bāwa	*mau bayah pa-da*	... will or must bring.
,, ,,	*pag-pa-da*	... will or must bring.
Bāwa lah	*da tah*	... bring thou.
Biar dia bāwa	*bīa na sila doma**	... let him bring.
Mem-bāwa-kan	*mag-da-han*	... to cause to be brought or taken.
Mem-bāwa-i	*pag-da-i, pag-da-a*	... to cause to be brought or taken.

* Another form of *da*.

MALAY.	SULU.	
Bāwa-an	*da-an*	... that which is brought.
Di bāwa nia	*pa da-an nya, sia*	... is, was, etc.,
	da-a.	brought by him, her, or them.
Ter-bāwa	*nug-da*	... brought.
	Ambil, *kawa*, take.	
Sāya ambil	*aku kawa, kawa ku*	... I take.
Meng-ambil	*mug-kawa, mang-*	... take, to take.
	awa	
Sūdah ambil	*bakas na kawa*	... has or had taken.
Telah ambil	*na kawa na*	... had taken.
Handak ambil,	*mau bayah komawa,**	shall take or
māū ambil	*pug-pa-kawa*	about to take.
Ambil lah	*kawa tah*	... take thou.
Biar dia ambil	*bial na sia komawa*	... let him or her take.
Handak di am-	*mau bayah kawa*	... he must take,
bil nia	*nya, pŭg-pa-*	or intends to
	kawa nya	take.
Peng-ambil-an	*pang-awa-an*	... the act of taking.
Di ambil-nia	*kiawa nya*	... is, or was, etc., taken by him, her, or them.
Ter-ambil	*nug-kawa*	... taken.
	Sūruh, *dāk*, order.	
Sāya sūruh	*aku dāk, dāk ku*	... I order.
Men-yūruh	*mŭg-dāk*	... to order.

* Another form of *kawa*.

MALAY.	SULU.	
Telah sūruh	*na dāk na*	... ordered.
Māu sūruh	*mau bayah dāk*	... will order.
Handak sūruh	*pūg-pa-dāk*	... shall order.
Sūruh lah	*dāk tah*	... order thou.
Biar dia sūruh	*bial na sia dāk*	... let him order.
Men-yūruh-kan	*mūg-dāk-an*	... to issue orders.
Ter-sūruh	*nūg-dāk-an*	... ordered, having been ordered.
Di sūruh nia	*diak nya*	... is, or was, etc., ordered by him, her, or them.

VI.—ADVERBS.

The Adverbs in most current use are as follows:—

Adverbs of Time.

MALAY.	SULU.	
S'kārang, k'īni	*bīh'aun, sin-īni-īni*	... now.
Tādī	*kaina*	... very lately.
Dahūlu	*nakauna*	... before, formerly.
Sa-bantar lagi	*dai-dai dakoman*	... presently.
Sa-bantar	*dai-dai*	... presently.
Jūga, jūa	*īsab*	still.
Balūm	*wala*	... not yet.
Kamadīan	*ulih-an*	... afterwards.
Pāgi-pāgi	*māināt-māināt*	... early.
Esok, besok	*kinsūm*	... to-morrow.
Kalmārīn	*kahāpun*	... yesterday.
Lūsa	*kunīsa*	day after to-morrow.
Tatkāla	*pa-bīla*	... when.

MALAY.	SULU.	
Kamudian	*ka-ulih-an*	... afterwards.
Pernah	*tiâd, tap-tap*	... ever.
Ta-pernah	*di-tiâd*	... never.
Sedang	*ampa*	... while.
Kādang	*mahang*	... sometimes.
Apa-bīla	*ka-ūno*	... when ?

Adverbs of Place.

Sīni	*di, ha īni*	... here.
Sītu, sāna	*ietu, dūn*	... there.
Māna	*dien*	... where.
Di-māna	*ha-dien*	... where ?
Dekat	*ma-sŭk*	... nigh.
Hampir	*hampil*	... nearly.
Lūar	*ha-gūah*	... outside.
Dālam	*ha-lŭm*	... inside.
Sabrang	*ang-sipak*	... beyond.
Jāūh	*māioh*	... far.
Di-ātas	*ha-tās*	... above.
Di-bāwah	*ha-babah*	... below.
Sa-blāh	*āraig*	... beside.
Di-blākang	*ha-likŭd*	... behind.

Miscellaneous.

Bagīni	*bī-ha-īni*	... like this.
Bagītu	*bī-ha-ien, bīa-itu*	... like that.
Bagi-māna	*bīa-dien*	... how ?
Yā	*hŭ*	... yes.
Tīdak	*di*	... no.
Būkan	*būkŭn*	... it is not.
Sāja	*sāja, lūal*	... only.

VII.—PREPOSITIONS.

MALAY.	SULU.	
Di	*ha*	... at, in, on.
Ka	*pa*	... towards.
Deri	*dien*	... from.

These connected or compounded with adverbs, &c., form many words which are employed as prepositions :—

MALAY.	SULU.	
Di-ātas	*ha-tās*	... on the top of.
Ka-ātas	*pa-tās*	... to the top of.
Deri ātas	*dien-ha tās*	... from the top of.
Di-dālam	*ha-lŭm*	... in the interior of.
Ka-dālam	*pa-lŭm*	... to the interior of.
Deri dālam	*dien-ha lŭm*	... from the interior of.
Di-blākang	*ha-likūd*	... at the back of.
Ka-blākang	*pa-likūd*	... to the back of.
Deri blākang	*dien-ha likūd*	... from the back of.
Di-sabrang	*ha-ang-sīpak*	... on the farther side of.
Ka-sabrang	*pa-ang-sipak*	... to the farther side of.
Deri sabrang	*dien-ha ang-sīpak*	... from the farther side of.
Di-bāwah	*ha-babah*	... at the bottom of.
Ka-bāwah	*pa-babah*	... to the bottom of.
Deri bāwah	*dien-ha babah*	... from the bottom of.
Di hadāp-an	*ha harāp-an*	... in the front of.

MALAY.	SULU.	
Ka hadāp-an	*pa harāp-an*	... to the front of.
Deri hadāp-an	*dien-ha harāp-an*	... from the front of.
Di-lūar	*ha-gñah*	... at the outside of.
Ka-lūar	*pa-gñah*	... to the outside of.
Deri lūar	*dien ha-gñah*	... from the outside of.

The preposition *dien* (from) is generally followed by the preposition *ha* (at, in, on), but there are exceptions to this rule, as—

Dien dien na kau? ... From whence have you come?

Dien dān.   ... From yonder.

The preposition "deri" (from) is likewise followed by the preposition "pada" (at, in, on, to), when placed before nouns or verbs, as—

Deri-pada* lāngit, from the sky.

Deri-pada sebab ītu, from that cause.

Deri-pada meng-ābis-kan arta nia, from having consumed his property.

Dien-ha* *lāngit*, from the sky.

Dien-ha sebab iaun, from that cause.

Dien-ha pa hobūs-an in alta nya, from having consumed his property.

The preposition "ka" is, in a similar manner, frequently followed by "pada;" but *pa*, its equivalent, is not followed by *ha* the equivalent of "pada."

* "Deri" or "deri-pada," and "*dien*" or "*dien-ha*" are specially employed in forming the comparative degree of adjectives and adverbs.

EXAMPLES.

Ka-pada rūmah, to the house.

Ka-pada tepī āyer, to the water's edge.

Pa bāi, to the house.

Pa hēgad tūbig, to the water's edge.

Of the other prepositions the following are the principal :—

MALAY.	SULU.	
Pada, ka-pada	*pa*	... at, to, on, towards.
Deri-pada*	*dien-ha*	... from, than.
Akan	*kan, ha*	... to, for, as to, as for.
Ulih	*iban, sin*	... by.
Atas	*tās*	... on, upon.
Dātang	*dātang*	... until, as far as.
Sampei	*sampai*	,, ,,
Hingga	*hingga-an*	,, ,,
Antāra	*ūt, gītong*	... between.
Samantāra	*āmpa*	... until.
Ganti	*ganti, subli*	... instead of.
Bālik	*lio*	... behind.
Serta	*salta, iban*	... with.
Sāma	*iban, kan*	... with, to.
Dengan	*dangan*	... with.
Dālam	*ha-lūm*	... in.
Lepas	*ha-ulih-an*	... after.
Kārna	*kalna*	... on account of.
Sebab	*subab*	... ,, ,,

* The Sulus sometimes use "deri-pada" instead of *dien-ha*

MALAY.	SULU.	
Sa-kadar	*kadal*	... according.
Demi	*sin*	... by.
Dekat	*sŭk*	... near.

VIII.—CONJUNCTIONS.

The following is a list of useful conjunctions : —

MALAY.	SULU.	
Dan	*īban*	... and.
Atau	*atawa*	... or.
Kalau, jikalau	*bang*	... if.
Antah, kunun	*indai*	... perhaps.
Sopāya	*agas, agar*	... in order that.
Pūla	*maien*	... also, again.
Sambil, selang	*in-ka*	... whilst.
Serāya	*hati*	... then.
Tambah-an	*but maien*	... furthermore.
Kārna, sebab	*kalna, sabab*	... because.
Serta	*salta*	... and also.
Asal	*asal*	... provided that.
Tetāpī	*bŭt, sa-guah*	... but.
Me-lain-kan	*ma-lain-kan*	... except.
Hānia	*bŭt, lŭal*	... but, except.
Kelak	*lulus perakal*	... forsooth.
Jūga, jūa	*īsab*	... also.
Sāja	*sāja*	... only.
Lagi	*na mayen*	... again, even.
Lagi pūla	*na mayen īsab*	... again too.
Seperti	*sapalti*	... as, like.
Laksāna, bagei	*bīa*	... like.
Iya-ītu	*iann*	... that is to say.
Lamun-kan	*mīsan*	... although.

IX.—INTERJECTIONS.

MALAY.	SULU.	
Hei! ya!*	aia!*	O! oh!
Adōhi	arōhi	oh!
Niah	segah!	begone!
Ai! wah!‡	abah!‡	alas! oh!
Ayo! ayohi!		ah! (affection)
Chih!	are!	fie!
Wallahi!	wallah!	by God!
Nah!	nah!	there! take it!

X.—PARTICLES.

Although examples of the application of most of the particles have been given already, there are several which require special mention.

Tah or *ta* (" lah ") is an emphatic particle that may either follow or be affixed to words employed in asking a question, or expressing a command, as— *mai-tah*, " meng-apa " tah, wherefore? *pa-ka-ien tah*, " ka-māna tah," whither? *Katoh tah*, " pergi lah," go; *pa guah tah*, " ka-lūar lah," go out. The elimination of *tah*, or " lah," would not affect the meaning of any of these words, but it would make them less emphatic. *Tah* is also used euphoniously.

Bah (" lah ") is an expletive that may either follow or be affixed to nearly all kinds of words. It is also employed as a particle of intensity.

Dah seems to be a modification of *bah*.

* *Aia Tuhan ku*, oh my Lord!   † *Ya Tuhan ku*, oh my Lord!

‡ Astonishment or affection.

Kah and *tah*, in both dialects, are interrogative particles that may either follow or be affixed to words in any part of speech that may become the subject of a question, as—*rāja-tah*, " rāja-kah," is it the king? *pūtih kah*, "pūtih-kah," is it white? *iaun tah*, " ītu kah," is it that? *Kah* is in less general use than *tah* in the Sūlū, whilst the reverse is the case in the Malay.

Na is an intensive particle and an expletive. It also denotes the past tense.

Di, the particle of negation, generally precedes the nominative in a sentence, as—*di aku maka tūm-tūm*, I do not remember; *di aku maka panau*, I cannot walk. *Di*, no; *di tūd*, never.

Tūd denotes the superlative degree of adjectives and adverbs.

Hi ("si") is a particle that is prefixed to proper names, and sometimes to verbs.

Ma is an inseparable prefix. Its functions have been noticed under nouns and verbs; nevertheless, it may be remarked here, when adjectives follow their substantives *ma* is generally omitted. It is never prefixed to *dākolah*, great; or, *asīvī*, small.

Pieg, a form of the prefix *pūg*, is employed together with the affix *an* in the formation of substantives from verbs. It is also prefixed to verbs.

An, as a transitive suffix, seems to be a contraction of *han*. A little care is necessary in distinguishing it from the particle *an* which is employed in the formation of substantives from verbs, &c.

Kia seems to be a modification of *ka*.

Sa (se) is an adverbial sign. The same effect is produced by *sa* following an adjective as by adding **ly** to an adjective in English : e.g.. *bunal sa,* " se benar," truly from *būnal* or benar. It will be observed that " se " precedes the adjective in the in the Malay.

ORTHOGRAPHY.

This Introduction would not be complete without some notice of the orthographical vagaries of many Sūlū words. These vagaries are frequently attributable to dialectical differences, which are best exemplified in those words adopted from the Malay, but in the majority of cases they are due to the love the Sūlūs have for euphonious expressions.

The euphonious changes are effected (1) by the aid of mutable letters, and (2) by the interpolation of an additional syllable immediately after the initial letter or syllable of a word; e.g., *k* is changed into *l*, as *kāngoy, lāngog* ; *p* into *m*, as *māgoi, pāgoi,* etc.; *tumpang* into *tumumpang* ; *gāban, gomāban* ; *mūi, minui* ; *bāgit, biagit* ; *tābang, tomābang* ; *dāg-an, domāg-an.* etc. *D,* when it comes between two vowels, is frequently changed into *r,* as *edok, erok* ; *taud, ka-taur-an* ; *sūd, pa-sūr-an.*

The beginner, at first, may find these seeming inconsistencies somewhat troublesome, but with a little practice in the language any difficulty in the matter will disappear.

W. C. C.

ENGLISH-SULU-MALAY.

ENGLISH.	SULU.	MALAY.
A (an, one)	*īsai, sa, angka, ang,*	sa, suata,
	īsa, hambok,	suatu, sātu
Abaft	*habūli, di-burīt-an*	di-blākang
Abandon	*biugit*	tinggal-kan
Abandoned	*pŭg-biugit*	ter-būang
Abate (in force)	*gam-gam*	tūrun
,, (in price)	*tāwal*	tāwar
Abdomen	*tīan, ka-mamāw*	prut, are-are
Abet, to aid and	*tābang-manābang*	tōlong-
		menōlong
Abhor	*būnshi, binchi*	īri, binchi
Abhorrence	*ka-būnshi-an*	ka-binchi-an
Abide (wait)	*tŭgad*	nanti
Abide (dwell)	*hūlah*	dīam, dūduk
Ability (power)	*ka-gaus-an*	ka-kuasā-an
,, (clever)	*ka-pandai-an*	ka-pandei-an
Abjure	*taubat*	taubat

C

2

ENGLISH.	SULU.	MALAY.
Able	*būsag, basag, maka,-jādī*	kūat, bulih men-jādī
Ablution	*pieg-paigoh-an, pieg-pairoh-an*	ka-mandī-an, ghasil
Abode	*tingūd hūlah*	tampat dīam
Abominable	*halam*	haram
Abortion	*ka-pakpak-an*	gugūr-an anak
About	*mare*	kadar
,, (more or less)	*kīla-kīla*	lebih-korang
About, round	*lībūt*	kolīling
Above	*atās, ha-atās*	atas, di-ātas
Above all (first)	*tagnah, wāi-na-lio*	pertama
Abroad (outside)	*ha-guak*	di-lūar
Abscess	*bahū-ūtūt*	bīsol
Abscond	*māgoi, pāgoi*	lārī
Absent	*wāi, wāi-na, wala di*	tiāda, t'āda
Absolute	*mūtalak*	mūtalak
Absolutely (fact)	*būnal-būnal*	sūngoh-sūngoh
Absolve	*ampūn-an*	ampūn-kan
Absorb	*sūp-sūp*	īsap
Absurd	*kāngog*	babal
Abundance	*ka-tāud-an, ka-taur-an*	ka-banyak-an, ka-limpā-an
Abundant	*matāud, tāud, sakīan*	bānyak, lampau, sakien
Abundantly	*mūg-dūang-dūang*	ber-tambah-tambah
Abuse (to rail at)	*peninggad*	mākī

2

ENGLISH.	SULU.	MALAY.
Accept	*taīma*	terīma
Acclamation	*sñalak*	sūrak
Accommodated	** numpang, tumpang*	tumpang
Accompany	*mŭg-dăngan-dŭn-gan, pieg-ībun-an, ībun-an*	ber-sama-sama, meng-āwan, ber-kāwan
Accomplice	*ībun*	kāwan
Accord (agree)	*muwáfakat*	pakat, sūdi
,, (harmonize)	*sāli, sa' palti*	sapŭrti
,, (concede)	*magad*	men-ūrut
Accordingly	*bī-ha-icn*	bagītu jūga
Accost (speak to)	*pamong*	meng-āta
Account	*ītong-an, kīla-kīla*	bīlang-an, kīra-kīra
,, (news)	*habal, baita*	khabar
Accountant	*pandai mŭg-kīla-kīla*	tūkang meng-'īra-'īra
Accumulate	*tipān, pūn, himpān*	kumpul, tambun
Accurate	*amūna, āmŭ*	betul
Accursed	*halam, intok-an sin Tuhan*	īang di kutōk-ī Allah
Accuse	*tăgha-an, yen-an, ma-baita*	tūdoh-kan, chīmā
Accustomed	*bīaksa*	bīāsa
Ache, to	*sakit, ma-sakit*	sakit, ber-sakit
Acid	*ma-asin, māslom*	asam, masam
Acknowledge	*ātās*	akū

* To be accomodated with a passage in a vessel or with lodgings.

4

ENGLISH.	SULU.	MALAY.
Acquaint, to	*baita, malūm*	brī tāhu
Acquainted, to be	*kīlohan*	kanāl
Acquaintance	*ka-paham-an*	peng-anal
Acquiesce	*tūgūt, sālūt*	tūrot, īkot
Acquit	*ēg, pa-eg-an*	lepas
Acrid	*ma-pait, pait,*	pait,
	ma-harat, pūkat	padas
Across (athwart)	*babag*	lintang
Act (to do)	*hīnang*	būat
,, (to play)	*pa-naiam-naiam*	ber-māīn
Action (act)	*peig-hīnang-an*	per-būat-an
Active	*sāmūt, buskai,*	chapat,
	kasai	pantas
Acute (cunning)	*mūg-akal*	ber-akal
Add	*dūang*	tamba
,, (to reckon)	*jūmlah-an*	jumlah-ī
,, up	*mūg-jūmlah*	jumla-kan
Address, to	*tagha*	tagar
Address, an	*alamat*	alamat
,, (application)	*sambah*	sambah
Adept	*pandai*	pandei
Adequate	*ganap, abut,*	chūkup,
	sarang	sedang
Adhere	*pīkit, mīkit*	lekat
Adjacent	*masūk*	dekat
Adjourn, to	*tumanggo*	tangguh
Adjudge	*mūg-hūkūm*	ber-hūkum
Adjust, to	*sālasai*	salesai
Administration	*palentah*	parentah

ENGLISH.	SULU.	MALAY.
Administration, letters of	*sulat kuāsa*	surat kwāsa
Admirable	*maraiau* *maka-kŭg-kŭg*	bargŭs skali, ĕlok
Admiral	*panglīma*	panglīma lāŭt
Admit (enter)	*picg-sād-i*	bre-māsok
,, (allow)	*bīal*	bīar
Adopt, to (a child)	*pŭg-īpad*	pīarah
Adopted child	*anak pŭg-īpad*	anak-angkat
Adorn, to	*pŭg-daiau, darhauan*	hiñs-i
Adrift	*hiānād, anād*	āniut, ānyut
Adulterate (mix)	*lamūd*	champor
Adultery	*jīnah*	zinah
,, , to commit	*mŭg-jīnah*	ber-zinah
Advantage	*pāidah, hasil-hasil, pus-pus*	faidah, ontong, lāba
Adventure (to try)	*solaī*	chūba
Adventure (dare)	*ma-īsog*	berānī
Adversity	*sangsāh*	sangsāra
Advice, to ask	*mangaioh nasīhat*	minta nasīhat
Advise, to	*dumīhil nasīhat*	bre nasīhat
Advocate, to	*tabang bechala-an*	gāwam
Adze	*bansing, banshing*	banchī, papātil
Afar	*māioh, lāioh*	jāuh
Affable	*chumbū*	sūpan
Affair	*pali-hāl*	pri-hāl
Affection	*ka-lasa-an, ka-kasih-an, kiă-ulŭng-an*	pa-rasā-an, kasīh-an, sāyang

ENGLISH.	SULU.	MALAY.
Affectionate	*ūlŭng-olŭng*	kāsih-kāsih
Affiance, to	*mŭg-tūnang*	ber-tūnang
Affirm, to	*mam-baita*	meng-atā-kan
Affix	*būtang*	būboh
Affliction	*ka-susah-an*	ka-susah-an
Affluence	*dayah-an, lāngkc*	ka-kayā-an
Affright, to	*kieblahan, kīgnŭt, kia-kang-an*	meng-ajŭt, gantar-kan
Affrighted	*kiang-kang-an*	ter-kajŭt
Affront	*ka-sīpŭg-an*	brī mālū
Afloat	*lantop*	timbul
Afraid, to be	*ma-bōga, bōga*	tākut
,, (fearful)	*dīamag*	chabar
Afresh	*bāgū*	bāhrū
Aft	*ha-bāli*	di-burīt-an
After (in place)	*ha-būli*	di-blākang
After (in time)	*ka-ulih-an, mahūli*	kamadīan, telah
Afternoon	*lohol, asal*	berāleh hārī
,, , late in the	*mahapun*	patang
Afterpart	*bāli*	blākang
Afterwards	*ka-ulih-an*	kamadīan
After that	*,, dien-dān*	di-blākang ītu
Again	*balek, īsab, dakoman*	kambāli, lāgi, pūla
Again and again	*mahang-mahang*	ūlang-ūlang
Age (term of life)	*āmol*	ūmor
,, (period)	*kāla, abad, waktā*	māsa, zemān, dīwāsa
Aged	*mās*	tūah

ENGLISH.	SULU.	MALAY.
Agent	*wakīl*	wakīl
Agent (substitute)	*wali*	gantī
Agent (attorney)	*wakīl mūtalak*	wakīl mūtalak
Agile	*ûs-ûs*	pantas
Agitate (shake)	*hibal, kimabal*	kiber
,, (stir up)	*mŭg-hīlo-hāla*	hīru-harā-kan
Agony	*sangsāh*	sangsāra
Agree	*mŭg-janjī*	ber-janjī
Agree (friendly)	*pŭg-bagāi*	ber-sohbat
Agreeable	*maraiau, maka-jarī*	jadī-la
Agreement	*pŭg-janjī-an*	per-janjī-an
Aground	*sanglad, sankut*	sakat, kāndas, sangkut
Ague, fever and	*kura, tiandŭg*	demam kura
Ague (fever)	*demam, heng-law*	demam
Ah !	*arē*	iā, adōhī
Ahead	*ha-dong-dong, ha-dong, ha-unah-an*	di-aluan, di-mūka, di-adāp-an
Aid (assistance)	*pŭg-tābang-an*	per-tolong-an
Aim (to direct)	*tūjū-han kītal-an*	tūjū-kan, tunjuk
Aim at	*kītal-an*	tūjū, mītar
Ajar	*ma-kiput*	renggang
Akimbo	*mang-hawak*	tangan di pinggang
Akin	*tau-tai-anak*	ber-sānak
Alacrity	*ûs-ûs*	chapat
Alas !	*arōhi*	adōhī

ENGLISH.	SULU.	MALAY.
Albino	*ûgis, ûgis*	baler, sopak
Albumen (of a cocoa-nut)	*ûnûd nîog*	isī kalāpa
Alert	*buskai*	chākap
Alien	*tau dowāin, tau doāin*	ōrang-asing, ōrang gherīb
Alight	*timapok, dumaggut*	angkap
Alike	*angka rûgbus, sali*	sa'rūpa, sama
Alive	*boheh*	hīdop
All	*ka-tān, ka-tan-tan, lûn-lûn*	samūa, segala, sakali-an
Alligator	*būaya*	būaya
Allot (to share)	*bahāgi*	bhāgi
Allow (permit)	*bīal, bīa*	bīar
Allowance	*balanja*	balanja
Ally	*bagāi, salanga, makiwan*	sohbat, kāwan, stiwan
Almighty	*nûg-kuāsa*	mahā-kuāsa
Almighty, the	*Alah-tāla*	Allah-tàñla
Almost (time)	*mare*	hampir
Almost (place)	*ma-sûk, apit*	dekat
Alms	*sadakah*	sadakah
Aloes-wood	*gāhrū*	gàhrū
Aloft	*ha-atās ha-tās*	di-ātas
Alone	*īsa-īsa, angka-tau*	s'ōrang
Also	*īsab, dakoman*	jūga, pūla
Alter	*sālin, gomanti*	ūbah, gantī
Altercation	*kakat*	per-bantāh-an
Alternate	*ganti-mûg-gomanti*	ganti-ber-gantī

ENGLISH.	SULU.	MALAY.
Although	*mīsan*	maskī
Alum	*tāwas*	tāwas
Always	*tap-tap, abaran, hawa*	s'lalu, santiāsa
Am (be)	*aun*	ada
Amazed	*hḯilan*	heirūn
Amanuensis	*jūlo-tūlis*	jūro-tūlis
Ambassador	*dāk-an, ganti, utūs-an*	surūh-an, gantī, utūs-an
Ambush, to lie in	*homapa, tapok*	meng-ādang
Amen	*āmīn*	āmīn
Amend (mend)	*pŭg-daiau-i*	bāik-ī
Amicable	*pŭg-taimanghud*	ber-sohbat
Amid	*ha-gītong*	di-dalam
Amidst	*ha-tingah, ha-gītong*	di-tengah
Amiss	*sāh*	sālah
Amongst	*halŭm*	antāra
Amputate	*ūtūd, ūtūr-an, ma-manggol*	pōtong, kūdong
Amuck, to	*mŭg-āmok*	meng-āmuk
Amuck (holy war)	*mŭg-sabil*	prang-sabil
Amulet	*ajīmat, hajīmat*	azīmat
Amuse one's-self	*naim-naim, naiam-naiam*	māin-māin, ber-māin
Amusement	*pieg-naim-an*	per-maīn-an
Anarchy	*hīlo-hāla*	hīrū-hāra
Ancestors	*ka-apoh-an, ka-mās-an*	nēnek mōyang
Anchor, an	*bāoji, bōji*	sāuh

ENGLISH.	SULU.	MALAY.
Anchor, to	*pieg-lawig*	ber-lābūh
Anchor, to weigh	*bongkal-an,ōtong-an*	bongkar sāūh
Anchorage, an	*lawig-an*	labūh-an
Ancient	*sa-logai-logai*	zeman, lama
,, (old)	*mās*	tūah
Ancients	*tau nakauna*	ōrang dāūlu
And	*ĭban*	dan
Anew (new)	*bāgū*	bhārū
Angel	*malaĭkat*	malāikat
Anger	*gama.*	ka-gusār-an
Angle (to fish)	*bingit, mamingit*	mem-anching
Angle (corner)	*pījū, dugu*	sīkū, penjūru
Angry	*magama, mabungīs, molka**	marah, bāngīs, morka*
Anībong †	*anībong*	nībong
Animal	*haiop*	benātang
Ankle	*būkū-būkū-sīki*	māta-kākī
Annex	*sambong*	ūbong
Annihilate	*lag-lag, na-āis*	men-īāda-kan
Annoy	*mang-ūsih, ūsibah-an, sasat*	ūsik, gāduh, bīsing
Annual	*ha-mūsim ha-mūsim*	tīap-tīap-mūsim
Another	*doāin, dowāin*	lāin
Answer (reply)	*sambag, samambag, jawab, asip*	sāhut, jawāb, men-īāut

* Molka and Morka are used only when speaking of high personages.

† *Caryota urens:* a palm tree much used by the natives for house building purposes, etc.

ENGLISH.	SULU.	MALAY.
Ant, red	*sanam*	semut merah
Ant, large black	*salinbara*	,, ītam
Ant, white	*anai*	anei-anei
Antics	*tinggah dawa*	tingkah
Anus	*jubol*	tumbong
Anvil	*landāsan*	landāsan
Anxiety	*sinta*	chinta
Any	*mănga, dien-dien*	sa-bārang
Anywhere	*ha-dien-dien*	di-māna-māna
Apart (separate)	*ha-ang-sīpak*	di-sa-blāh
Apartment	*bīlik*	bīlēk
Apartment, small	*tamboh*	anjong
Ape (monkey)	*amok*	mūniet
Apologize, to	*mīki ampūn*	minta ampūn
Apology	*ampun-an*	ampūn-kan
Apostle	*rasūl*	rasūl
Apparel	*tāmūngan, kakāna*	pakāi-an
Apparition	*lōtaw*	hantū
Appeal	*na-ra in bechala*	bāwa bechāra, meng-ādū
Appearance	*rūgbūs, dūgbūs, bantok*	rūpa, paris, sikap
Appease	*sabal, pūg-dami*	sabar-kan, per-damei-kan
Appelation	*ingān, tāg-an*	nāma
Appertaining	*in ka-nya*	iang ampūnia
Appoint	*būtang*	men-jādi-kan
Apprehend (seize)	*sagau*	tangkap
,, (understand)	*maka-hāti*	meng-arti

ENGLISH.	SULU.	MALAY.
Apprise	*mŭg-baita,*	brī-tāhu,
	gāwi-han	khabar-kan
Approach, to	*pa-sūk-an*	ampīr-kan
,, (sidewise)	*ma-tapil, tampil*	tampil
Apt (fit)	*sarang*	pātut
Apt (clever)	*pandai*	pandei
Aquatic	*tubig*	ayer
Arab ; Arabian	*Arab*	Arab
Arabic	*bhāsa arab*	bhāsa arab
Arabia	*Benña-arab*	Negrī-arab
Arable-land	*ūma-an*	bendang
Arduous	*sūkal*	sūkar
Are	*aun*	ada
Areca (green)	*būnga*	pīnang mŭda
,, (ripe)	*pāla*	pīnang
Argue (wrangle)	*pailo-mamailo*	ber-bantah
,, (discuss)	*mŭg-bechala*	per-bechāra
Argument	*bechala*	bechāra
Arise	*bangūn*	bangun
Arm, fore	*tataklāi-an*	lāngan, tangan
Arm (upper part)	*būktŭm*	,,
Armour	*lamīna* *	bājū rantei *
Armpit	*elok*	katīak
Arm-rings	*galāng*	galang
Arms, side	*takŭs*	sinjāta
Arms, fire	*sanjata*	snapang
Arms, to bear	*mŭg-takŭs*	pakai sinjāta
Aromatic	*ma-lara, māla*	padās

* Coat of mail.

ENGLISH.	SULU.	MALAY.
Around	*lībut*	kolīling
Arrack	*ālak*	arak
Arrange	*hatol, mūmūs*	atōr
Arrest	*sagau*	tankap
Arrive	*sampai, ābūt*	sampei, tība
Arrow	*anakpānah, bawang*	anak pānah
Arsenic	*walāngan*	warāngan
Art (science)	*ilmu*	ilmu
,, (cunning)	*akal*	akal
Artery, main	*ñgat dakolah*	ūrat nādī
,, (a vein)	*ñgat dūgūh*	ūrat darāh
Articles (goods, property)	*alta, kakāna*	arta, bārang-bārang
Artifice	*akal-an*	tīpu
Artificer	*tūkang, pandai*	tūkang
Artist	*pandai*	pandei
Artless	*būnal*	benar
,, (simple)	*dōpang*	bōdoh
As	*bīal, sali*	bagei, sapūrti
,, much as	*bīha ter-tāud*	sa-baniak
,, quickly as possible	*samut-tūd*	sa-brāpa lakas īang bulih
,, well as you can	*bīa raiau*	sa-brāpa bāīk īang bulih
,, yet, not	*dī-pa*	būlom
Ascend	*gāban, sakat*	nāik
,, a tree	*domag, rāg, dūg*	panjat
,, a river	*sūmūd, sūd*	mūdik
,, a hill	*tumūkad, tūkad*	mendāki, dūki

ENGLISH.	SULU.	MALAY.
Ashamed	*ma-sīpŭg, sīpŭg*	mālū
Ashes	*abū*	abū
Ashore	*ha-lopa*	di-dārat
Aside	*ha-ang-sīpak*	di-sa'blah
Ask (beg)	*pangaioh, mangaioh*	minta, pohon
,, (inquire)	*ūmāsubū, asūbū*	tānia, sīdik
Askance	*lībat in māta*	junlīng, jūlīng
Asleep	*ma-tōg, tōg*	tīdor
Assault, to	*langgal*	langgar
Assemblage	*tīpun-an, ka-tāud-an, ka-taur-an, mairan, majēlis*	himpūn-an, ka-banyak-an, mēdan, mējēlis
Assemble	*tīpūn, hīpūn*	himpūn
Assist	*tābang,*	tōlong, bantū
Assistance	*tabāng-an, ma-tabāng-an*	tolōng-an, ka-tolōng-an
Associate	*īban*	taman, kāwan
Astern	*ha-būli*	di-burīt-an
Asthma	*sāngot, siāngot*	sesak dāda, īsak
Astonish	*hāilan*	hēiran
At	*ha*	di
,, first	*tagna*	mūla-mūla
,, home	*ha-bāi*	di-rūmah
,, last	*mah'ulih*	akhir
,, present	*bi-h'aun*	skārang
Astray	*nalīng*	sasat
Attack, to	*langgal*	langgar
Attempt, to	*sōlai*	chōba
Attend upon	*suapan*	layānī

ENGLISH.	SULU.	MALAY.
Attendant	*īban*	kāwan, būdak
Attest	*picg-saksi*	brī sahādat
Attest (subscribe)	*nŭg-būtang sāp*	būboh chāp
Attire	*tāmūgan*	pakāi-an
Auction	*mang-hīlāgi*	lēlong
Audience(atcourt)	*majēlis*	mējēlis
Auger	*barīna*	gurdi
Aunt	*īnah-an*	ma'kechil
Authentic	*būnal-būnal*	benar
Authority	*kñasa*	kwāsa
Avaricious	*lōba*	kīkir
Avenge	*maus*	bālas bhaya
Averse(unwilling)	*ma-hūkau*	tīāda māū
Avert (ward off)	*tangkis, tomangkis*	tangkis
Await	*tūgad, tumūgad*	nanti, tunggū
Awake	*jāga*	jāga
Away	*batē*	nialang
,, (direction)	*matū*	sana
Awe	*maka-hailan*	ka-takūt-an
Awful	*ajaib, maka-hailan, maka-bōga*	heibat sūanggī
Awning(canvas)	*haima*	chatri
Awning(palmleaf)	*kajang*	kajang
Awning, side	*pūrdah*	pūrdah
Awry	*ka-king*	īrut
Axe	*kāpah*	kāpak
Axe, a native	*patōk*	belīong
Axis (nave)	*bujal*	pusat
Azure	*walna sali langit*	bīru langit

ENGLISH.	SULU.	MALAY.
Babies	*anak-anak-an*	anak-anāk-an
Baby	*anak asīvī*	anak kechil
Bachelor	*bujang*	bujang
Bachelor, young	*sūbūl*	būyong
Back, the	*taīkād*	blākang
Back (of a knife)	*sālig*	sālig
Back, to draw	*bieng*	undur
Back-again	*mūī*	pūlang
Backside	*būlī*	ponggong
Backward	*ha-būlī*	di-blākang
Bad	*mang-i, ngi*	jāhat
Bad (decomposed)	*haloh*	būsok
Badinage	*bechala wāi tantu*	jenāka
Badge	*tanda, sāp, indahan*	tanda
Bag, a	*karot*	kārong
Baggage	*alta, līan-an*	arta, barang
Bail (surety)	*ātas-an, tanggong-an*	peng-ākū, jamin
Bait (for fish)	*ompān*	ompan
Bake (broil)	*dang-dang*	panggang
Bajau (sea gipsy)	*samal-laud, bajau*	bajau, baju
Balance (scales)	*timbāng-an*	timbāng-an
,, (remainder)	*kapin*	baki
Balcony(in front)	*hīgad sēngan*	barāndah
,, (at the end)	*hīgad sōngan*	barāndah
Bald	*bangkulik*	bōtak
Bald (forehead)	*āngas*	sūlah
,, (crown)	*āpau*	gundul
Bald, pie-	*lang*	balang

ENGLISH.	SULU.	MALAY.
Bale of goods	*bandala*	bandella
,, out water, to	*lelēmas tūbig*	men-imba ayer, chedok
Ball (bullet)	*pūngloh*	pelūrū
,, (wicker)	*sīpah*	raga
,, of tobacco	*būngkal tabākū*	bīji tambākū
,, of opium	*limping marat*	bīji afyūn
Ballast	*tōlah-bāla*	tōlak-bāra
Bamboo (large)	*pātong*	būlūh, bambū
,, (small)	*dabong*	rebong
,, (utensil)	*dagtong* *	tābong *
Banana	*sāin, sāing*	pīsang
Bandage, to	*balut, kubut*	balut-kan
Bandy-legged	*kabig in sikī*	īrut kākī
Banish	*bingit*	būang
Bank (border)	*hēgad*	tabing, tepī
Banner	*panji*	panji, tunggal
Banquet	*ñira-an*	jamū-an
Banter	*ōlah-ōlah*	men-yindīr
Bar (shallow)	*babau*	tōhor
Barber	*tūkang bagūng*	tūkang chūkor
Bare (naked)	*hūboh*	talanjang
Bark of a tree	*pāis kāhoī*	kūlit kāyū
,, of a dog	*tanghol*	salak
Barrel	*tōng*	tōng pīpa
,, of a gun	*būlū*	laras
Barter, to	*sēmbi, sāmbi*	tūkar
Bashful	*sīpūg, sanūnoh*	mālū

* Utensil for holding water—made of the large bamboo.

D

ENGLISH.	SULU.	MALAY.
Basket	ambong,	karanjang,
	bakol	balātak
,, (for cotton)	salingkat	bakŭl
,, (for fruit)	sūgñb	rāga
Basin	bātil	bātil
Bastard	halam bīcra	anak gampang,
		haram zada
Bat, a	kabīlau	kalāwar
,, (largest	kābūg	kalūang,
species)		kalāmbit
Bath	maigoh-an	per-mandī-an
Bathe	maigoh, māiroh	mandī
Bath-room	bilik maigoh	bīlik mandī
Batter (paste)	kanjī	kanjī
,, (beat down)	langgal	rōboh
Battle	parang, bunohan	prang
Bawl, to	sual	terīak
Bay (of the sea)	lōk	telūk
Bay-colour	pūla	mērah-kŭning
Bazaar, coast	parīan	pāsar, pŭdian
Bazaar, hill	taboh	pāsar
Be	aun, jādī, jārī	ada, jādī
Beads	manī, manik	mānī-mānī
Beak (of a bird)	tūka	pāroh
Beam (of wood)	hanglad, anglad	galagar
Beans (pulse)	bātong	kāchang
Bear (ursus)	baruang, baluang	brūang
,, on the head, to	lūtoh	junjong

ENGLISH.	SULU.	MALAY.
Bear (carry)	*balong*	pīkul
Bear on the shoulders, to	*balong*	pīkul
,, (to support)	*tanggong*	tanggong
,, (with poles)	*tanggong*	ūsong
,, children, to	*pieg-anak*	ber-ānak
,, children in the arms, to	*pīpi, tagung*	dukong
,, on the bach, to	*babah*	dukong
,, arms, to	*mäg-takūs*	pakāi sinjāta
,, fruit, to	*mäg-būnga*	ber-būah
Beard	*janggot*	janggot
Beast (unclean)	*bīnāt·ing*	benātang
Beast, wild	*satua*	satua
,, (cattle)	*haiop*	benātang
Beastly	*sali bīnātang*	seperti benātang
Beat, to	*lobak*	pūkul
,, (chastise)	*binasa*	gasak
,, with a hammer, to	*pokpok*	banting
,, a gong, to	*lesag*	pukol, gambang
,, with the fist, to	*suntok*	gōchok
Beat, to (as in washing clothes)	*dak-dak*	sesah
Beaten (overcome)	*sumang*	kalah
Beautiful	*maraiau, madaiau*	misai, mūlek, chantek

ENGLISH.	SULU.	MALAY.
Because	*kalna, sabab, sabab-kalna*	kārna, sebab, kārna-sebab,
Béche-de-mer	*bāt*	trīpang
Beckon	*kāmai, kāmbai*	lambei, brī-isarat
Become	*maka-jādī, man-jādī*	jādī, men-jādī
Bed (dais)	*kūlang-an*	tampat tīdor
Bedstead	*kantīl*	katīl or kantīl
Bed-cover	*sīob*	salīmut
Bee	*pūchūkan, pūsūkan*	lebah
Beef	*ūnūd sāpī, sāpī*	daging lembu
Befall	*jādī*	kunjōng
Beetle	*mñat kūbing*	kumbang
Before (time)	*nakauna*	lebih dahūlu
Before, to go	*mūna*	dahūlu
,, (a place)	*ha-halop-an*	di-hadap-an
,, the wind	*angin ha-būlī*	angin blākang
,, (in front)	*ha-dong*	di-mūka
Beg (ask)	*pangaioh, mīki*	minta, pohon
,, alms	*pangaioh sadakah*	minta sedekah
Begin	*tagnah-i*	mulā-i
Beginning	*tagnah, awal*	mūla, awal
Begone	*sōng, sēgah, shegah*	pergi, inchit, niah
Beguile	*man-īpū*	būjok
Behead	*ma-manggol-ū, panggol-ū*	panchong-kapāla
Behind	*ha-likūd, ha-lio, ha-būlī*	di-blākang, di-būrit-an

ENGLISH.	SULU.	MALAY.
Behold (look)	*kīta bah*	tengoh la
Being (existence)	*ka-aun-an*	ka-ada-an
Belch	*simigub, sigñb*	sirdawah, blahak
Believe (trust)	*halap, andal, perachaya, agad*	harap perchāya
,, (think)	*pīkir*	fikir
Bell	*bagtiny*	lōching
,, , small	*kong-kong*	,, ketchīl
Bellows	*pātput-an, popot-an*	hambūs-an
Belly	*tīan*	prot
Belonging	*kan, ka*	pūnia
Beloved	*parñka*	padūka
Below	*ha-babah*	di-bāwah
Belt, a	*kandit, jimpau*	tālī pinggang
Bench	*bangkoh*	bangkok
Beneath	*ha-bābah*	di-bāwah
Benefit	*ka-sudah-an, hasil-hasil, pus-pus*	ontong, hasil, laba
Benediction	*salāmat*	slāmat
Bent	*bengkok, kalok*	bēngkok, bantok
Best	*in maraiau tūd*	īang bāik sakālī
Bestow	*anūghara*	anugrah
Bet, to	*tauhan, palis*	tāroh
Betel (piper betel)	*būioh*	sīrih
Betel-leaf	*dahun būioh*	dāhūn sīrih
Betel-box	*salapa*	bakas sīrih salapa

ENGLISH.	SULU.	MALAY.
Betel-nut (green)	*bānga*	pīnang mūda
,, (ripe)	*pāla*	pīnang tūah
Betroth	*tūnang*	tūnang
Better	*lebih maraiau*	lebih bāik
Better, to make	*mūg-daiau-i*	mem-bāik-i
Between	*ha-tingah-tingah, ha-gītong, ha-üt*	di-tangah, antūra
Beverage	*minom-an*	mīnom-an
Bewail	*nūg-tangīs*	men-angīs-kan
Beware	*jāga-jāga*	jāga
Bewitched	*pangun-ōbāt*	kenū hōbāt-an
Beyond (across)	*ha-ang-sipak*	di-sabrang
,, (behind)	*ha-lio-lio, ha-lio, ha-līkūd*	bālik sāna, di-blākang
Bezoar	*gūlīga*	gūlīga
Bid (to request)	*dāk*	sūroh
Big	*dākolah, māslūg*	gadáng, besár
Bill (account)	*kīla kīla*	kīra kīra
,, (of a bird)	*tūka*	pāroh
Billet (firewood)	*kāhoī dongol*	kāyū āpi
Bill-hook	*gōk*	golok
Billow	*bōmbang, alun*	galombang
Bind	*hiūkit, hūkit*	īkat
,, up, to	*bagkut, baggut*	bābat, barot
,, the hands, to	*gīapūs*	īkat tāngan
Bird	*manōk-manōk*	būrong
Bird's-nest	*pūgad manōk*	sarang būrong
Bird's-nests (edible)	*salang*	sarang

ENGLISH.	SULU.	MALAY.
Birth	pieg-anāk-an	ber-anāk-an
Biscuit	bāng-bāng	bisquit
Bit, a (piece)	ang-ūtūd	sa'potong
,, (of bridle)	bāsī sin kakang	lāgam
Bitch	erok babai	anjing betīna
Bite, to	tūkūb, kūt-kut, man-ūtkūt	gīgit, men-gīgit
,, the lips, to	mang-ūtom, kebam	meng-atam
Bitter	ma-pait, pait	pait
Blachan *	bāling	blachan
Black	ītam, itūm	hītam
Blacksmith	tūkang bāsī, pandai bāsī	tūkang besī pandei besī
Blacksmith's craft	sasal-an bāsī	pe-karjā-an besī
Blade (of a knife or weapon)	sīlab, lāding	pīsau, sakin
Blade, edge of a	māta	māta
Blade-bone	kūka	balīkat
Blain	bahū ūtāt	bīsol
Blame, to	mūg-sāh	men-iālah
Blanket	sīob	kamli
Blaze	laga	niāla
,, , to	ma-laga	ber-niāla
Blear-eyed	māta bīlas	māta nīlas
Bleed	nūg-dūrāh	ber-dārah
Blemish on the eye, a	būlag	balālak, kalābū

* " Blachan " is a kind of Caviar made of dried shrimps.

ENGLISH.	SULU.	MALAY.
Blind	*būta*	būta
Block (pully)	*tīmūn-tīmūn*	kapī, karī
,, (chock)	*kalang-an*	kalang-an
Blockhead	*babal*	bŏdoh, bingong
Blood	*dūgūh*	dārah
,, , of noble	*bangsāwan*	bangsāwan
Blossom (flower)	*sumping*	būnga
,, (bud)	*pusud, būkūl*	kūtum
Blossom, to	*nūg-būkūl*	ber-būnga
Blow, to	*tīop, kīop* *	tīup, humbus *
,, , to	*tūnga-tāmūnga* †	mangah †
Blow-pipe	*sūmpitan*	sūmpitan
,, dart	*bawang*	bawang
Blue	*bīlu*	bīrū
,, , dark	,, *itūm*	,, ītam
,, , light	,, *pūteh*	,, pūteh
Blunt	*tūmpāl,*	tūmpūl,
	di-mūk	kōrang tājam
Boar	*baboi mandangan*	bābi jantan
,, wild	,, *katīan*	,, hūtan
Board, a (wood)	*digpi*	pāpan
Boat (European)	*bōtī*	bōtī
,, (dug out)	*gōbāng*	sagor
,, (outrigged)	*dāpang* ‡	praū
,, (large dug-out)	*bāngka*	bīduk

* To blow with the mouth, or as the wind. † To blow as a porpoise.

‡ The *dapang* is almost universally used by the natives in the Sulu Archipelago.

ENGLISH.	SULU.	MALAY.
Bob up and down, to	*kirut*	timbul ting-glam, goyang
Body	*baran, badan*	tūboh, badan
Boil, to	*tognah, tolah*	rebūs
,, rice, to	*pāngaiū, pangaiū*	men-ānak
,, , a	*bahū ūtūt*	bīsol, bāra
Boiling, to be	*būkal*	men-dīdik
Boisterous	*hūnūs, tampīas*	tampīas
Bold	*ma-īsūg*	barāni
Bolster (pillow)	*ū-an*	bantal, sāraga
Bone, a	*būkog*	tūlang
Bonnet	*kopīa, tūdong*	kopīah
Book	*sūlāt*	sūrat
,, (religious)	*kītab*	kītab
Booty	*lampas-an*	rampas-an
Border, a (edge)	*hīgad, pigi, bīring*	tepī, bībir, pinggīr, bīrih
Borer (auger)	*jalah kīna*	jalah chīna
Bore, to	*barenahan*	gērek
,, the ears, to	*tugsukan bolah*	ber-tīndek
Born	*pieg-anak*	ber-ānak
Borneo	* Pūlo ka-lamantah-an	
,, (city)	*Būnai*	Brunei
Borrow, to	*būs, mūg-būs, mūs*	pinjam
Bosom (pectus)	*dagha*	dūda
Both	*ka-dūa-dūa, ka-rūa-rūa*	ka-dūa

* The Sulus have no name for the whole of the Island.
" Pulo ka-lamantah-an " means Sago Island.

ENGLISH.	SULU.	MALAY.
Bottle, a	*kācha, kāsa*	bōtol, būlī
Bottom	*būlī*	pantat
,, (anus)	*jubol*	tumbong
,, (hips)	*opoh*	ponggong
,. of the sea	*ha-babah dagat*	dī-bāwah lāūt
Bough	*sanga*	chābang, tārok
Bow (for arrow)	*pānah*	pānah, būsor
Bow-string	*lubid pānah*	tālī būsor
Bow (to make obeisance)	*hāmūboh, hūboh*	tunduk
,, the head, to	*māndok, āndok*	layah
Bowels	*lingan lingan tīan*	īsī prot
Bowl, a	*pinggan,* batil*	mangkok
Bowsprit	*jūnyal*	jonggor
Box (blow)	*sontok*	gōchoh
Box, to	*nūg-sontok*	ber-tampar
,, (chest)	*balolang, bilolang, baul, tong, pati*	petī balolang, petī, bākas
,, , a musical	*salindo*	petī salindo
,, , a sirih	*salapa*	salapa
Boy	*bata-bata ūsog*	būdak lāki
Brace (a couple)	*angka-pāsang*	sa-pāsang
Bracelet	*gālang*	galang, pontok
Brackish	*ma-bāngog, ma-asin*	pāyau, māsin
Brains	*ūtāk*	ūtak, benā
Branch (a bough)	*sanga*	chābang, dāhan
Brand, a	*sāp*	chop, chāp
,, (mark)	*tanda*	tanda

* " Pinggan " in Malay means plate.

ENGLISH.	SULU.	MALAY.
Brandish	*sāyāng, sinlog*	balāyam, āchu
Brass	*tambāya, tūmbāga*	tambāga
Brass-tray	*talam*	talam
Brave	*ma-īsñg*	barānī
Brawl	*hīlō-hāla*	hīrū-hāra
Bray (to pound)	*bāioh*	tūmbūk
Bread	*lītī*	rōtī
Breadth	*lūkbang*	lēbar
Break, to	*bag-bag*	pechah
,, off, to	*baleh, mūtus*	pātah, pūtus
,, a promise	*munkir*	munkir
,, wind, to	*utut*	kuntut
,, (smash)	*ma-tūmā*	hanchor
Break-of-day	*sūbāh-sūbāh adlau*	dīnī hārī
Breakers (surf)	*ma-alun*	ombak
Breast (pectus)	*dāgha*	dāda
,, (mammæ)	*dūrūh*	titī, sūsū
Breath	*napas*	nafas, hawā
Breathe	*mūg-napas*	men-afas
Breech	*būlī*	burīt
Breeches	*sāwal*	saluar
Breed, to	*pieg-anak*	ber-ānak
Breeze	*hangin*	angin
,, , land	*hangin ha hīgad*	angin darat
,, , sea	*hangin ha lāūd*	angin lāūt
Bribe	*suāb*	suāb
Brick	*bātu nūg-hinang bāi*	bātu bākar
Bride, a	*pengantin babai*	mampilī perampuan

ENGLISH.	SULU.	MALAY.
Bridegroom, a	*pengantin usog*	mampilĭlakĭ
Bride's-maid	*pandala*	pengapit
Bridge, a	*taitaian, titi-an*	jambātan
Bridle, a	*kakang*	dras, kang
Bright (shining)	*sāia*	chāia
,, (clear)	*ma-sawa*	trang
Brilliant	*sāia pakaraiau*	chāia benār
Brimstone	*mailang*	balĕrang
Brindled	*patikan*	īram
Brine	*tubig ma-asin*	āyer māsin
Bring	*da, doma, da-han*	bāwa
,, (imp.)	*pakaria-an, pakaria*	,,
,, here	*da-mārĭ, da-han mārĭ*	bāwa sīnī
,, up, to	*ĭpat, paliara*	piāra
Brink	*hĭgad*	tepī, tabing
Briny	*ma-asin*	māsin
Brisk (active)	*biskai, buskai, mikang·*	rājin, pantas, chapat
Brittle	*putuk-putuk*	rāpoh
Broad	*lŭkbang, lŭag*	lĕbar, lŭas
Broadcloth	*sakelāt*	sakelāt
Broil	*dang-dang*	panggang
Brooch	*karosang*	krosang
Brood (offspring)	*kānak-kānak*	kānak-kānak
,, (to sit on eggs)	*mŭg-gaham*	meng-aram
Brook (ditch)	*gāta*	pārit
,, (stream)	*anak sŭbah*	anak sŭngei
Broom, a	*sa-sāpŭ*	peniāpŭ
Broth	*sābau*	kŭah

ENGLISH.	SULU.	MALAY.
Brother	*taimanghūd*	sudāra
,, , younger	*manghūd*	adek
,, , middle	*ha-gitong-an*	per-tengahan
,, , elder	*magolang*	abang
,, , ,, (or sister)	*kakah*	kakah
Brother-in-law	*īpag*	īpar
Brow	*ha-gītong-an*	kening
Bruise, to	*pipis*	pipis
Brunette	*mairùm*	ītam mānis
Brush, to	*sāpū*	sāpū
Brush-wood	*katian*	samak
Brute (animal)	*haiop*	benātang
Brutal	*sali bīnātang*	seperti benātang
Buck, (male deer)	*ūsa ūsog*	rūsa jantan
Bucket (zinc)	*mītal*	timbā besī
,, (wood)	*baldī*	baldī
Bucket, small	*gayong*	gayong
Buckle, to	*sabit-an, sambat*	meng-anching
Bud (blossom)	*mūkūl, būkūl*	kūtum
Buffalo, water	*kābau*	karbau
Buffalo-pool	*lublub-an*	kūbang-karbau
Bug	*bāngking*	pīnding, pījad
Build, to	*nŭg-bangun*	bangun-kan
Bull	*sāpī mandangan sāpī ūsog*	lembū jantan sāpī jantan
Bullet	*pangloh*	pelūru
Bullock	*sāpī kabīli*	lĕmbu kāsīm
Bundle,	*pātūs*	bŭngkūs

ENGLISH.	SULU.	MALAY.
Bundle of grass	*bātok*	barkas
,, of rotans	*gālong*	gālong
Bung	*dabus-an tōng*	sŭmbat tōng
Buoy, a	*lintang, pilampōng*	lampōng
Buoyant	*liantop*	timbul
Burden, a	*bābah-an*	bāban
Burlesque, a	*tinggah dawa*	tingkah
Burn, to	*sānog*	bākar
,, (scald)	*na lŭs, hanglŭs*	hāngus
,, (clear land)	*mŭg-lāb*	bākar
,, (to flame)	*ma-laga*	ber-niāla
Burst	*bustak*	tatas, belāh
,, (blow up)	*lupot, bagbag*	malŭpop
,, (as a boil)	*mŭstik, mŭstig*	bŭrut
Bury	*mŭg-kŭbŭl*	kubŭrkan
Burying-place	*kūbŭl*	kubŭr
,, (ancient)	*tampat*	krāmat
Bushes	*katian*	samak
Business	*ka-hīnang-an*	pe-karjă-an
Busy	*wāi sanang,*	ta'senang,
	tŭga ŭsaha,	ăda ŭsaha,
	wāi ka-tauam-an	bāniak karja
But (sed)	*bŭt, bŭt meyen,*	tetāpī, tŭpī,
	bŭt maier	lakin
Butt, to	*mŭg-tandok*	men-andok
,, (cask)	*tōng*	tōng pīpa
Butter	*lanah sāpī,*	mīnyak sāpī,
	mantagelia *	mantēga *

* Spanish, "*mantequilla* and "manteca."

ENGLISH.	SULU.	MALAY.
Butterfly	kaba-kaba	kūpū-kūpū, rāma-rāma
Buttocks	opoh, būlī pong-pong	gadipong
Button, a	tambākū	kanching
„ , to	tambūkū-han	meng-anching
Button-hole	māta-lamboh, pakaw	lobang „
Buttress (of a tree)	dālig	banir
Buy	bī, mī	bilī
„ (offer)	tāwal	tāwar
„ (wholesale)	tughan-an	pajak
By	īban, dien-pa	ūlih, deri-pada
„ , near	masūk	dekat
„ , to put	tīau, tāu	simpan, tāroh
By-and-bye	dai dai dakoman, yana-gana,	sa-būntar lāgi, nanti dahūlu

---

Cabal	ka-rapāt-an	peng-ūbong
Cable (chain)	gandāwalī bāoji	rantei sāūh
Cage	kōng-an	sangkar-an
Cajole	pamong manīpu	mem-būjok
Cake, a	paniam	pengan-an
Cake (Chinese)	garati	bīpang *
Calabash	kābāsi	labū
Calculate	nug-kīla-kīla	ber-kīra-kīra
Calf	anak sāpī	anak lembū
„ (of the leg)	butug butug bitis	jantong betis
Calico, brown	gajah helau	kāin blachau
Calico, red	koko pāla	kāin merah

* Chinese, " bi phang."

ENGLISH.	SULU.	MALAY.
Calico, white	*koko puteh*	kāin puteh
Calk	*hulat-an, gūlam*	pakkal
Call	*tāwag, tāg*	panggil
,, at, to	*hāpit*	singgah
Calm	*limbuh, lēnau*	tenang, tedoh
Calumniate	*mang-ompat*	niāya
Camel	*onta*	unta
Camphor	*kapol*	kāpūr
Camphor-tree	*kāhoī kapol*	kāyū kāpūr
Can (able)	*maka-jārī, man-jādī*	bulih, jādī
Cancer	*lāstong*	rāstong
Candle	*lansok*	lilin
Candlestick	*ka-dādūkan lansok*	kākī dīan
Cane (arundo)	*pātong*	būluh
,, (calamus)	*wāi*	rōtan
,, , walking	*tongkūd*	tongkat
,, , sugar	*tubu, tabu*	tebū
Cannon	*espil*	marīam
Cannot	*di maka-jādī,*	tiada būlih
	di man-jādī	ta' būlih
Canopy	*kālambū, lohol,*	kalambū,
	lāngit-lāngit	lāngit-lāngit
Canvas (sailcloth)	*kākāna lāig*	kāin lāyar
Caoutchouc	*tāgoh litahan*	getta līchah
Cap (head-dress)	*kopīa*	kopīah
,, (percussion)	*kīp, batil-batil*	kēp
Capacious	*hāyang, ma-lūag*	lāpang, lūas
Capacity (talent)	*akal*	akal, budī
Cape (head-land)	*tandok, tandoh*	tanjong

ENGLISH.	SULU.	MALAY.
Capital (stock)	pūhūn, mōdal	pōkōk, mōdal
Capon	manok kabīli	āyam-kabīrī
Capsicum	lāra pula	lāda mērah
Capsize	rāub	jūkang
Captain (European)	kapitan *	kapītan
Captain (Native)	nakora	nakoda
Captive	tawan	tawan
Captivity	tāwan-an	tāwan-an
Carcass	bangkai	bangkei
Care; diligence	usaha	usaha
Care, to take	jaga, daiau-daiau	jaga
,, (trouble)	sūsah	sūsah
Care of, to take	kumītak	tengok
Cargo; freight	lūan-an	muāt-an
Carnage	lampas-an	per-būnoh-an
Carpenter	tūkang-kāhoi, pandai-kāhoi	tūkang-kāyū
Carpet	pelmadanī, hampalan	permadānī
Carriage (vehicle)	karosak	krētā
Carry	hākūt	pīkul
,, ; convey	hīatud	antar
,, on the back	bābah	dūkong
,, on the hip	pīpi	gandong,
,, under the arm	sipit	kepit
,, on the head	lutoh	junjong

* Spanish, "Capitan."

ENGLISH.	SULU.	MALAY.
Carry with the fingers	*pindit*	bibit
,, on the open hand	*tiataiak*	tatang
,, on the shoulder	*pasan*	kilik
,, a person	*balong*	dukong, pīkul
,, outside	*dahan haguah*	bawa klūar
Cart, a	*karosah* *	pedātī, krētā
Cartridge	*kaluchucho* +	petron, tam-pang, pompas
Cartridge-pouch	*abah-abah*	kerpēi
Carve	*ākil*	ūkir, tūrī
Cascade	*togpa in tūbig, busai, tubig-nñg-togpa*	panchoran āyer, āyer terjun
Case; sheath	*tagōban*	sārong
,, (for trial)	*bīchala, dawa*	bichara, dawa
Cash (money)	*pelak*	wang
,, (Chinese)	*kushing pitis, kushing tūmbaga*	pītis
Cask	*tong*	tong
Cassia	*pais lawang*	kūlit lawang
Cast (throw)	*tēlo, tēloh*	limpar
Cast anchor, to	*biugit bāoji*	būang sūah
Cast off	*biugit lubid*	lepas tālī
Cast (of the eye)	*jūlīng*	jūlīng
Caste (tribe)	*bangsa*	bangsa

* Spanish, "Carreza.
"Cartucho."

ENGLISH.	SULU.	MALAY.
Casting-net	layah	jāla
Castor-oil plant	tangan tangan pala	pōkῑ jārak
Castrated	kabīli, kasī	kāsīm, kabīrī
Casuarina	arau	arau
Cat	kūting	kūching
Catechist, a	mamum	mamum
Catch, to	sagau, sambut	tangkaꜩ
Catch in the hand, to	timaboh	sambut
Catch hold of, to	kimaput, kaputan	pegangkan
Cattle (cows)	sāpī	sāpī, lembū
Cattle (animals)	haiop	benātang
Catty (1½ lbs.)	katī	katī
Caulk, to	hūlat-an, gūlam	pakkal
Cause	sabab	sebab
Caution, to	māg-hindoh	meng-ājar
Cave	liang	guah
Cavity	lungag	lobang
Cease	dūmahong	berhinti
Ceiling	langit-langit, lohol	langit-langit
Celebrated	māshol	ter-nāma, mashūr
Celerity	ma-būskai, ma-ragan	lākū-pantas, lājū
Centre	ha-gitong-tīⁱl	tengah-tengah
Centre (of a gong)	bujal	pūsat
Centipede	laihīpan, alaīpan	halīpan

ENGLISH.	SULU.	MALAY.
Ceremony	*hādat*	ādat
Certain	*tantā*	tantu
Certainly	*būnal-būnal*	sūnggoh-sūnggoh
Certificate	*sāp*	chāp
Chaff (of grain)	*hapa*	sekam, ampa
Chagrin	*sāsah-atāi*	sūsah hāti
Chain, a	*gandāwalī*	rantei
Chain (necklace)	*bilanggok*	ūtas
Chain (fetters)	*ikang-ikang*	lunggū
Chair	*sīa* *	krosī
Chamber	*bilik*	bilek
Change (to alter)	*ūbah, salin*	ūbah
,, dress, to	*salin tāmūgan*	sālin
,, houses, to	*pindah*	pindah
Chapter	*jūd, pasal*	juz, fasal
Character (letter)	*hulup*	huruf
Charcoal	*papau*	ārang
Charge, to (accuse)	*tāgha, yen-an*	tūdoh
Charge (price)	*halga*	harga
Charity	*raka*	sadaka
Charm, a (spell)	*ajimat*	azīmat
Chart; map	*patā*	pātah, kart
Chase, to	*hiapas*	kejar
Chase, the (hunt)	*panhūt-an*	būrū
Chastise, (to correct) ·	*anad, binasa*	ajer, gāsak

* Spanish, " Silla."

ENGLISH.	SULU.	MALAY.
Chat; banter	kong-kau	banchang, kechĕ-kechĕ
Chattels	álta, átu	árta
Chatter (talking volubly)	kaibah	bīsing, chūra, lītar
Chatter (teeth)	galeteh	galetek
Cheap	mohaī	mūrah
Cheat, to	panipu, tīpu, pieg-akal-an, lĕgau	tīpu, berakal, kīchū
,, ,, (trick)	kejib	kĕchoh
Cheek	pisni	pīpī
Cheerful	senang-atāi	senang hāti
Cheese	kīsō*	kĕjū
Chest (of opium)	pāk	pāk
,, (of tobacco)	bakag	petī
,, (breast)	dagha	dāda
,, (box)	bilolang	peti balolang
Chew, to	māmah	mämah
Chew, a (quid)	sopah	sepah
Chew, to (the cud)	māg-sopah	mamah bīak
Chicken	anak-manok, impis	anak-āyam
Chide (correct)	anad	ajar
Chief	tau-dakolah	ōrang-besar
Child	batah, anak	anak
Child (firstborn)	anak sūlong	anak sūlong
Child (lastborn)	bongsu	anak bongsu
Child, with (pregnant)	būrus	bunting

* Spanish, "queso."

38

ENGLISH.	SULU.	MALAY.
Children	*kānak-kānak, batah-batah*	kānak-kānak
Chilli; cayenne	*lara-pula*	lada-mērah
Chin	*takū*	dāgū
China	*Song-song, banña Kīna*	negri China
Chinaman	*Lanang*	Orang-chīna
Chinese	,,	,, ,,
Chintz	*kalangkali*	kalankāri, chīt
Chisel, a	*sangkap*	pāhat
Chock, a	*kalang-an*	kalang-an
Chocolate	*sūkalāti, sūkūlati*	chocōlāt
Choice	*pehpeh-an*	pilīh-an
Choke, to	*biungkūl, kia-būkog-an*	chokek, lemas
Choler (anger)	*ma-gama*	marah
Choleric	*ma-bīngis*	bīngis
Cholera	*sāka-intahu*	waba
Chop, a (seal)	*sāp*	chop, chāp
Chop: to hack	*tūis-tūis*	tatak
Chop; to cut	*tūgbas*	potong
Chop; to chip	*bas-bas* *	potong
Chop, to	*jug-jug*	sumpil
Chopper	*ūtak*	kapak
Choose, to	*peh-peh*	pilih
Christ	*Nābi-īsa*	Nābi īsa
Christian	*Bisaya*	Sarānī
Church	*baī mūg-doa*	grēja

* " Bas-bas " means to dress wood.

ENGLISH.	SULU.	MALAY.
Cicada	*dahu-rahu*	riang-riang
Cigarette	*sigarīllio* *	rokō
„ , cover	*dahun toak*	dahun rokō
Cinnamon (wild)	*pais lawang, mana*	kāyū mānis,
Circle	*tībok*	būlat
Circumcise, to (a male)	*mäg-islam*	ber-sūnnat
Circumcise, to (a female)	*mäg-sunnat*	ber-sūnnat
Citadel	*kōta banūa*	kōta negrī
Citron	*līman*	līmau karbau
City	*banūa*	negrī
Citizen	*tau banūa*	ōrang bendar
Civit-cat	*tinggālōng*	tinggālōng
Civil	*ma-ingat hadat*	sūpan
Civility	*arab*	adab
Clamour	*hībok, būkag*	gampar
Clamp-shell	*manangkai*	kīma
Clasp, to (embrace)	*dakap*	dākap, pelūk
Clasp (fasten)	*sābit-an*	sambat
Claw, a	*kūkū, tiandoy*	kūkū
Clay	*lopa līat*	tanah līat
„ ; earth	*lopa*	tānah
Clean	*lunoh*	brīseh
„ , to	*tīmūr-an*	sūchi, chūchi
Clear, (transparent)	*ma-lchau, masawa*	trang, jerneh

* Spanish "Cigaro."

ENGLISH.	SULU.	MALAY.
Clear, to (a plantation)	*lāpa,* hawan-i †*	tābas, siang-i
,, (open)	*ma-hawan*	trang
Cleave (to split)	*belah*	belăh
Clerk	*klanī*	kranī
Clever	*ma-pandai*	pandei
Cliff, a	*dalas*	tāpat
Climb (a tree)	*rāg, dag, domay*	panjat
,, (a stair)	*sākat, samakat*	nāīk
,, , to (a hill)	*tūkad, tumukad*	dākī
Clip, to	*gūnting-an*	gunting-kan
Clitoris	*tū-tūi*	kalinti, kalintat
Clock	*lēlōs ‡*	jām
Close, to (to shut)	*tambal, tāmbūl*	tūtup
,, (touching)	*ma-lāpat*	rāpat
,, (as folds)	*kūmūt*	rapat
Closet	*tamboh*	anjong
Closet, water	*bilik mīhi*	jamban
Cloth	*kākānu*	kāin
,, , woollen	*sakelāt*	sakelāt
,, , white	*koko putih*	kāin putih
,, , red	*,, pula*	,, merah
,, , black	*,, itum*	,, hītam
,, , sail	*kakana layog*	,, layer
,, a (to hide the nudities)	*sūlit*	kāin chawat

* To clear the ground of Brushwood, long Grass &c.

† To free from Creepers, Weeds &c.

‡ Spanish, " Reloj."

ENGLISH.	SULU.	MALAY.
Clothes	támüngan, pakai-an	pakāi-an
Cloud	áwan	áwan, mēga
Clouds (white and fleecy)	īnák ámbūn, aso	tāi hāngin
Clown	tau babal	bedāwi
Clove (spice)	bunga láwang	chengkē
Cluster, a (of fruit)	raug, bālig, tūndūn	tindan, sīkat
Coagulated	ma-tūg	bakū
Coal	būling-bátu, bátu bāling	árang-batu, batu-árang
Coarse (in texture)	rápau	kásar
Coarse (in language)	sáplah, k īsáp	kasar, kásáp
Coast, the	lípá, hīgad, bēd	dárat, tepī laūt
Coat, a	bájū	bájū
Cobble	tampal	menampal
Cobweb	láwai láwa-láwa	sárang lába-lāba
Cock, a	manok ūsog	ayam jantan
Cock, a jungle	labuyuk	ayam ūtan
Cockscomb	dáling	bālūng
,, fight (with gaffles)	bālang	sábūng
,, ,, (without gaffles)	takbi	meniábūng
Cockroach	kūk	lipas

ENGLISH.	SULU.	MALAY.
Cocoa	*kākāw*	kŏkāu
Cocoa-nut	*nīog, lāhing*	nīor, kalāpa
,, ,, husk	*bānāt*	sābūt
., ,, shell	*hungut, ugab*	tempūrong
Coffee (coffee arabic)	*kawah, kahāwa*	kawah
Coffin	*lālong, kaban*	long, kafan
Coil up, to	*nāg-lingan*	lingkar
Coincide	*sālāt*	tūrut
Coition	*pieg-īut-an*	se-tubōh-an
Cold	*haykut, haggut*	sejuk, dīngin
Collide	*langgal, dogtol*	langgar
Colleague	*īban*	kāwan
Collect	*tīpun, napun, pun*	kumpul
Colour	*walna*	warna
Colt	*kāra-sābāl*	anak kūda
Column (pillar)	*tiang*	tiang
Comb	*sādlai*	sīsir, sīkat
Combine, to	*pākat*	pākat
Come	*domatang, maka-di, maka-ri,*	dātang
,, (imperative)	*mārī, di, kari,*	mārī
Come and go, to	*mātoh mārī*	pergi pūlang
Comet	*bālākau*	bintang ber-ekor
Comfort, to	*tībau*	hibor
Command (of a Chief)	*dīak, tītah*	tītah
Commander	*panglīma*	pangūla

ENGLISH.	SULU.	MALAY.
Commerce	pieg-dagang-an	per-niagā-an
Commit (murder)	būnoh	būnoh
,, (perpetrate)	hīnang	būat
,, a crime, to	dōsa	ber-dōsa
Common people	layat	rayat
Communicate	pieg-baita, ma-maita	brī-tāhu, malūm-kan
Companion	īban, abai	kāwan, taman
Compare, to	singur-an	banding-kan
Compass, mariner's	padōman	padōman
,, points *	māta-padōman	māta padōman
Compassion	ka-lasah-an	kasīh-an
Compel, to	paksa, gāgah	paksa
Complain, to	mang-āru	meng-ādū
Complete	ganap, ma-katō	ganap
Completion	ka-sūdah-an	ka-sūdāh-an
Compliments	selam-dōa	tābek
Comply	agad, sūlūt, tūgūt	ikot, tūrut
Compos mentis	saioman, saioi	siyuman
Compound, (to mix)	lāmūd	champor
Comprehend	maka-hāti	meng-artī
Compress	gipit	apīt
Compute	bīlang, nãg-ītong	ber-itong
Conceal	tapok	sembūnī
Concede	tūgūt	tūrut
Concha de nacar	pais tīpai, tīpai †	kulit muntīara

* See Table.   † M.O.P. Shell.

ENGLISH.	SULU.	MALAY.
Conclude	*hobus-an*	ābis-kan
Concluded	*tammat*	pūtus-sūdah
Concertina	*ambag-ambag*	ambag
Concubine	*sandil, bagai*	gundik
Concupiscence	*lasig, nafsu*	ka-ingīn-an
Condemn	*măg-hukum*	meng-hukum
Condiment	*lamai, pāmāpa*	lauk, hulam, sambal
Conduct, to	*hiatud*	antar
„ by the hand	*ambit*	pimpin
Conduct (manner)	*ka-lāku-an*	ka-lākŭ-an
Conduit	*selūran tūbig*	panchūr-an
Conference	*beshala, bechāla*	bechāra
Confess (to own)	*mang-akū*	meng-akū
Confide	*hālap*	per-chāya
Conform	*tūgūt, sūlūt, agad*	tūrut, īkot
Confuse	*bingong*	kachau
Conjecture	*agah, agau*	sangka
Conjuncture	*abīla*	katīka
Connect	*măg-sambong*	meng-ūbong
Conquer (to win)	*gimaug*	menang, sumauk
Consanguinity	*tau tai-ānak*	dūs-ānak
Consciousness	*simangat*	semangat
Consider, to	*pīkil-pīkil, isūn*	fikir, sangka
„ (lit. to weigh)	*timbang*	timbang
Constantinople	*Istambul, Stambul*	Istambul
Constantly	*mahūmu*	santiāsa
Construct	*hīnang*	būat, bekin

ENGLISH.	SULU.	MALAY.
Contain (to hold)	luan	mūat
Content	puas	puas
Contents	lūan-an	mūat-an, īsī
Contest, to (to dispute)	dāwa	dāwa
,, (to quarrel)	bantah	bantah
Contraband	contrabando, lāng-an	larāng-an
Contract, to	kumut-an	memendek-kan
Convalescent	ma-gām-gam in sakit, nauam	sumboh, betah, niāman
Convention	janjī-an	per-janjī-an
Conversation	beshala	bechāra
Converse (to talk)	măg-bishala	ber-bechāra
Convey (bring)	hiatud, pāg-da	antar
,, (send)	pa-lā, pa-rā	kīrim
Convulsions	sāuran	sāwan
Cook, to	lutoh, pangāiñ	memāsak
Cooking-place	kosina,* dapol-an	dapor
Cool	haggut ·	sejuk
Copper	tūmbāga	tambāga-mérah
Copra (sp.)	lahing-tahai	īsī-nīor
Copulate	măg-īut, măg-kindoh, kioh	hamput, sa'tūboh
Copy	sālin	sālin
Coral	sahasah	kārang
Cord	lūbid	tālī
Cork (stopper)	hūlat, dabus-an	sumbat, prop
Corn (maize)	gandom	jāgong

* Spanish, "Cocina."

ENGLISH.	SULU.	MALAY.
Corner (inward)	*pēju*	sīkū
,, (outward)	*dugu*	penjūru
Corpse	*maiat*	mayit
Corpulent	*tambăk*	gumok
Corrupt (bribe)	*dīhil sāăb*	bri súāb
Cosmetic	*burak*	badak
Cost (price)	*hāga*	harga
,, (prime)	*puhun*	pōkō
Costly ; dear	*m·thonet*	mahal
Cotton (bush)	*gāpas*	kāpas
,, (tree)	*kāpok*	kāpok
,, thread	*tingkal*	benang
Couch, a	*kolang-an*	tămpat-bāring
Cough, a	*ūbuh*	batok
Coulter (of a plough)	*sūlab, sēlab*	pisau tanggāla, nājam
Council (assembly)	*maupakat*	himpūn-an
Count, to	*hītong*	bilang, hītong
Countenance	*bāihu, bāihok*	mūka
Country	*banūa, lopa, hulah*	negrī, tānah
,, (interior)	*gimbah*	ūlu
Countryman (rustic)	*gimbahan-an*	orang-ūlu, ōrang-dūsun
Couple, a (pair)	*angka pāsang*	sa`pāsang
,, , a married	*dua mñg-tiaun*	laki-bīni
Course (direction)	*tūju*	tūju
Course (way)	*rān, dān*	jālan
Court-yard	*halāman.*	alāman

ENGLISH.	SULU.	MALAY.
Courteous	*tangkai, suman*	sūpan
Courtesan	*sundal*	sundal
Cousins	*tungad minsan*	sa'pupu
,, , second	,, *maka ruā*	dua sa'pupu
Cover, to	*tirong*	tūdong, tūtup
,, , a	*tirong-an*	tūtup-an
Cow	*sāpī ōmagak*	lembū betīna
Cowardly	*sabol*	chābar
Crab	*kagang*	ketam
Crack, to (the joints)	*lagupuk*	lantik
Crackers (fire works)	*tembak-tembak*	merchun
Crackle	*kūlapi*	latop, latos
,, (as wood in a fire)	*laginit*	,.
Cradle (suspended from a beam)	*buahan, buah-buah*	buayan
Craft (cunning)	*akal*	tīpū
,, (vessel)	*prau, sakai-an*	prau
Crank (of an engine)	*king-king*	uling
Crawl (on all fours)	*mananap*	merangkok
,, to (creep)	*kura kura*	me-lata
Crease, a	*ilah-an*	kedut
,, , to fold	*ilah*	lipat
Create	*men-jadi*	men-jadi-kan
Creator (God)	*Tuan Allah*	Tuan Allah

ENGLISH.	SULU.	MALAY.
Creek	*anak sobah, trusan*	anak sungi, trusan
Creep, to	*mananap*	rayap
Crescent	*būlan langkong*	būlan lang-kong
Crew (of a vessel)	*sakai*	awak, klassi
Cricket, a	*tŭgad tŭgad*	chingkrek
Crime	*sāh, dosa*	sālah, dōsa
Cripple	*tongkah*	ōrang tempang
Crisp (as dry leaves)	*lapok*	misi, kring
Crocodile	*būaya*	buāya
Crooked	*kabig-kabig*	bengkok
Crop	*umā-han*	per-umā-an
Cross (crucifix)	*salib*	salib
Cross over, to	*humuntas, limiu*	meniabrang
Cross-road	*sempang*	sempang
Crow	*wāk*	gāgak
,, to (as a cock)		kŭkuk
Crowd, a	*tau-sākien*	kumpūl-an ōrang
Crowded	*ma-simbūl*	ramei
Crown, a	*karūna*	makuta
,, (of the head)	*umbun-umbun-an*	ūbun-ūbun
Crude	*hālan*	mantah
Cruel	*bīngis*	bīngis
Crush	*na-liumbut*	tindis
Crush (to pieces)	*ma-tūmū,*	hanchur
Cry (to weep	*tangis*	menangis

ENGLISH.	SULU.	MALAY.
Cry (to shout)	sūalak	sūrak
Cucumber	maras	tīmon
Cud	sopah	bīak
Cud, to chew the	mŭg-sopah	mamah bīak
Cultivate	tianam, mŭg-āma	tānam
Cunning	akal	àkal
Cup, a	sāwan	chāwan
,, (a bowl)	pinggang *	mangkok
Cur	edok	kūyuk
Cure (to heal)	nŭg-obat, ka-huli	men-iumboh
Curly (as hair)	kŭlong-kŭlong	kerenting
Current (tide)	hāus, sūg	hārus
Curse (impreca-tion)	sŭgnah, intok	kūtok, lanat
Curse, to	nŭg-intok	meng-utok-i
Curtailed	tipukol	pendek
Curtains	kulambau, langsei	kulambū
Cushion	ō-an	bantal
Custard-apple	atis	serī-kāya
Custom (practice)	hadat, ādat, tabiat,	ādat, chāra
Customs (excise)	sūkai	chūkei, bēs
Cut, to	hoyah, utud	pōtong
,, (hack)	tigbas	tatak
,, in two, to	sīpak	panggal
,, off	utud, utur-an	meng'rat
Cuttle-fish	kula-butan	īkan-gorita
Cylindrical	tībok	būlat, pāras
Cymbals	tinting	charachak

* A *pinggang* in Malay is a plate.

ENGLISH.	SULU.	MALAY.
Dagger	*kalīs, takus*	krīs, sēwā
Daily	*hadlau-hadlau*	hārī hārī
Dam, to	*tambak*	bandung
Damaged	*kangi*	rōsak
Damascened	*lūmah*	ber-pāmor
Damp	*ma-himil*	langas
Damsel	*būjang*	būjang
,, (virgin)	*dāgah*	anak dārah
Dance	*pengālaī, mengālaī, mūg-jōgīt*	menārī, tārī jōgēt
Dandruff	*hāgikhik*	dākī, gūrak
Dandy, a	*helbat*	hebat
Dangling	*juntai*	berjuntei
Dare, to	*maka-aisṅg*	barānī
Dark	*tigidlam*	galáp
Darling	*ka-kāsi*	ka-kāsi
Dates (fruit)	*kolma*	khurma
Dash down	*ampas, bingit*	ampas, būang
Daughter	*anak babai*	anak peramp-ūan
Daughter-in-law	*anak-an babai*	menantū perampūan
David	*Dāud*	Dāud
Dawn (sunrise)	*sābūh-sūbūh-adlau*	dinī-hārī
Dawn, before	*lapit adlau*	pāgi-pāgi-scali
Day	*adlau*	hārī
Day, mid	*ogtoh sūgah*	tengah hārī
Dazzling	*kanau-kanau*	gomīlang
Dead	*matāi, miatai*	māti

ENGLISH.	SULU.	MALAY.
Dead	marihang *	mampus
,,	ma-lindong †	mangkat
,,	malohom ‡	marhum
Deadly	bīsa	bīsa
Deaf	bīsu, tūlī	pukak, tūli
Deal (to traffic)	mãg-dagang	men-iiga
Dear (expensive)	mahonet	mahal
Dearth	gutom	ka-lapār-an
Death	ka-matāi-an	ka-matī-an
Debate, to	beshala	mem-bechāra
Debt	ātang	hūtang
,, (time to pay)	tanggoh	tanggoh
Debtor	in tūga ātang	īang berūtang
Decant, to	mãg-hain	salin
Decayed	haloh	būsuk
Decease	lindong	mangkat
Deceive, to	haianat, mãg-tali, mãg-akal, mãg dapat	tīpu, mem-būjok, semū-kan, menīpu
Deception	ka-rapat-an, ka-akal-an	ka-tali-an, dāya, semū
Deck (of a ship)	lantai, dẽk	tingkat, dek
,, (of a prau)	lantai	jūbong, lantai
Decree	tītah	tītah
Deduct	dag-dag-i, kolang-i	korang-kan
Deep	mālim	dālam

* Used when speaking of Unbelievers.

† Used when speaking of personages of Royal Blood.

‡ Used when speaking of Sultans only.

ENGLISH.	SULU.	MALAY.
Deeply-laden	*tugub*	sarat
Deer	*āsa*	rūsa
Defend	*mŭg-sagak*	lindong-kan
Deficient	*kōlang*	kōrang
Deflower (rape)	*tangkog, īusibah*	rūgūl
Deformed	*kāng-kāng, māpīo*	chāpik
Defray	*mŭg-dihil bālanja*	bāyer blanja
Defy	*meng-ātu, omātu*	melawan
Degrade	*mŭg-bukog*	pīchat
Delay, to	*lalai, hali*	lalei, līna
,, payment. to	*tanggoh*	tanggoh
Delirious, to be	*mŭg-līgau-lēgau*	ber-īgau-īgau
Deliver (release)	*tabus*	lepas
Deliver, to	*dumihil*	sarah-kan
Deluge	*dūnok*	āyer bah
Demand (ask)	*mangaioh*	minta
Demand, a	*pangaioh-an*	per-mintā-an
Demise	*malohom*	murhum
Demolish	*lābuh*	rōboh, runtoh
Demon	*sāitan, jin, hantu*	shētan, hantū
Dented	*sŭmbing*	sŭmbing
Deny	*mŭngkil, lŭkoh*	mungkir
Depart	*katoh, ēg, mēg*	pergi
Depart (return)	*mūi, mināi*	pūlang
Depth	*halŭm*	dālam
Derange, to	*jag jag*	rōsak, kachau
Deranged (mind)	*gīla*	gīla
Descend	*mānog*	tūrun ·
,, a hill, to	*lumūd*	,,

ENGLISH.	SULU.	MALAY.
Descend a tree, to	*lumurus*	turun
Desert, to	*bingit-an*	tinggal-kan
Desire, a	*kahandāk*	kahandak
Desire, to	*bimbang*	bimbang
Desist	*dūmahong*	berhentī, dīam
Despair	*gūmon-tūd in atāi*	pūtus-asa
Destiny	*sūkūd*	nasīb
Destitute (bereft)	*wāi-run mās-an*	būlus, piātū
Destroy	*na-larak*	rosak
Detain	*ka-put-an,ha-wir-an*	men-āhan
Detest	*binshi*	binchi
Deviate	*sigpang, tālibas*	simpang
Devil	*shaitan, sāitan, jin*	shētan, iblis
Dew	*aloh*	āmbun
Dewlap	*lingayat*	jūmbul
Dhotu	*sūlit*	chawat
Dialect	*bahasa, lagam*	bhāsa
Diamond	*intan*	intan
Diarrhœa	*picg-intahu intahu, chāyar*	gāchar, chīrit lindir
Die (death)	*matāi, lindong, malohom*	mātī, mangkat, marhum
Differ (difference)	*doain, bīdah, basalah*	chidera, bīdah, ber-selīsih
Differently	*doain-doain*	lāin-lāin
Difficult	*ma-honet, payah*	sūsah, payah
Difficulty	*ka-sūkal-an*	ka-sūkar-an
Dig	*kali, kīalut*	gāli
Digitus	*tudloh*	jarī

ENGLISH.	SULU.	MALAY.
Dilatory	ma-bus-kaw	lambat
Diligent, to be	ūsaha, biskai	ūsaha, rājin
Dim	mŭg-ābun	rābūn, kābur
Dimensions	lagkŭ, laggŭ	ukūr-an
Diminutive	asiī	kechil
Dimsighted	mŭg-ābun in māta	māta kābur
Din	latah, bukag	gamaratak
Dine, to	santap	santap
Direct, to	hindoh, tudloh-a	tunjuk, tūjuk
,, (straight)	tulid, tāi	lūrus, trūs
Direct, to go	limaus	menōtong
Dirt	sagbut, kāput	sampah
,, (mud)	pīsak	lūmpor
Dirty	lōbag, ŭmēh	kōtor
Disagree	nŭg-sagah	ber-selīsih
Disappear	lainap	linniap
Discard	biugit	būang
Discharge a gun, to	tembak	pūsang, tembak
,, cargo, to	hāwas	ponggah
Disciple, a	mūlīd	mūrīd
Discontent	sākit hatai	sākit hāti
Discuss	mŭg-bechala	per-bechāra
Disease	sakit	pen-iākit
Disease, skin	ugihap	korap
,, (scrofula)	īkat	peniākit-baka
Disembark	ma-nog dien ha kapal, ma-nog pa lōpā	tūrun deripada kapal, naik dārat

ENGLISH.	SULU.	MALAY.
Dish (plate)	*lāi*	pinggan
Dish, a brass	*talam, dulang*	talam
Dish, a wooden	*bintang*	dulang
Dish, a square	*suntai* *	talam
Dishes (for food)	*ka-k'aun-an*	ka-santap-an
Disloyal	*dūlaka*	dūraka
Dismount	*ma-nog dien ha kūra*	tūrun
Dispatch	*pa-samut-an*	me-lekaskan
Displace	*pindah-an*	ūbah-kan
Displease	*bāngis*	bāngīs
Displeasure	*gūsar-an*	gūsar-an
Disposition	*palāngai*	parāngi
Dispute	*buntah*	tangkar
Disrespectful	*wāi rūn adat*	tiāda tāu ādat
Dissimilar	*doain-doain*	tiāda sāma
Dissolve	*ma-tīnoh*	anchur
Distant	*māioh, lāioh*	jāuh
Distress	*ka-sukal-an*	ka-sukār-an
Distribute	*nūg-bahagi-bagi*	mem-bhāgi
Disturbance	*hīlō-hāla*	gampar
Ditch	*gāta*	pārit
Dive	*lerop, limūrop*	men-yelam
,,	*mūg-sāp* †	,, ,,
Diverse (various)	*ginis-ginis*	jenis-jenis
Diversion	*naiam-naiam-an*	māin-māin-an
Divide	*bahagi*	bhāgi
,, (halve)	*sīpak*	bhāgi dua

* Made of brass.

† To dive for pear shell.

ENGLISH.	SULU.	MALAY.
Division	bahagi-an	bhāgi-an
,, (of a house)	selangan	ruang
Divorce	biugit, butas, bātan-an	talāk, cherai, lepas
Dizzy (to rock)	goyang	goyang
,, (giddy)	na-abong in māta	pening
Do, to	hīnang	būat
,, -not	aiāu	jāngan
Docile	tutut	jīnak
Dock (to crop)	tŭp-tŭp	rāgas
Doctor	tabib, mediko doktol	tabib, dūkŭn, bomo
Doe	ūsa ōmagak	rūsa betīna
Dog	crok, cdok	anjing, kŭyuk
Dog-vane	tanggal	tanggal
Dole-out	pansing	tupūd
Dollar	pelak	ringgit
Dollar, a gold	dūblūn	,, mās
Domesticated	tutut, ma-am	jīnak
Dominion	palentah	parentah
Donation	sampang, sadakah nŭg-dihil-an	pem-brī-an, sadakah
Done (finished)	hobus, bakas	habis, sudah
Don't	aiāu	jangan
Doomsday	adlau kiamat	hārī-kiāmat
Door	lawang	pintu
Double	dua ang lapis	dua lapis
Down(of animals)	būl-būl *	būlū *

* Also applied to hair on the body of persons and to feathers.

ENGLISH.	SULU.	MALAY.
Down (of plants)	*dapau, rapau*	būlū
Down-below	*ha babah*	di bawah
Down, to go	*ma-nōg*	tūrun
Downright (fact)	*būnal*	benar
Dowry	*dīhil-an*	brī-an
Drag, to (pull)	*utŭng, utny*	tarek
,, (anchor &c.)	*liad, liar-an*	lārat
,, after, to	*guiud, guiur-an*	īrit, hīrit
Dragon	*naga*	naga
Dragon-fly	*dahu-rahu*	bari-bari
Drake	*itek-ŭsog*	itik jantan
Draw (pull)	*hela*	tārĕk, hela
,, out, to	*larut*	chabut
,, (a curtain)	*lais-an, giais-an*	sangkap
,, (back)	*sñlŭt*	undur
,, (delineate)	*tūlis*	tūlis
,, (design)	*lūkis*	lūkis
Drawer	*ongsud-ongsud,*	lachi
	kūndīsa	
Drawers	*sawal*	serawūl
Dream	*na-naga inop, inop*	mimpī
Dregs (leavings)	*tuah-tuah*	kruh
,,	*tāi, lindang*	tāi, chīrit
Dress, to	*mam-akai*	pākei
Drift, to	*hianad, anud, pielis*	hānyut
Drink	*hinom, minom*	minom
Drive away, to	*duiu*	halau
,, a nail, to	*mŭg- lansang*	mem-akū
Drop, a	*angka tō*	tītek

ENGLISH.	SULU.	MALAY.
Drop, to	*tanak*	lūroh
Drown	*lunud, lūmūs*	tinggalam, lemās
Drowned	*matāi lunud*	māti lemas
Drowsy	*kierroh*	antuk
Drugs	*obat*	obat
Drum	*gāndang*	gandarang
Drunk	*heloh*	mābok
Dry	*tahai, ma-tahai*	kring
Dry, to	*nug-tahai*	kring-kan
,, (in the sun)	*buhad, buhar-i*	jemur
Duck, a	*itek*	itek
Due (debt)	*ūtang*	hūtang
Dugs	*pungau duruh*	māta sūsū
Dūkū (fruit)	*buahan*	lansat
Dull	*bingong*	bingong
Dumb	*āmahu*	bīsū, kelū
Dun, to	*samukut ūtang*	men-āgi-ūtang
Dunce	*dopang*	bodoh
Dung	*tāi, tāhī*	tāi, tāhī
Durian	*dūīan*	durīan
Durian, preserved	*likin dūīan*	
Dusk	*tigidlam, klam*	sīlam, kābus
Dust	*lumbut, tūmū, bā-gūnbun, maagbon*	ābū, duli, lubu, lūmat
Dutch	*Holanda*	Blanda
Duty (revenue)	*sūkai*	chūkei, hasil
Dwell	*hūlah*	tinggal, dīam
Dwelling	*bāi*	rūmah

ENGLISH.	SULU.	MALAY.
Dysentery	*pieg-intahu dūgūh*	chīrit dārah
Dye	*walna-han, palang*	chelap

Each	*tiap tiap*	tiap tiap
Ear	*tāīnga*	telinga
,, -ring	*bang*	krabu, sūbang
,, ,, pendant	*anting-anting*	anting-anting
Early (in the day)	*lapit adlau, sūbūh-sūbuh-adlau*	pada siang hārī, dinī hārī
,, (before)	*kaina*	dahulū
Earnings	*tangdīn*	gājī
Earth	*lopa*	tānah
Earth, the	*būmi, duniā*	būmi, duniā
Earthquake	*linog, jāgjag in lopa*	gumpah
Earthenware pot	*anglit lopa*	qualī tānah
Ease	*ka-sanang-an*	ka-senang-an
Easily (easy)	*mohai*	mudad-mudah, gampang
East	*tīmol*	tīmor
Eat	*ka-aun, ka-maun*	mākan
,, (repast)	*santap*	santap
Eatables	*ka-aun-an*	makān-an
Eaves (of a house)	*sengan*	berandah
Ebb-tide	*hūnas, lāng*	sūrut
Ebony	*āta-āta*	kāyū ārang
Echo, an	*ulangig*	bālas būnyi
Eclipse (sun)	*līahoh in sūga*	garahan
,, (moon)	*,, in bulan*	,, būlan
Economical	*hēmat*	hēmat

ENGLISH.	SULU.	MALAY.
Eddy	*leloh, limbuh*	ūlei, hārū
Eddying	*nŭg-pusal in tubig*	pusār āyer
Edge	*hegad*	tepi
,, , teeth on	*mang-īloh*	mjīlū
Edict	*tītah*	tītah, sabda
Educate(instruct)	*mŭg-hindoh, pŭg-anad*	meng-ājar
Eel	*kasih, kasil*	balūt
Efface, to	*nalawa*	meng-ilang-kan
Effects	*ata, ka-kana*	harta
Effort, to make an	*solai*	chūbā
Egg, an	*eklog*	tulor
,, -shell	*pais-eklog*	kūlit tulor
,, -plant	*tālong*	trōng
Egypt	*Banua Mīser*	Negrī Mīser
Eight	*wālŭ*	dūlāpan, lāpan
Eighteen	*hangpoh-tug-wālŭ*	lāpan-blas
Eighty	*ka-wālu-an*	lāpan-pūloh
Either	*atawa*	atau
Eject	*biugit, būgit*	būang
Elbow	*sīku*	sīku
Elder	*magolang*	lebih tūah
,, -brother	*magolang*	abang
,, -sister or brother	*kākah*	kākak
Elect, to	*peh-peh*	pileh
Elephant, an	*gājah*	gājah
Elephant's tooth	*gāring*	gāding
,, trunk	*mayong*	balālei

ENGLISH.	SULU.	MALAY.
Elephantiasis	ipol, bunta	ūntūt
Eleven	hangpoh-tīg-īsa	sa'blas
Elope	magoi	lārī
Eloquent	pandai mäg-pumong	pandei berkata
Else	malainkan, atawa	malainkan
Elucidate	mahawa-an	trang-kan
Emaciated	ma-kaiñg	kūrus
Emancipate	mahal-dika-an, sūd- an ha tan maraiau	brī-mardika, me-lepas
Embark, to (ship)	nñg-gaban ha kapal	nāik kāpal
„ „ (praū)	„ -sumakat	nāik praū
Embers	bāga	bāra
Emblem	indahan	upāma
Embrace	dākap, dākup	dākap
Embroided	puntas	sūjī, sūlam
Emetic	obat sūka	obat mūntah
Emigrate	pindah banūa	pindah negrī
Emissary	dāk-an	surūh-an
Emolument	ontong	ontong
Employ, to	mäg-tangdan	ber-ūpah
Employment	ūsāh-an	ūsāh-an
Empower	peig-kuasa, pia-palok	menguāsa
Empty	wai lñan, apā	kōsong, ampa
Emulsion (of the cocoa-nut)	gata-lahing	santan
Enamoured	lāsig	āsik
Enclosed (fenced)	pieg-ād	ber-pagar
End (point)	dōhol	ūjong

ENGLISH.	SULU.	MALAY.
End (of time)	*ahil*	akhir
End (of the world)	*hadlau-ahil*	hārī-kiāmat
Endeavour, to	*solai*	chūba
Endure	*sandal, maka-kaya-han, kamdus*	tāhan, derīta
Energetic	*kasai*	rājin
Enervated	*ma-lema*	leteh, lusū
Engine	*makīna* *	jentra, pesāwat
England	*Banua Anggalis, Lopa* ,,	Negrī Inggris, Tānah Inggris
English	*Tau Anggalis,*	Orang Inggris
Engrave	*ūkil*	ūkir
Enigma	*penalka*	penarka
Enlighten	*hawan-a*	trang-kan
Enough	*sarang, ganap, jukop*	sedang, ganap, chukop
Enquire	*asābū*	tānia
Enraged	*magama*	mārah
Enraptured		berāhī
Ensign (flag)	*panji*	bandēra
Enslave	*hinang-an īpun, īpun-an*	menjadi-kan hamba
Entangle	*sagnat*	meng-ūsut
Enter, to	*sūd, samub*	masok
Entertain (feast)	*piey-oira-han*	men-jāmu
Entrails	*lingan lingan, unud tīan*	īsī prot, tāli prot
Entrance (door)	*lāwang*	pintū

* Spanish ' Maquina."

ENGLISH.	SULU	MALAY.
Entreat	*pangaioh, mīki*	pohon, minta
Enumerate	*ītong*	bīlang
Envelope, an	*putas-sūlat*	sarong sūrat
Envoy	*dāk-an*	surūh-an
Epilepsy	*pūg-bāboi-baboi*	pētam bābī
Epistle	*sūlat*	sūrat
Equal	*salī-salī, salī*	sāma
Equal, to	*singud*	tāra
Equip, to	*paniap, chakap*	me-langkap
Equipment	*ka-paniap-an*	ka-langkāp-an
Equity	*sūlāh*	ādil
Era (Mahome-dan)	*hajerat*	hejerat
Erase	*kagis*	kīkis, hāpus
Erect (set up)	*pieg-bangun*	men-dīrī-kan
Err	*pieg-sāh*	ber-sālah
Eruct, to	*sigub*	blahak
Eruption, skin	*ūgūd*	kūdis
Escape, to	*pagoi, magoi*	lārī, lūput
Eschar	*kūgang*	salaput
Escort, to	*hiatud*	antar
Espy, to	*hengon, hēng-an*	tintang
Essence (sub-stance)	*unul*	ūjūd
Essential	*sobai*	wājib
Ethiopian	*habsh*	habshī
European	*Tau-pūteh*	Orang-pūteh
Even (level)	*dātag*	rāta, datar
,, (number)	*ganap*	ganap

ENGLISH.	SULU.	MALAY.
Evening	*mahapun*	patang
Event (affair)	*palkala*	perkara
Ever	*tap-tap*	pernah
Every	*ka-tan-tan, lun-lun, sakali-an*	sagala, skali-an se-ganap
Evil	*mang-i*	jāhat
Evil-spirit	*jin*	jin
Ewe	*bili-bili ūmagak*	bīrī-bīrī-betīna
Exact	*āmūna, āmū*	betul
Exalt, to	*mam-gālār-kan*	mem-besār-kan
Examine	*paleksa*	pareksa
„ closely, to	*dūmāban*	pilat
Example	*lanjawan*	telādan
Exceed	*pakarāiau, tūd*	lampau
Excellent	*marāiau-marāiau*	baik skali
Except	*lual, ma-lain-kan*	hānia, me-lain-kan
Excessive	*lando*	terlālu
Exchange	*sambi, sumambi*	tūkar
Exclaim	*man-yabut*	meng-ūchap
Excrement	*tāi*	tāi
Excuse (pardon)	*ampūn-an, maaf-kan*	meng-ampūn, maaf-kan
Exert (one's-self)	*kasai kasai*	rājin-kan
Exhausted	*hiāpus, mahaẓus*	lētek
Exist (to live)	*boheh*	hīdop
Exist (to be)	*aun*	ada
Exorcise	*biugit sāitan*	būang sētan
Expand (dehisce)	*muskag*	kumbang

ENGLISH.	SULU.	MALAY.
Expect	*agan-agan*	me-nanti
Expedite	*pa-seyla-han*	segrā-kan
Expel, to	*biugit, hālau*	ālau, būang
Expend	*peg-balanja*	ber-balanja
Expense	*balanja*	balanja
Experienced	*biaksa*	biāsa, marāsa
Expert	*pandai*	pandei
Explain	*mam-baita*	trang-kan
Expose (to the sun)	*buhad*	jumor
Express (squeeze)	*mulajut, gipit*	prah
Expunge	*kagis*	hāpus
Exquisite	*maraiau pakaraiau*	ēlok, nàmat
Extend (the legs)	*ma-bing-kang*	kang-kang
Extensive	*hayang, lñag*	lāpang, lūas
Exterior	*ha-guah*	di-lūar
Extinguish	*pōng, pohong*	pādam
Extremity	*ñgbūs* *	gintas *
,, (extreme point)	*dohol*	ūjong
Eye	*māta*	māta
Eye-ball	*āgong-āgong māta*	bījī māta
Eye-brow	*kīlai*	kening
Eye-lashes	*pelok-māta*	būlū māta
Eye-lid	*takolaub māta*	kalūpak māta
Eye, pupil of the	*tau-tau māta*	anak māta

Face	*baihok, baihā*	mūka
Fade (as leaves)	*lāyū, lūmanñs*	lāyū
Fag-end of a cigar, the	*pūpūd dubla*	

* Used when speaking of branches, twigs, and plants.

ENGLISH.	SULU.	MALAY.
Fail (in business)	*holog,*	jātoh,
	*bag-bag in kongsi**	pechah kongsi*
Faint (swoon)	*pieg-baboi-baboi*	pangsan
,, (fatigued)	*lema-lema*	lelah, leteh
Fair (handsome)	*ma-pūtih*	permī, člok
Faith (religion)	*īmān*	īmān, dīn
Fall, to	*holog, hōg, legad*	jātoh
Fall, to (as leaves)	*pak-pak*	lūroh, gūgor
,, off, to	*tanak*	tanggal
False	*dusta, pūting*	dusta, bōhong
Family, a	*angka bāi*	īsī rūmah
Famine	*ka-gātom-an*	ka-lapār-an
Fan	*kab-kab*	kīpas
Far	*māioh, lāioh*	jāūh
Fare (passage money)	*chukai*	tambang, sewa
Farewell	*māī na aku,*	tinggal-lah,
	mārī na kāmi,	salāmat-
	mātoh na kāmi	tinggal
Fashion	*ādat, tabīat*	ādat, tabīat
Fast (quick)	*samut, ma-samut,*	lekas, pantas,
	buskai, ma-buskai,	lājū,
	dāgan, ma-rāgan	bāngkat
Fast, to	*puāsa*	puāsa
Fasten, to	*hiukut, hiugut,*	īkat, ūbong,
	būkū-han	tambat, ūlas
,, (as a sarong)	*man-amang, tamong*	īkat
Fat (corpulent)	*ma-tambuk*	gumok

* " Kongsi "—co-partnership.

ENGLISH.	SULU.	MALAY.
Fat (grease)	*daging, ma-raging*	lemak
Father	*amah*	bāpa
Fathom	*dupa, dapa*	depa
Fatigued	*hiapus*	panat
Fault	*sāh*	sālah
Favour	*kāsih-kāsih*	kāsih
Fear (dread)	*ka-boga-an*	ka-takut-an
,, (to be afraid)	*ma-boga*	tākut
Feast	*oirah-an*	jamū-an
Feast, to	*māg-oirah*	ber-jāmū
,, (festival day)	*hai-lāya*	hārī rāya
Feather	*bul-bul*	būlū
Features	*rūgbus, dagbus*	pāras
Feeble	*lema-lema*	lemah
Feed, to	*ka-maun, ka-aun*	mākan
Feel (touch)	*dimupun*	jāmah, jābat
Feeling	*pa-lasa-an*	rasa-an
Feet	*siki*	kākī
Feign	*āla-āla*	pūra pūra
Fell (cut down)	*pīla, mamīla, lapa**	tebang
Fellow (chum)	*īban, abai*	kāwan
Female	*babai* †	perampūan †
Female	*omagak* ‡	betīna ‡
Fence	*sasak, ād*	pāgar
,, in, to	*māg-ād, ād*	ber-pāgar

* " Lapa " means to cut and clear away undergrowth, bushes, grass, &c.

† Generally used when speaking of human beings.

‡ Generally used when speaking of animals.

ENGLISH.	SULU.	MALAY.
Fence (parry)	tangkis	tangkis
Fern (edible)	pakis	pākū
Ferocious	talon	gārang
Fester	mǎg-nānah	ber-nānah
Festival-day	hai-lāya	hāri-rāya
Fetch	dāhan mārī	bāwa
Feted	haloh	būsok
Fetters	ikang-ikang	rantei
Feud	bantah-an	per-bantah-an
Fever (calentura)	henglaw	damam
,, (ague)	tianding	kura
Few	tioh-tioh	sedīkit
Fiddle, a	bīola	bīola
Fibre	āgat	ūrat
Fickle	bimbang	bimbang
Fie	are!	chih!
Field	pantai	pādang
Fiend	sāitan	sētan
Fife	suling, hoinp-hoinp	sūling, bangsī
Fifteen	hangpoh-tug-līma	līma-blas
Fifth	in ka-līma	īang ka-līma
Fifty	ka-ima-an	līma-pūloh
Fight (to kill)	nǎg-būnoh	ber-bunoh
,, (contest)	nǔg-lorai	ber-klāhī
,, (to war)	nǔg-parang	ber-p'rang
,, cocks, to	takbi, būlang *	sabong
Fight,to(as cattle)	mǎgumagak,daukad	laga
Figure (of speech)	ibarat, upama	ibarat

* " Bulang " is the term to apply when gaffies are used.

ENGLISH.	SULU.	MALAY.
Figure (form)	*dugbus*	rūpa
Filigree	*lūkat-charo*	karāng-an
File, to	*kīkig*	kīkir
File, to (the teeth)	*lagnas*	dābōng
Fill, to	*lūan*	īsī
Fillip, to	*lugpi, labtik*	jintik
Filly, a	*kura daga-daga*	kuda gadis
Film	*lākāp*	kābur māta
Filter, to	*sāh-an*	tapis
Filth (rubbish)	*sagbut*	sampah
Filthy	*ma-umep*	chumar
Fin	*kapai, sik*	sīrip, sisik
Final (last)	*āhil*	akhir
Find, to	*ka-abāk, bāk*	dāpat
,, (look for)	*ka-put-an, pit-an*	chāri
Fine, to (mulct)	*nǎg-sāh, ma-sah*	denda
,, (in texture)	*lanoh*	hālus
Finger	*gālamai ha līma*	jārī
,, (fore or index)	*tudloh*	jārī tunjak
,, (middle)	*lusoh*	jārī tengah
,, (third)	*jali mānis*	jārī mānis
,, (little)	*kingking*	kalingking
Finis	*tammat*	tammat
Finish	*hōbus-an, puas-an, timus-an*	ābis-kan, pūtūs-kan,
Finished	*hōbus*	ābis
Fire	*kāyu*	āpi
Fire (flame)	*ma-lāga*	niāla
,, a gun, to	*tembak*	pāsang

ENGLISH.	SULU.	MALAY.
Fire, to set on	*butang-an kāyu*	pāsang-āpi
„ , to be on	*sūnog-an*	hangus
Fire-arm	*sanapang*	bedil
Fire-place	*ka-dapol-an*	dāpor
Fire-fly	*lambitong, klip-klip*	kūnang
Fire-wood	*kahoi dongol*	kāyū āpi
Fireworks	*tembak-tembak*	merchum
First	*tagnah, māna, ūna,*	pertāma, mūla-
	ha-ūna-han, ka-īsa,	mūla, jōlong,
	āwal	āwal
First-born	*ka-magōlang-an*	sūlong
„ and the last, the	*āwal ahil* +	āwal dan ākhir
Fish	*istā*	īkan
„ (dried)	*istā tahai*	īkan kring
„ , to catch	*bingit, ma-mingit*	panching
„ with nets, to	*mug-layah*	men-jāla
Fish-trap	*sangban* *	bubu *
Fish-hook	*bingit*	kail
„ , large	*kawil*	kail besár
Fish-spear	*sapang*	sarampang
Fishing-line	*hapūn*	tāli panching
Fishing-net	*pūkūt*	pūkat
Fish, to (M.O.P.	*mūg-bajah,* (dredge)	
Shells)	*mug-sāp, manuntong* (dive)	
Fist	*kūm-kūm*	ganggam, tēnjū
Fits	*sawan, baboi-baboi,*	sawan, pitam,
	gīla-baboi	gīla-babī

† Alpha and omega.

* Made of wicker-work.

ENGLISH.	SULU.	MALAY.
Five	*līma*	līma
Flabby	*lunyut*	lunak
„ (pendulous)	*buyog-buyog*	kupak
Flag	*pangi*	bandērā
Flagstaff	*tarok pangi*	tīang bandērā
Flame	*ma-lāya*	niāla
Flank	*kēd*	lambong
Flash (as lightning)	*mag-kīlat*	ber-kīlat
Flask, powder	*puntuk*	puntuk
Flat (smooth)	*punyah*	pīpeh
„ (level)	*dātay, rātag*	rāta
Flavour	*lāsa, anam*	rāsa
Flea, a	*kūtū-edok*	kūtū-anjing
Flee, to	*pāgoi*	lārī
Flexible (soft)	*lūnuk, lūmit, buyog-buyog*	lambēk. līat, lumbut
Fling, to	*teloh, paneloh, siapud, hiambat*	limpar, champak, lontar
Flint	*bātū āpī*	bātu āpi
Float, to	*liantop, lantop*	timbul
„ (drift)	*hianad, pielis,*	hānyut
Flood	*dunuk*	āyer-bah
Flood-tide	*tanb*	āyer-pāsang
Floor	*lantai*	lantei
„ , plank	*lantai digpi*	lantei pāpan
Flour (wheat)	*talīgū, tilīgū*	tepong
„ (rice)	*tapong*	tepong
Flower	*sumping*	būnga
Fluent (in speech)	*pandai mag-pamong*	pandei berkāta

ENGLISH.	SULU.	MALAY.
Flushed (face)	*ma-pūla in baihok*	mūka mērah
Flute	*pulautu*	sūling
Fly, to	*lōpad*	terbang
,, (musca)	*pīkit*	lālat
,, (large fly)	*langau*	pikat, langau
Flying-fish	*bingkis, tikbi*	īkang terbang
Foal	*anak kūra*	anak kūda
Foam	*būkal*	būhī
Fog (mist)	*gabun*	kābut
Foiled (worsted)	*tīwas*	tiwas
Fold, a	*ang lapis*	sa'lapis
,, , to	*lopī*	lipat
,, (enclosure)	*pagal*	kandang
Follow, to	*āgad, bunyog, urol, turol*	īkot, tūrut, īring, kajar
Follower, a	*īban*	kāwan
Fond (fondness)	*kasih-kasih*	ka-kasih-an
Food	*ka-aun-an*	makān-an
,, , cooked	*lutoh-an*	īmei, nāsī *
Fool	*babal, kāngog, dopang, bīngong*	babal, bōdoh, gīla, bīngong
Foolish, to be	*māg-lāngog, hasmak*	māīn bōdoh
Foot	*sīki*	kāki
,, (sole of the)	*pād sīki*	tāpak kāki
Foot-mark	*limpa sīki, bekas sīki*	bakas kāki
Foot-path	*dān, rān*	jalan
For	*būt-kalna*	kerna
Forbid	*lāng*	lārang

* Cooked rice.

ENGLISH.	SULU.	MALAY.
Forbidden	*halām*	harām
Force (strength)	*ma-tras, ka-gaus-an*	ka-kūat-an
Ford, a	*ka-lang-an, dasal*	langdai
„ (to wade)	*ūbog*	merandau
Forecastle	*dong-dong, dohong*	haluan
Foreign	*dowain*	asing
Foreigner	*tau dowain*	ōrang asing
Forefathers	*ka-āpō-apo-an*	nōnek mōyang
Forefinger	*tudloh*	jārī tunjuk
Forehead	*tuk-tūk*	dāhī
Fore-mast	*tārok ha-dong*	tīang tūpang
Foremost	*in ha-ūna-han*	īang dahūlu
Foreskin	*mūmūd*	kūlop
Forest	*kātian, golangan*	ūtan, rimba
Forever	*sa-logai-logai-nya*	salamalamanya
Forget	*lūpa, ka-lūpa-han*	lūpa
Forgive, to	*mūg-ampūn*	meng-ampūn
Fork, a	*tūksūk, tūgsūk*	garfū
Forked	*sāpan, sanga*	chābang
Form	*rūgbus*	rūpa
Former	*in ka-ūna-han*	īang dahūlu
Formerly	*nakauna, kaina*	dahūlu
Formidable	*ajaib*	heibat
Fornication	*pūg-bais-an*	per-sundal-an
„ (to commit)	*mūg-sundal*	ber-kendak
Forsake	*biugit, ēg-an*	men inggal kan
Fort, a	*kōta*	kōta
Fortune	*sūkūd*	nesīb
Fortunate	*maraiau sūkūd*	nesīb baik

ENGLISH.	SULU.	MALAY.
Forty	*ka-opat-an*	ampat-pūloh
Fosse	*gāta*	pārit
Foster	*īpat, palihula*	pīāra, paliara
Foul (as cables)	*sagnat*	sangkūt
„ (dirty)	*mumi*	chumar
Founder(as a ship)	*lūnūd, langkat*	kāram, gullā
Fountain	*tubur-an*	māta āyer
Four	*opat*	ampat
Fourteen	*hangpoh-tūg-opat*	ampat-blas
Fowl (bird)	*manok-manok*	būrong
„ (domestic)	*manok*	āyam
„ (wild)	*labuyoh*	āyam-ūtan
Fragrant	*ma-hamut*	harūm, wāng-ī
Fraud	*manīpā*	tīpū
Freckles	*intik-intik*	tāi lālat
Free (manumitted)	*mahaldīka*	mardīka
Freeman, a	*tau maraian*	prīnan
Freight	*lūan-an*	muāt-an
French	*Francis*	Orang-francis
Frenzy	*biñlākan*	kheialī an
Frequently	*abaran, ma-hūmū, mahang-mahang*	terkādang, ūlang-ūlang
Fresh (new)	*bāgū*	bāhrū
„ (not brackish)	*tabang*	tāwar
Freshet	*dunuk*	āyer bah
Friday	*adlau jamahat*	hārī jumāt
Friend	*bagāi, taimanghūd*	sohbat, sahabat
Friendly	*mug-selām dua*	ber-sohbat
Fright (fear)	*ka-boga-an*	ka-takūt-an

ENGLISH.	SULU.	MALAY.
Fringe	*jambā*	jala-jala, rambū
Frivolous	*ūla-ula*	olok-olok
Frog	*ambak*	kōdok, kātak
From	*dien*	deri
Front	*ha-rāp-an, ha-lop-an*	hadāp-an
Froth	*būkal*	būhī, ārū
Frown	*kimānāt, kānāt*	krot, karnyīt
Fruit	*bānga-kāhōi*	būah-kāyū, būah
Fruitless (in vain)	*kiog-an, sangsah*	sīa-sīa
Fry, to	*dang-dang, giuling*	gōring
Fuel (firewood)	*kāhōi-dongal*	kāyū-tambun
Fugitive	*tau māgoi*	ōrang-lārī
Full	*hipoh*	punoh
,, (satiated)	*kien subahan, puas*	kenniang
Full-moon	*būlan-damlag*	būlan-pernāma
Fun	*nāim-an*	gūrau, sanda
Fundament (anus)	*jubol*	tumbong
,, (bottom)	*būlī*	pantat
Fundamental	*asal*	asal
Funeral	*pag-kubal-an*	per-tanām-an
Funnel	*put-put-an*	chorong
Furl	*lunan*	golong
Furnace	*dapol-an*	dapor, tanūr
Fye	*chih*	cheh

Gable (of a house)	*songan*	songan
Gad, to	*lonsol-lonsol*	meng-ombāra
Gain (profit)	*untong*	lāba, ontong
Gaffles	*bulang*	taji

ENGLISH.	SULU.	MALAY.
Gain (to win)	*gimang*	menang
Gale (tempest)	*hūnus*	rībut
Gall (bile)	*apdu*	ampadū
Gallant (brave)	*pa-lāwan*	pa-lāwan
Gallop	*passo*	ūnggul
Gallows	*giantong-an*	peng-antong
Gambier	*gata-gambīl*	gambīr
Gamble, to	*mŭg-salah,*	māin-puakau,
	mŭg-gip-po,	māin-jūdī,
	mŭg-shugal	mang-sugal
Game	*pa-nāim-an*	māin-an
Gander	*āngsa ūsog*	āngsa jantan
Gape (to yawn)	*mang-iyab-an*	ganggang
,, , to	*ngānga*	ngānga
Garden	*kabūn*	kabūn
Gardener	*tūkang-kabūn*	tūkang-kabūn
Gargle, to	*mamai-mŭg-mŭg*	kūmor
Garlic	*bāwang pūtih*	bāwang pūtih
Garment	*tamūng-an*	pakāi-an
Garnet	*iākūt*	iākūt
Garrison	*tau sin kōta*	ōrang kōta
Gash (wound)	*pali*	lūka
Gate	*lāwang*	pintū
Gather (as fruit)	*ma-pūt, pūt-an*	pūngut
Gay (in dress)	*ma-jantih*	chantek
Gaze	*hangat, dūmūlag,*	pandang,
	man-dūlag, mang-alī	renong, amat
Geld	*kabīli-han*	meng-āsīm
Gem	*palmāta*	permāta

ENGLISH.	SULU.	MALAY.
Generous	*maraian hatāi*	mūrah hāti
Gentleman (sir)	*tūan*	tūan
Gently (slowly)	*ananai-ananai*	perlāhan-pālan
Get (obtain)	*kabak, bak*	dāpat
,, up, to	*bāngun*	bāngun
,, out	*pa-guah*	ka-lūar
Ghee	*lanah kābau*	mīnyak karbau
Ghost	*lōtau*	hantū
Giddy	*na-abong in māta*	pening
Gift	*būdī, bakti, sam-* *pang, kasih-kasih*	hadiah, sampa-na, pem-brī-an
Gills (of fish)	*asang*	īsang
Ginger	*loiah*	alīa
Girdle	*kandit, jimpau*	tālī pinggang
Girl	*bata-bata babai*	būdak-perampūan
,, (mistress)	*sandil*	gundik
Girth (of a saddle)	*bandot*	sabok
Give	*di-hil, domīhil*	kāsih, brī
,, back, to	*iulih-an, ūlih-an*	mem-balīk-kan
Glad	*senang-atāi*	senang-hāti
Glade	*pantai*	pādang
Glass	*kāsha, kāsa*	kācha
,, (mirror)	*sāmin*	chermin
,, (telescope)	*talompong*	trōpong
Glitter, to	*maidlap*	gomirlap, kīlū
Globe, the	*būmi, duniā*	būmi, duniā
Globular	*tībuk*	būlat
Gloom	*tigidlim*	kalám

ENGLISH.	SULU.	MALAY.
Glove	*tagoban-līma*	sārong-tāngan
Glue	*pīkit-an*	prakat
Glutton	*lagak, kalāgto, dahal*	glōjoh, tama, mājoh
Gnat	*hamah*	āgas
,, (mosquito)	*hilam*	niāmok
Gnaw	*tūkab*	kīkil
,, (to bite)	*man-ātkāt*	gīgit
Go	*katoh*	pergi
Go, to let	*ēg*	lepas
Go (proceed)	*song*	sorong
Go (to walk)	*panau*	jālan
Go in, to	*sūd, sūmūd*	māsok
Go up, to	*sakat, samakat, gaban, gomaban*	nāik, dāki
,, (to climb)	*rāg, dāg, domāg*	panjat
Go down, to	*nōg, ma-nōg*	tārun
Goat, a	*kāmbing*	kambing
God	*Allah-tàāla*	Allah-tāāla
,, (the Lord)	*Tūhan*	Tūhan
Goggle-eyed	*pirat in mātu*	māta bīlas
Gold	*balāwan*	amas, mas
., (dollar)	*dūblān*	ringgit-mas
Gone	*mināi-nah, bakas mināi, bakas panañ*	sudah pūlang, sudah jālan
Gong	*agōng, samarang*	agōng, chanang
Good	*maraiau, madaiau*	bāik
Good-bye	*mūi-nah kāmi, mūi-nah aku*	salāmat tinggal pūlang-lah

ENGLISH.	SULU.	MALAY.
Good for nothing	*wai gūna-gūna*	tīāda ber-gūna
,, , to make	*pug-daiau-i*	bāik-i
Goods	*ātu, altu*	harta, bārang
,, (merchandise)	*dagāng-an*	dagāng-an
Goose	*āngsa*	āngsa
,, (gander)	,, *asog*	,, jantan
Gore, to (to butt)	*man-andok*	menāndok
Gorgonia	*akal abahal*	akar albahar
Gormand	*lagak, kalagto*	glōgoh
Gourd, a	*lābā*	lābū
Govern	mam-alentah	mem-arentah
Governor	*gubirnārol,*	gubernor
Gown	*hujalat*	kabāya
Graceless	*chelāka*	chelāka
Gracious	*ka-lāsa-han*	kāsih, srī
Grade	*pangkat*	pangkat
Grain (seeds)	*bīgi-bīgi, binhih*	bīji, benih
Grand (great)	*dakolah*	kāya, besár
Grand-child	*anak-apoh*	anak chūchū
Grand-father	*apoh*	nēnek-lāki
Grand-mother	*apoh-babai*	,, perampūan
Grasp, to (in the hand)	*kam-kum-i*	ganggam
,, (in the arms)	*hakap-an*	peluk
Grass (generic)	*sagbut*	rumput
,,	*parang,+ bailī *	lālang †

* "*Bailī*" is a long creeping kind of grass which makes excellent fodder for cattle.

† "*Parang*" or "lalang" is a long and rank kind of grass.

ENGLISH.	SULU.	MALAY.
Grasshopper	*ampan*	belâlang
Grateful (thankful)	*tāima-han-ku*	īang trīma kāsih
Grating (lattice)	*sāisīk, sāisīy*	kīsī-kīsī
Gratis	*kāsih-kāsih*	sa-kāsih-kasih
Grave, a	*kūbūl*	kubūr
Gravel	*pāsil, karsik*	bātu klikid
Gravy	*sābau*	kūah
Graze	*māg-ka-aun sagbut*	mākan rumput
Grease	*dāging*	lemak
Greasy	*ma-raging*	ber-lemak
Great	*dākolah, ma-lāgkū*	besár, gadáng
Green (colour)	*gādong*	hījau
,, (unripe)	*būlak*	mūda
Greens	*sāyol*	sāyor
Green-snake	*hās gādong*	ūlar ijau
Greet, to	*man-āyina*	brī-tābek
Grey	*walna ūban-an*	warna karabau
Grey-hair	*ūban*	ūban
Grief	*ka-sūsah-an, ka-rūka-an*	ka-sūsan-an, dūka
Grit	*karsik*	pasīr
Grieve	*ma-sūsah*	me-rasā-i dūka
Grind (to whet)	*mang-āsah*	meng-āsah
Grind-stone	*bātu-āsah-an*	bātu-āsāh-an
Groan, to	*māg-ālōhi, kaloh*	mengrang
Groin	*ītah*	konchī pāuh
Groom	*sāis kūra, syce*	sāis kūda, syce
Groom's man	*pandala-ūsoy*	pungapit-lāki

ENGLISH.	SULU.	MALAY.
Grope	*ma-nanau, măg-sănau*	rūba, korek *
Ground (earth)	*lōpah*	tānah
Grow	*tābāh, tumābăh*	tumbuh
Growl	*ăgol*	ngarōng
Gruel	*mīstang*	āyer kanjī
Guana	*bībang*	bīāwak
Guard (to watch)	*tūnggū, jāga*	menunggū, jūga
„ (watchman)	*jāga-jāga*	ōrang-jāga
Guava (fruit)	*bīabas, makopa*	jāmbū
Guess, to	*tūkăd-tūkăd*	sangka, agak
Guide (to conduct)	*hīātud*	antar
„	*āmbit-an* †	pimpin †
„ (conductor)	*mālim*	màlim
Guilt	*ka-săh-an, dōsa*	ka-salāh-an
Gullet	*tūn-tūn-an, gūng-an*	korong-kūngan
Gulp (swallow)	*tāan, tūn*	talan, gōgau
Gum	*tāgok*	getah
Gums	*ngīloh*	gūsī
Gun	*bedil*	bedil
„ (musket)	*sanāpang*	snāpang
„ (ordnance)	*espil*	marīam
Gunpowder	*ōbat-sanāpang*	ōbat-bedil
Gush	*pānchōl*	panchor
Gutta	*tāgok*	getah
Gutta-percha	*kālāpīa*	getah merah
Gutta-percha tree	*ngatu* ‡	ngatu, balan
Guzzle	*la-lăk-lăk*	chāruk, īrup

* To find by probing; to clear or make a hole by poking.

† To lead by the hand.   ‡ Dich opsis gutta..

H

ENGLISH.	SULU.	MALAY.
Habit (custom)	*hadat, ādat*	ādat
,, of, in the	*bīaksa*	bīāsa
Hack (to chop)	*tūis-tūis*	tatak
Haggle (to bargin)	*tāwal-tāwal*	tāwar-tāwar
Hail, to	*tāg, ūlang, gāsūd* *	ruwah, sarū
Hair (of the head)	*būhōk*	rambūt
,, (of the body)	*bahīboh*	būlū, rūma
,, , fair-	*būlahau*	rambūt kūning
,, , grey-	*ūban*	ūban
,, , fine-	*būl-būl* +	būlū +
,, , to cut off the	*ūtūd, ūtūr-an būhōk*	rāgas
Hair-pin	*sāsūk-sanggol*	chūchūk-sanggol
Hair-less	*bangkulit*	bōtak
Hairy	*tūg-būl-būl*	ber-būlū
Half	*sīpak, tingah*	tengah, sapārō
,, (a part)	*ang-ūtūd*	sa-potong
Hall (public)	*bālai*	bālei
Halt (to limp)	*tōngkah*	pinchang, tempang
,, (to stop)	*dumuhong*	ber-hentī
Halve, to (divide)	*bahāgi dūa*	bhāgi dūa
,, , to (cut)	*ūtūr-an*	pōtong dūa
,, , to (split)	*sīpak-an*	blāh dūa
Hammer, a	*tūtukol, tūkol*	pemūkol, pūkol besī
,, , to	*puk-puk*	timpa, pukol
Hamper, a	*ambong*	karanjang

* To hail with the characteristic Sulu whoop.

† Applied also to feathers and the hair of animals.

ENGLISH.	SULU.	MALAY.
Hand	*līma*	*tāngan*
„ , at	*ma-sūk*	dekat
„ , palm of the	*pād-līma*	tāpak tāngan
„ , be led by the	*āmbit-an*	pimpin
„ , left	*līma ha lawa*	tāngan kīrī
„ , right	*līma ha tō*	tāngan kānan
Handkerchief	*sāpū-tāngān*	sapū-tāngan
Handle (of a kris)	*dāngān-an*	ūlū
„ (of a barong)	*pōhān*	ūlū
„ (of a hammer)	*tāngkai*	ūlū
„ (of a spear)	*ālisi*	ūlū
Hand's-breadth, a	*ang-pād*	sa' tampak
Handsome	*dūgbūs maraiau*	bāgus rūpa
Hang	*giantong, bītai-bītai*	gantōng
Happen	*man-jādī, man-jārī*	jādī
Happy	*senang-atāi*	senang-hāti
Harbour (bay)	*lōk*	telok
„ (anchorage)	*lāwig-an*	labūh-an
Hard	*ma-tras, ma-landoh*	kras, tegar
Hardship	*ka-sūkāl-an*	ka-sukār-ān
Hardy (bold)	*ma-īsūg*	barānī
„ (stout)	*tagoh*	tagoh
Harlot	*babai ka-lūgah-an, mabiga*	sundal, pendāyang *
Harmonious	*mālōi*	mardū
Harrow	*sūdlāi*	sīsir tānah
Harsh (severe)	*bīngis, bāngis*	bīngis, kras
Harvest	*mūg-ānī pāi*	per-umā-an

* Commonly used in Brunei.

ENGLISH.	SULU.	MALAY.
Haste, to	*ūs-ūs, sēgla, sāmūt*	gūpoh, segra, pantas
Hat, a	*sārōk*	chapīau, tōpī
„ (straw)	*sāpūio*	kōpīa
Hatch, to	*ma-mūsah, piusah*	men-atas
Hatchet	*kampak, kāpah*	kāpak
„ (native)	*patōk*	belīong
Hate, to (detest)	*bānshi*	binchi
Hatred	*ka-bānshi-an*	ka-binchī-an
Haul	*hēla*	hēla, tārek
Haunted	*tūga saitan*	ber-hantū
Have, to	*aun, tūga*	ada
Hawk, to (spit)	*mūg-kāhāk*	gārut
„ , a	*sambūlan, lāng*	wālī
Hay	*sagbut ma-tahai*	rumput kring
Haze	*gabun*	kābut
He	*sia, nia, sila, nila*	dia, ia, nya
Head	*ō*	kapāla, ūlū
„ (crown of)	*ūmbūn-ūmbūn-an*	ūbūn-ūbūn
Headache	*sākit-ō*	sākit kapāla
Head-dress ·	*pīs, būlang-būlang*	singal, destar
Headland	*tāndoh*	tanjōng
Headlong	*tīmōngke*	pūkang
Head-wind	*angin ha baihok*	angin di mūka
Heal	*ka-huli, mūg-obat*	men-iumboh
Health	*nanam*	nyāman, afīat
Heap (a pile)	*tabun-an, mīnd*	tambun
Hear	*dūngag, rūngag*	dengar
Heart	*jantong*	jantong

ENGLISH.	SULU.	MALAY.
Heart (spiritual)	*hatai*	hāti
,. (of wood)	*īsok*	tras
Heat	*ka-pāso-an*	ka-panās-an
Heave (throw)	*tēlo, lapud*	champak
,, up (weigh)	*bongkal-an, ōtong-an*	bongkar
Heaven	*shōlya, sōrga, sōga*	surga, shorga
Heavenly	*bidādāli*	bidādarī
,, beings	*anak* ,,	anak ,,
Heavens (sky)	*lāngit*	lāngit
Heavy	*ma-bōgat, bōgat*	brat
Hedge	*ād*	pāgar
Heed	*ingat, daiau-daiau*	īngat
Heel	*tīkūd-tīkūd*	tūmit
,, (to incline)	*ma-kīng*	singīt, mīring
Height	*tās*	ka-tinggī-an
Heir	*wāris, walis*	wāris
Heir-apparent	*lāja-mura*	rāja-mūda
Heir-loom	*pāsaka*	pusāka
Hell	*nālka*	nārka, narāka
Helm	*bānsan*	kamūdī
Helmsman	*jūlo mūdī*	jūro-mūdī
Help (to assist)	*tābang*	tōlong
Hem, to (fell)	*kēkēm*	klem
Hemp-plant	*lānāt* *	pīsang tālī
Hen (domestic)	*manok ōmāgak*	āyam betīna
Her	*sia, nia, sila, nila*	ia, dia, nya
Hers	*kan sia*	dia pūnia
Here	*dī, di-ha-īni*	sīni, di-sīni

* Musa textilis: Bisaya, "abaka."

ENGLISH.	SULU.	MALAY.
Heretic	*mūltad* *	murtadd *
Hernia	*mustik*	būrut
Hermaphrodite	*bāntūt, papua*	pāpak, banchī
Herself	*īsa-īsa-nya,*	dia sindīri
	bārān-nya	
Hiccup	*sioklah, siokloh*	sedū
Hide, to (conceal)	*tapōk, timapok, libun*	sembūnī-kan
,, (take shelter)	*selong, mug-hali*	ber-selindong
,, (skin)	*pais*	kūlit
High	*ma-tās*	tinggī
High-spirits	*gumbīl-an*	gambira
High-water	*taūb dākolah*	hābis pāsang
Highway	*dān dākolah*	jālan rāya
Highwayman	*shugarol*	peniāmun
Hill	*bād*	būkit
,, , ant-	*banki, bōki*	pusu
Hilt	*pōhan, tāngkai*	ūlū
Hilly	*ma-bād-bād*	ber-būkit
Him	*sia, nia, sila, nila*	dia, ia, nya
Himself	*baran-nya,*	dia sindīri
	īsa-īsa-nya	
Hinder, to	*hāwid-an, hawir-an*	tegah-kan
Hinder-part	*būlī*	būrīt
Hip (haunch)	*pigi*	pangkal pāha
Hire (of labour)	*tangdan*	ūpah
,, (of a house)	*chukai, sūkai*	sēwa
His	*kan nia*	dia pūnya
,, own	*kan nia īsa īsa nya*	dia sindīrī pūnya.

* Applicable to Mahomedans only.

ENGLISH.	SULU.	MALAY.
Hit	*kiĕgdān*	kena
,, (strike)	*lobak*	pŭkul
Hither	*ka-rī*	ka-mārī,ka-sīni
Hitherto	*āmpā bi-h'aūn*	sampei skārang
Hoarse	*līagāñ-an*	pāro, gāro
Hoe	*sāngkol*	changkol
Hog	*baboi*	bābi
Hoist	*būhat*	angkat
Hold (grasp)	*ma-pūt, kaput*	pegang
,, (stop, retain)	*bŭg-bŭg*	tahan
Holdout (endure)	*maka-kaya-han*	tahan
Hold (of a ship)	*lūang*	polka, pĕtak
,, one's peace	*dāmahong, duhong*	diam
Hole	*lūngag, līang*	lōbang, liang
,, , buffalo-	*lublub-an*	kubang
Holiday	*adlau hai lāya*	hārī rāya
Holland	*Banūa Holanda*	Negrī Blanda
Hollow, a	*lūbak*	lakok
Homage	*hōlmat, sambah*	hormat
Home (house)	*bāi*	rūmah
,, , at	*ha-kāmoh*	di-rūmah
Hone	*bātu-āsāh-an*	bātu-āsah
Honest	*tūlid*	lūrus
Honey	*tūnōb, tūnŏp*	madū
Honour (respect)	*hōlmat*	hormat
,, (dignity)	*ka-mulī-an*	ka-mulī-an
Honourable	*dākolah*	ter-nāma
Hoof	*kuku sīkī*	kūkŭ
Hook, a	*bīngīt*	kāīl

ENGLISH.	SULU.	MALAY.
Hook, a (large)	*kāwīl*	kāīl besár
,, , to	*sābit*	kāyit
,, , bill-	*ûtak*	pārang
Hoop, a	*būka*	simpei
Hop, to	*laksû*	lompat
Horizon	*hīgad lāngit*	tepī lāngit
Horn	*tandok*	tandok
Hornbill	*tāūsi*	būrong enggan
Horse	*kūda, kūra*	kūda
Horse-race	*māg-lōmba kūra*	ber-lomba kūda
Hot	*pāso*	pānas
Hour	*jām*	jām
House	*bāi*	rūmah
How	*bīadien, bīardien*	bagimāna
,, many or much	*pēla*	brāpa
,, long	,, *in hābah*	,, panjang
,, long (time)	,, *lōgai*	,, lāma
,, often	*māka pēla*	,, kāli
,, do you do	*maraian na kah*	ada bāīk
However	*sāgūah*	akan tetapi
Hue	*wālua*	warna
Hug	*nāg-gūlgūl*	pelūk, dākap
Huge	*ma-luggû pakaraia*	uter-lālu besár
Hull (of a vessel)	*baran kapal*	badan kapal
Hum, to (as bees)	*lagunglung*	ber-dengong
Human	*mānusīa*	mānusīa
Hump	*pūgau*	kandūng
Humpback	*būgol*	bongkok
Hundred	*rātus, gātus*	rātus

ENGLISH.	SULU.	MALAY.
Hunger	*hiāpdi*	lāpar
Hunt, to	*pānhut*	būrū, bārah
Hurl	*tēloh*	limpar, **lūtar**
Hurly-burly	*hīlo-hālo*	hīru-bīrū
Hurricane	*hunus*	rībut, tūfān
Husband	*ebāna*	lāki, swāmī
Husk (of paddy)	*hāpa*	sekam
,, (of cocoanut)	*būnāt*	sābūt

I	*aku, pātek, kāmi*	aku, pātek, **sāya**
Ice	*ayel bātu*	āyer bakū
Idea	*āgī, sāmbat*	akal, sangka
Idiot	*dōpāng, gīla, babal*	bōdoh, gīla
Idle (indolent)	*ma-huskau*	mālás
,, (negligent)	*lalai*	lālei
Idol (spirit)	*bāla*	berāla
If	*bāng, pabīla*	jekalau, kālau
Ignite	*sōh-a*	pāsang
Ignorant	*dōpāng*	bōdoh
Ill (sick)	*mangi-lasa, sākit*	sākit
Ill-bred	*wāi ma-ingat hadat*	kōrang bhāsa
Illegal(forbidden)	*hālam*	hāram
Illicit (trade)	*lāng-an*	lārang-an
Illness	*sākit*	peniākit
Illuminate	*ma-sawa-han*	trang-kan
Image (likeness)	*pātā*	gambar
Imbricated	*sūsūn-sūsūn*	tindeh
Immediately	*bīh'aūn, bihaiaun*	s'kārang īni
Immense	*dākolah tūd*	besár s'kali

ENGLISH.	SULU.	MALAY.
Immodist	*wāi sīpŭg*	kŏrang mālŭ
,, (obscene)	*sābŭl*	chābul
Impede	*sankut*	sangkŭt
Implements	*ka-pāniap-an*	pukākas, ālat
Impossible	*di tŭd man-jādī*	ta'buli s'kali
Impossible!	*mūstahil!*	mŭstahil!
Impost	*chūkai, ñsōl, bea*	ūsōr, chukei
Impotent	*līogbai*	lemah zakar
Improper	*būkŭn maraiau*	kŏrang pātut
Improve	*pūg-daiau-i*	mem-bāīk-i
In	*halŭm, halam*	dālam
Inactive	*ma-lulai*	lālei
Incest	*sūmbang*	sūmbang
Inclination	*ka-baya-an*	ka-andak-āti
Inclosure (fence)	*pāgal, kāndāng*	kandang, pāgar
Incomplete	*kīlang ganap*	kŏrang ganap
Increase	*dūang, sūmūnūh*	tambah
,, (to add)	*pa-lebih-lebih-an*	me-lebih-kan
Incurable	*di-maku ka-ulih-an*	tiāda de per-sumboh
Indecent	*sābul*	chābur
Indeed	*būnal-būnal*	sunggoh-sunggoh
Indian	*Kaling*	Kling
Indian-corn	*gāndom*	jāgong
India-rubber	*tāgok litahan*	getah līchah
Indigent	*miskin*	meskin
Indigo	*anjibi*	nīl, tārŭm
Indolent	*ma-huskau*	mālás
Inebriated	*hēloh*	mabok

ENGLISH.	SULU.	MALAY.
Inexperienced	*būkūn bīaksa*	ta' biāsa
Infant	*anak-asīvī*	anak-kechil
Inferior	*kōlang maraiau*	kōrang bāīk
Infidel	*kāpil, tāu lanat*	kāfir
Inform (instruct)	*anad, hindoh*	ājar
,, (acquaint)	*baīta-i*	brī tāhu
Inheritance	*pāsaka,paniggal-an*	pusāka
Ink	*dāwat*	dawāt, tinta
Inkstand	*pa-rāwat-an*	tampat dawāt
Inland (interior)	*ha gimbah, ha-ō*	darat, di ūlū
Innocent	*wāi dōsa*	tiāda sālah
Inquire	*asūbu, mang-asūbu*	tānya
Insane	*gīla*	gīla
Insect	*bōk-bōk* *	bubok *
Inside	*halūm*	dalam
Insincere	*būkūn bānal*	būkan benar
Insolent	*ma-ninggad*	mākī, kāchak
Instant	*sa-sāat*	sa-sāat
,, (this moment)	*angka dāi-dāi īni*	sa-banter īni
Instead	*sūbli*	ganti
Instruct	*mug-hindoh*	meng-ājar
Insufficient	*wāi gānap, di abut*	tiāda chūkop
Insupportable	*di na ma-sindal*	ta' tāhan
Insure	*pōkē*	popia
Intellect	*akal, pāhām, budī, budiman*	ākal, pāhām, budī,budiman
Intelligence	*gāwi*	khabar

* This insect is very destructive to the wood and bamboo-work of
  houses.

ENGLISH.	SULU.	MALAY.
Intelligent	*tāga-akal*	ber-budī
Intention	*māksūd, sangajā*	maksūd, hājat
Inter (to bury)	*kābūl*	tānam
Interest(of money)	*anak-an, anak*	būnga wāng
Interior	*ha-lùm*	di-dālam
„ (of a county)	*gimbah, ō*	ūlū, pāsak
Interpret	*sālin*	sālin
Interpretation	*ībārat*	ībārat
Interpreter	*jūlō bāhāsa*	jūro bhāsa
Intersperse	*mūy-ūt-ūt*	selang-selang
Interview	*pūg-baīhok*	per-temū-an
Intestines	*lingan-lingan*	tūlī prot
Intoxicated	*hīloh*	mābok
Intrepid	*ma-īsog*	barānī
Investigate	*paleksa*	pareksa
Invulnerable	*kābūl, panglias*	kabal
Iris (of the eye)	*bīngkōl māta*	bingki māta
Iron	*bāsī*	besī
Irreparable	*di maka daiau*	ta' jādī lāgi
Is	*aun*	ada
Is not	*wāi*	tiāda
Is not, it	*būkùn*	būkan
Island	*pō*	pūlau, pūlo
It	*sia, nia*	dia
Itch	*ūgūd*	kūdis
Itchy	*gātal, gātùl*	gātal
Itinerant	*mūg-lonsol-lonsol*	ber-jalan-jalan
Itself	*īsa-īsa-nya*	dia-kindīrī
Ivory	*gāring, gāding*	gāding

ENGLISH.	SULU.	MALAY.
Jack-fruit	*nāngka*	nangka
Jacket	*bājū*	bājū
Jail	*pānjāla, jēl*	panjāra, jēl
Jambs (of a door)	*hīgad lawang*	janang
,, (sill & lintel)	*langkahan*	chupu
Jar (vessel)	*pūgah, būyong*	tampayan
,, (small)	*kībut*	taker, kībut
,, (flower pot)	*pasu*	pasu
Jatropha manihot	*panggi kahoi †*	ūbī kāyū
Java	*Jāwa*	Jāwa
Javanese	*Tau-jāwa*	Orang-jāwa
Jealous	*bāghoh*	chimbūru
Jevohah	*alah-talah*	āllah-tāāla
Jelly-fish	*bāngsābai*	ubor-ubor
Jesus	*Isa*	Isa
Jetty	*pantālan, pantān*	jambatan, tītī
Jew	*Iahudi*	Iahudi
Jeweller	*tūkang mas*	tūkang mas.
Jews-harp	*kūlaing **	genggōng *
Join (connect)	*sāmbong*	ūbong
Joint, a	*būkū*	sundi
Jostle, to	*dūgtol*	sontok
Journey	*ka-panau-an*	ber-jalān-an
Judge	*hākīm*	hākim
Judgement	*hukum-an*	hukum
Judgement-day	*adlau kīamat*	hārī kiāmat
Jump, to	*ma-ompat, laksū*	lompat
Jungle	*kātīan*	hūtan

* Made of bamboo.   † Tapioca.

ENGLISH.	SULU.	MALAY.
Jungle-fowl	*lābāyūh*	āyam ūtang
Jurisdiction	*pūg-palentah-an*	parentah
Just	*di mug dāpit*	ādil
Just now	*h'ēn dān, sin-īni-īni*	s'kārang īni
Just past	*kaina*	tādī
Juvenile	*bāta-bāta, sūbūl*	mūda

Kalong	*kābūg*	kalūang
Kamuning-wood	*bāntih*	kamuning
Keel	*lunas*	lunas
Keen (sharp)	*ma-hāit*	tajam
Keep	*itāu. tīau, tāu*	simpan
Keg, a	*pīpa*	pīpa
Kettle	*sīlī*	kendi, cherek
,, (earthenware)	*kāpsīo*	kipsiau
Kettle-drum	*gāndāng*	gandarang
Key	*chūchūk*	anak konchi
Key-hole	*tigbak-an*	lōbang ,,
Kick	*sīpah, simipah* *	sipak *
Kick	*man-akdūg, tākdūg* +	tendang +
Kid	*anak kambing*	anak kambing
Kid-nap	*man-īakau tāu*	menchūrī ōrang ,
Kill	*būnoh*	būnoh
,,	*sūmbai* :	sambilih :
Kin	*tāu-tāi-ānāk*	sānak
Kind (sort)	*gīnīs, ka-gīnīs-an*	macham, jinis
Kindle	*sōh, bōhe, lāga*	pāsang

* With the side or sole of the foot.   + With the sole of the foot.

: To kill animals for food with religious forms.

ENGLISH.	SULU.	MALAY.
Kindred	*kaum, tāi-ānāk*	dūsānak
King	*Lāja*	Rāja
King of spain	*Hari, Lāja Kastela*	Rāja Spaniol
Kiss	*sīum*	chīum
Kitchin	*kōsīna, dapol-an*	dapor
Kite, a (paper)	*tāgūri*	alang-alang
Kitten	*anak kūting*	anak kūching
Knee	*tūhūd*	lūtut
Knee-cap	*pinggan-pinggan-*	lūtut-
	tūhūd	tempūrong
Knife	*lāding, laring*	pīsau, lāding
Knife, clasp-	*laring piko*	,,
Knob (of a gong)	*būjal*	pūsat agōng
Knock against, to	*hāntak*	hantam
Knot, a	*biuku, būkū*	simpūl
Know	*ingat, maka-ingat*	tāhu
,, (understand)	*maka-hāti, hāti*	meng-arti
,, (acquainted)	*pahām, ka-ingat-an*	kanal
Know, I do not	*indai*	antah
Knowledge	*būdī, ilmu*	būdī
Knuckle	*būkū līma*	būkū jārī
Kris	*kālis*	kris

Labour (work)	*hīnāng-an*	karaja
Lad	*bātā-batā-ūsog*	būdak, būjang
Ladder	*hāg-dān*	tanggah
Lade out, to	*lelēmas*	men-imba
Ladle, a	*gāyong, hūnjūt,*	gāyōng,
	ūgah	tempūrong

ENGLISH.	SULU.	MALAY.
Lady	*dāyang*	setī, inchī
Lake	*lānau, dānau*	dānau, tūsek
Lamb	*anak bīlī-bīlī*	anak bīrī-bīrī
Lame	*singkang, bangkang*	tempang
Lament, to	*mäg-mātāi*	rātap
Lamp	*palītahan*	palīta
Lance (spear)	*bījāk*	limbing
Land	*lōpa*	tānah
Language	*bāhāsa*	bhāsa
Languid	*lema-lema*	leteh, lemah
Lantern	*tānglōng*	tenglōng
Lap	*gība*	pangkū, rība
Lap (lick up)	*dīlat*	jīlat
Lapidary	*pandai palmāta*	pandei permāta
Lard	*lānāh bābōi*	lemak bābi
Large	*dākolah, maslūg*	besár, gadáng
,, (spacious)	*lūag, ma-lūag*	lūas
Last	*in ha ulih-an tūd, ka-tapus-an, ahil*	īang di blākang s'kāli, ākhir
Last-born	*ka-bongsū-an*	bongsū
Last-night	*k'ābi*	sa'malam
Last-day	*adlau ahil*	hārī kīāmat
Last (to endure)	*sandal, kamdus*	tāhan
Late (in time)	*di sa-āt, ma-lālai*	lambat
Lately	*kaina, tāgua*	tādī
Lath (batton)	*būlah, banga †*	tatal
Lattice work	*saisik, sāisīg*	kīsī-kīsī
Laugh	*ka-tāwa, tu-tāwa*	tertāwa

* Made of bamboo.   † Made of anibong.

ENGLISH.	SULU.	MALAY.
Law	*hākām*	hukum
Lawsuit	*dawa, bechāla*	dawa, bechāra
Lay (to place)	*būtang*	tāroh, latak
Lay-by	*tiau, tāu*	simpan
Lay hold of, to	*sagau*	tangkap
,, eggs, to	*mang-eklog*	ber-telor
Lazy	*ma-hūskau*	malas, segán
Lead	*tinggah, tinkah*	tīmah-hītam
,, ,white (paint)	*sāt pūtch*	chat pūteh
,, , red (paint)	*sāt pāla*	chat mērah
,, (for sounding)	*prōm*	frōm
,, (to conduct)	*hīatūd*	antar
,, (by to hand)	*āmbit-an*	pimpin
Leader (chief)	*panghūlu*	pangūlu, kapāla
Leaf	*dāhūn*	dāun
Leak, to	*na hūd-hūd* *	mīris
Leaky	*tō*	tīris, mīris
,, (as a boat)	*būslot*	bōchor
Lean (thin)	*kāiüg*	kūrus
Lean against, to	*sāndig, sumāndig*	sandar
Leap, to	*laksŭ*	lompat
Learn	*ānād*	bel-ājar
,, the koran, to	*mang-āji*	meng-āji
Learned	*ālim*	ālim
Leather	*pāis*	kūlit
Leave, to	*maka-bīn, miaid* †	tinggal-kan
,, (permission)	*tūgāt, pasaran*	idzin, mōhon
,, (to sail)	*tumulak*	tōlak

*As grain from a torn bag. †"*Miaid*" is used by an inferior to a superior.

I

ENGLISH.	SULU.	MALAY.
Leavings	*tñah-tñah*	sīsa
Leach, horse-	*lintah*	lintah
Leach, land-	*limātōk*	achīh, pachat
Lecherous	*lasig, gātal*	kanjī
Lees (sediment)	*lidang, ākal*	chīrit, kruh
Leeward	*ha bābah hangin*	· di bāwah angin
Left (opposed to right)	*lāwa*	kīrī
Leg	*betis, pāhā, sīkī*	pāhā, kāki, betis
Leisure	*ka-tanam-an*	ka-senang-an
Leisurely	*īnūt-īnūt*	perlāhan
Lemon-grass	*sāi*	sarai
Lend	*bŭs-an, pǎg-bŭs*	me-minjam
Length	*hābā*	panjang
Lengthwise	*ōiun*	bujur
Lengthen	*ma-hābā-kan*	panjang-kan
Leprosy	*kūrō*	kūdal, kusta
,, (white spots on the skin)	*āp-āp*	panau
Less (in size)	*asīrī dien ha*	kechil deri-pada
,, (in number)	*kōlang dien ha*	kōrang deri-pada
Let (suffer)	*bīa, biah, bial*	bīar
Let go	*īg-i, butan-i*	lepas
Let (hire)	*sūkai*	sěwa
Letter (epistle)	*sūlat*	sūrat kirīm-an
,, (address of a)	*alāmat sūlat*	alāmat sūrat
,, (character)	*hūlup*	huruf
Level	*datāg*	rāta, dātar
Liar	*tau pūting-an*	pem-bōhong
Liberate	*īg-i*	lepas-kan
Licence (a permit)	*sāp bības*	chāp bības

ENGLISH.	SULU.	MALAY.
Lick, to	*dīlat*	jīlat, lūlum
Lid, a	*tūtŏp-an, tirong-an*	tūdong
,, , eye-	*takŏlaub mătu*	kalūpak mäta
Lie down, to	*kŏlang, kamŏlang*	bāring, limpang
,, on the back, to	*mŭg-duraiah*	talantang
,, , to (prone)	*nŭg-daraub*	tiārap
,, , a	*pūting*	bōhong
Life	*nīawa*	nīawa
Lift, to	*būhut*	angkat
,, (at one end)	*nagta, tŏngke*	jongkat
Light (opposed to dark)	*ma-sāwa*	trang, sīang
,, , day-	*sūbăh-săbăh-adlau*	sīang
,, (not heavy)	*ma-găban*	ringan
,, (to alight)	*timăpoh*	angkap
,, (as a lamp)	*sŏh*	pāsang
Lightning	*kīlat*	kīlat
Like (alike)	*salī, bīa*	sāma, bagei
,, (to desire)	*mŭg-ien, mau-bayak*	sūka, māu
Likeness	*ūpāma, pāntun*	upāma
,, (portrait)	*pāta tau*	gambar
Likewise	*dăkōman, īsab*	pūla, jūga
Limb	*anggăuta*	anggūta
,, (a haunch)	*pahā, pā*	pāhā, pauh
Lime (calx)	*bangkit*	kāpūr
,, (fruit)	*sñah manahut*	līmau nīpis
Limpid	*ma-lĕhau*	jernch, hening
Line (cord)	*lūbid*	tālī
,, (thread)	*saban*	benang
Lines of the hand	*gŏlis*	kōris

ENGLISH.	SULU.	MALAY.
Linger	*năg-hali, păg-hali-han*	ber-lengah
Lining	*lāpīs*	lapis-an, lāpis
Lion	*sīnga*	sīnga
Lip	*hĕgad sīmud*	bībir
Lisp, to	*kūtop*	gāgap
Liquid	*tūbig*	āyer
Liquor	*hinom-an, minom-an*	minom-an
Litigate, to	*măg-dāwa*	ber-dāwa
Little (small)	*asīrī*	kechil
,, (in quantity)	*tīoh-tīoh*	sedikit
,, while	*dāi-dāi*	sa-bantār
,, finger	*king-king*	kaling-king
Live (alive)	*bōhī*	hīdop
,, (dwell)	*hūlah*	dūduk, dīam
Livelihood	*ka-bōhī-an*	ka-hidōp-an
Lizard	*pinit*	chichak
,, , house-	*tōkĕ*	tōkĕ
Lo ! (behold)	*kītā-bah*	liat-lah
Load, to	*lāan*	mūat
Loadstone	*bātu balāni*	bātu b'rāni
Loaf of bread	*angka bīgī lōtī*	rōtī sa' būah
Lobster	*kañlang, kalīlang*	ūdang galah
Lock, a	*kānshi*	kunchi
Lock, to	*măg-kunshi, kiaunshi*	ber-kunchi
Log, a	*bātāng kāhōi*	bātang kāyū
Loiter	*măg-hāli-hāli*	ber-lengah
Loitering	*păg-hali-an*	lengah
Long	*hābah*	panjang
,, (time)	*mōgai*	lāma

ENGLISH.	SULU.	MALAY.
Long since	*mōgai-na*	sudah lāma
Long for, to	*lindang*	dindam
Look (to see)	*kīta, komīta*	lihat, tēngok
,, at, to	*hatud, pomʻio*	pandang
,, at indirectly, to	*mūg-lerong, harong*	meng-arling
,, at furtively, to	*heng, himeng*	
,, at earnestly, to	*man-dulag*	meng-āli
Looking-glass	*sāmin*	chermīn mūka
Loose (to unbind)	*ūbār-an, obad-an*	hūrei
Lord, the	*Tūhān*	Tūhan
Lose, to	*lāwa*	hīlang
,, (by gambling)	*sīang*	galah
,, (incur loss)	*lūgi*	rūgi
Louse	*kātu*	kūtū
Louse, to crack a	*hi mugbŭk, ūgbūk-an*	tindis
Love, to	*ma-lōi*	ber-āhī
Lovely	*maraian rugbūs*	élok pāras
Low	*bābah*	rendah
,, (in stature)	*pūndūk*	pendek
,, (in price)	*mohaī*	mūrah
,, water	*hūnas*	āyer timpas
,, (below)	*ha bābah, ha sūm*	di bāwah
Low, to (as cattle)	*mūg-mā*	meng-wa
Luck	*sūkūd*	nasib, mujur
Lucky	*maraian sūkūd*	nasib bāīk
Luminous	*sāia*	chāia
Lump, a	*kīumpul*	gompal
Lunatic	*gīla*	gīla
Lust	*lasig, hāwa, nāpsu*	hawā, nafsu

ENGLISH.	SULU.	MALAY.
Lustre	*sāia*	chāia, gamīlang
Lute, a	*sūling*	sūling
Luxuriant	*ma-lābong*	sūber, rampak

Machine	*makīna*	jantarā,pesawat
Mad	*gīla*	gīla
Maggot	*ûd*	ūlat
,, (wood worm)	*bōk-bōk*	bōbok
Magic	*hikmat*	hikmat
Magistrate	*hākim, māstirīb*	hākim,majistret
Mahomedan	*islām, slam*	islām
Maid (virgin)	*dāgā, būjang*	anak dārah
Mail, coat of	*lāmīna*	bāju rantei
Maimed	*pākōl*	kūdong
Maize	*gāndōm*	jāgong
Make, to	*hīnāng*	būat
,, (create)	*man-jādī*	men-jadī-kan
,, good, to	*mūg-daiau-i*	mem-bāīk-i
,, water, to	*mīhi, īhi*	būang āyer sinī
Malady	*sakit*	peniākit
Malay, a	*mālāyu, tāu mālāyu*	ōrang malāyū
Male	*ûsog, mandangan*	lakī-lākī,jantan
Malediction	*sūgnah-an,sāknah-an*	kūtok
Man, a	*tāu*	ōrang
Man-of-war	*kapal parang*	kapal p'rang
Mandate	*tītah*	tītah
Mane (of a horse)	*kābūlai*	gambong
Mango	*hāngtās*	kūrap binātang
Mango (large)	*wāni*	manggā

ENGLISH.	SULU.	MALAY.
Mango (small)	*mampalām*	mampalam
„ , horse-	*bāūnoh*	balūnuh
Mangrove	*bakaw, pagatpat*	bakaw, paratpat
Mangosteen	*manggis*	manggis
Mankind	*manūsia*	manūsia
Manner	*tābiat, ādāt*	chāra
Many	*ma-tāud*	bāniak
„ , how	*pīla in tāud nya*	brūpa bāniak
„ , ever so	*sākīan*	sekīan
Map, a	*pātā*	patah
Mare	*kūra omayak*	kūda betīna
Margin	*hīgad*	tepī
Mark	*īndān, gindān, sāp*	tanda, chāp
„ , foot-	*līmpa sikī*	bākas kāki
Market	*pārian, tāboh,*	pāsar, pakan,
	tīanggi	pudian
Marriage	*pieg-asawa, asawa-han*	kāwin
„ , rites of	*mūg-tiaun*	nīkāh
Marrow	*sûm-sûm*	ōtak tūlang
Marsh	*sāpa*	pāya
Masculine	*ūsog, mandangan*	lakī-lākī, jantan
Mash, to	*pipis-an*	pipis-kan
Mason, a stone	*tūkang bātu*	tūkang bātu
Massacre	*ka-būnōh-an*	ka-būnōh-an
Mast (of a ship)	*tarok*	tīang
Master	*tūan, tūg-īpun*	tūan, inchī
„ (of a ship)	*kapitan, nakōra*	kapītan, nakōda
Mat, a (of any sort)	*hānig*	tīkar, lampit
„ (made of pangdan)	*bāloi*	tīkar

ENGLISH.	SULU.	MALAY.
Mat (made of nipa)	*kājāng*	kājang
,, , ratan	*bûras*	tīkar rōtan
Matches	*bāgid-bāgid*	pendidip,maches
Mate (of a ship)	*malīm*	malīm
,, (companion)	*īban, abai*	kāwan, taman
Matter(substance)	*ānād*	zāt, ujud
,, (pus)	*nānāh*	nānah
,, , no	*di na āno, s'arī na*	tiāda mengāpa
Mattress	*tīlam*	tīlam, kasor
Mature (ripe)	*hīnōg*	māsak
May (can)	*maka-jādī*	būlih
,, be (possibly)	*kālō-kālō*	kālō-kālō
Me	*aku*	sāya, aku
Meadow	*pāntāi*	pādang
Mean (sordid)	*paisī*	kīkir
Meaning	*mānā, hatī*	ma'ana, artī
Measles	*sampal, ūtās*	chachar āyer
Measure, a (length)	*ākur-an*	hūkur-an
,, , to ,,	*māg-ākur*	hūkur-kan
,, a (capacity)	*sūkād-an*	sūkat-an
,, , to ,.	*mag-sūkād*	men-īukat
,, (one by one)	*tāpād*	sūkat sātu sātu
Meat (flesh)	*ānād*	dāging
Mecca (the city)	*Mūkkah*	Mekkah
Mechanic	*tūkāng*	tūkang
Meddle	*ūsībah*	ūsek,ūsah,jāmah
Medicine	*ōbāt*	ōbat
,, (remedy)	*tāmbal*	penāwar
Meditate	*pīkīl*	sangka

ENGLISH.	SULU.	MALAY.
Meet, to	*kiegdahan, bāk-an*	bertemŭ, jumpa
,, (proper)	*pātut*	pātut
Meeting	*kiegdahan-an*	ber-temŭ-an
,, (assemblage)	*ka-tāud-an*	ka-rapāt-an
Meliorate	*pīeg-daiau-i*	bāïk-i
Melodious	*ma-lōi*	mardŭ
Melon, water-	*tīmon*	mandīkī
Melt, to	*ma-ănchol*	anchor
Memory	*ka-tăm-tum-an*	ka-īngat-an
Mend (repair)	*pieg-daiau-i*	bāïk-i
,, a net, to	*pūnah*	bubul
Menial (slave)	*bata, īpun*	budak, hamba
Menstrual	*măg-dūgăh, dūgăh-an*	būlan-būlan
Mention	*sabūt, manyabūt*	sebut, meniebut
,, (relate)	*baita*	bilang, cherīta
Merchandise	*dagāng-an*	dagāng-an
Merchant	*saudāgāl*	sudāgar
Merciful	*ka-lāsa-han*	sāyang, kasīhan
Merely	*sāja*	sāja
Meridian	*ōgtoh*	rambang
Metaphor	*pāntun*	umpama
Meteor	*anŭnŭsol*	bintang ka-larāt-an
Method (mode)	*pāli-hăl*	pri-hal
Mew, to (as a cat)	*măg-īau*	meng-īau
Middle	*tengah, gītong, ŭt*	tengah
,, (the waist)	*hāwākan*	pinggang
Middle-finger	*jāī mānis*	jārī manis
Middling	*sārang*	sedang
Mid-day	*tengah-ādlau, ōgtoh*	tengah hārī

ENGLISH.	SULU.	MALAY.
Midnight	*tengah dūm*	tengah mālam
Midwife	*bāieran, man-ībau*	bīdan
Might (could)	*maka-jādī, maka-jārībūlih*	
,, (power)	*gaus, kūāsa*	kūāsa
Migrate	*pindah*	ber-pindah
Mild	*kapachut*	lembūt
Mildew	*kapu-kapu*	lapok
Milk	*gatas*	sūsū
,, , to	*kiawa gatas*	prah sūsū
Milliped	*labūd*	bagei halīpan
Mimic	*lūloi, uju-uju*	ajokan
Mina-bird	*tīong*	tīong
Mind (spiritual)	*hatāi*	hātī
,. (understanding)	*budī*	budī
Mine (possessive)	*ka-aku, kākū*	aku pūnya
	kan-patek	sāya pūnya
Minister (of state)	*mantīli*	mantrī
Mire	*pīsuk ma-habloh*	lichah, pichō
Mirror	*sāmin*	chermin
Miscarry (as a female)	*pak-pak in anak*	gugur anak
Miscellaneous	*īnda lopa*	macham-macham
Mischief	*kangī-an*	ka-jahāt-an
Misconstrue	*sāh in ka-hatī-an*	sūlah meng-artī
Miscreant	*jaulaka, daulaka*	se chelka
Miser	*tāu paisī*	ōrang kīkir
Miserly	*paisī, ma-ītong*	kīkir
Misfortune	*mangi sūkūd*	nasib jāhat
Miss (fail to hit)	*di kiegdahan*	tiāda kena
Mist	*gabun*	kābut

ENGLISH.	SULU.	MALAY.
Mistake	*sāh*	sālah
Mistress(concubine)	*sandil*	gundik
Mistrust	*di māg-andal*	kōrang perchāya
Misunderstand	*sāh in ka-hati-an*	sālah meng-artī
Mite (maggot)	*ūd*	ūlat
Mix	*lamād*	champur
Mixture	*ka-lamūr-an*	ka-champūr-an
Moan	*mūg-alohoi*	kāloh
Moat	*gāta*	pārit
Mock	*uju-uju, sumingut*	sindīr
Mode (method)	*pāli-hal*	prī-hal
„ (custom)	*hadat, tabiat*	ādat
Model	*sontoh*	telādan
„ (sample)	*lajawan, sontoh*	chontoh
Moderate(in price)	*būkun mahonet*	tiāda mahal
Molasses	*manīs-an tuak*	manīs-an tebū
Moment, a	*angka sāat*	sa'sāat
Monarch	*junjongan*	yang-de-per-tuan
Monday	*adlau isnin*	hārī isnin
Money	*pelak*	wāng
„ ready-	*tunai*	tunei
Monkey	*amok*	mūniet
Monopolize	*tūghan*	pājak
Monsoon (season)	*māsim*	mūsim
Month (moon)	*būlan*	būlan
Monthly	*ha būlan ha būlan*	būlan-būlan
Moon, the	*būlan*	būlan
„ , new-	*būlan bāgū*	būlan bāhrū
„ , full-	*būlan dāmlag*	„ pernāma

108

ENGLISH.	SULU.	MALAY.
Moonlight	ma-sawa in būlan	träng būlan
Moon (eclipse of)	līahoh in būlan	garahan būlan
Moon-rise	sumubang in būlan	būlan timbul
Moonless	kūp-an in būlan	tīdah būlan
Morass	sāpa	pāya
More	lebih, īsab	lagi, lebih
,, , no	wāi na īsab	tiāda lagi
Moreover	sahadan, īsab na	lāgī-pun
Morning	māināt, mahinat	pāgi
,, , early	māināt-māināt	pāgi-pāgi
Morrow, to-	kin-shūm	ēsok, besok
,, morning, to	kin-shūm māināt	besok pāgi
Mortar, a	lūsong †	lesong *
,, (cement)	bangkit	kāpūr
Moses (the name)	Mūsa	Mūsa
,, (the prophet)	nabī la Mūsa	nabī Mūsa
Mosque	masjid	mesjid
Mosquito	hilam	nyāmok
,, (gnat)	hamah	agas
Mosquito-curtain	kulambau	kulambū
Moss	lumūt	lumūt
Most	lebih-tūd	ter-lebih
Mother	īnah, indong	mak, ībū, bonda
,, , grand-	apoh babai	nēnek perampūan
Mother-in-law	ōgang-an	mertūa perampūan
,, -of-pearl-shell	pāis tīpai	kūlit mutīāra
Mould, a	tutuang-an	tuāng-an
Mouldy	kapu-kapu	lapok

* A wooden mortar, for holding paddy whilst being beaten to unhusk it.

ENGLISH.	SULU.	MALAY.
Mount, (to ascend)	*samakat, gomaban*	nāik, dākī
,, (climb)	*rāg, dāg, domay*	panjat
Mountain	*būd dākolah*	gūnong
,, (hill)	*būd*	būkit
Mountaineer	*tāu ha būd*	ōrang gūnong
Mouse	*ambāu asīrī*	tikus
Moustaches	*pāngōt*	mīsai, kūmis
Mouth	*sīmud*	mūlut
Much	*ma-tāud, ma-selūg*	bānyak
,, ? how	*pela in tāud*	brāpa bānyak
,, , very	*ma-tāud pakaraiau*	ter-lālu bānyak
Mucus	*sihpun*	īngus
Mud	*pīsak*	lumpur
,, , soft (mire)	*pīsak ma-hablo*	piche, lichak
Multitude	*ka-taur-an*	ka-banyāk-an
Mumble, to	*dub-dub*	rūngut
Murder (to kill)	*būnoh*	būnoh
Musa-textilis	*lānūt* *	pīsang tālī
Muslin	*kakana kāsa, kāsa*	kāin khasa
Must	*sobai*	hārus, paksa
Mustaches	*pūngōt*	kūmis, mīsai
Mustard	*sasāuri*	sesāwī
Must not	*aiau*	jangan
Mute	*di maka sabut or asip*	bīsū
Mutiny	*mug-hīlo-hāla*	gampar
Mutton	*ānūd bīlī-bīlī*	daging bīrī-bīrī
My (mine)	*ka-aku, kākū*	sāhya pūnya
Mysterious	*ajaib, gāib*	ghāib

* Bisaya " abaka."

ENGLISH.	SULU.	MALAY.
Nab	*sagau*	tangkap
Nacre	*tīpai*	kūlit mutīāra
Nacreous	*sāia tīpai*	chāia ,,
Naga	*nāga*	nāga
Nail (of iron)	*lansang*	pākū
,, screw-	*lansang siput, siput*	pākū skruf
,, (of the fingers)	*kūkū*	kūkū
,, , long finger-	*changgai*	changgei
,, , to	*lansang-an,*	pākū-kan,
	mag-lansang	lantak pākū
Naked	*hūboh*	talānjang
Nakedness	*ka-sīpāg-an*	ka-malū-an
Name	*ingān*	nāma
,, (title)	*gūlal, gālal*	gālar
Namesake	*īsai, angka ingān*	sa'nāma
Nape (of the neck)	*būkū-būkū pūgai*	tengkok
Narrow	*kūlang lukbang*	kōrang lēbar
,, (circumscribed)	*sigpit, sindat*	sumpit, sasak
Nation (race)	*bangsa*	bangsa
,, (country)	*banūa*	negrī
Natural (genuine)	*amuna, ma-tūd*	betul
Nature (disposition)	*palangai, tabiat*	parangi, tabiat
Nauseous	*ma-pait*	pahit, pait
Naval	*pūsud*	pūsat
Navigate	*mag-lāiag, lumāiag*	ber-lāyer
Neap-tide	*tubig-an, dagat-an*	āyer-purbani
Near (in place)	*ma-sūk, ārāig, sampig*	dekat
,, (in time)	*mārē*	hampir
Necessary-house	*pieg-intahū-an*	jamban

ENGLISH.	SULU.	MALAY.
Necessary, it is	*sobai*	hārus, patut
Necessity	*paksa*	paksa
Neck	*lēŭg, lēheg*	lēher
„ , having a long	*ma-tangkai*	jinjang
„ , nape of the	*būkū-būkū pūgai*	tengkok
Need (to want)	*kūlang*	kōrang
Needle	*jāūm*	jārum
Needless, it is	*s'āri na*	ta'usah
Neglect	*pa-sār-an*	tinggal
Negligent	*lalai*	lalei, alpa
Neigh, to	*īhīm, kīhīm*	ber-trīak, chārit
Neighbour	*iban nŭg-d'āraig*	ōrang sa'kampong
Nephew	*anak-an*	anak sūdara
Nerve (sinew)	*ūgat*	ūrat
Negotiate	*bechāla mŭg-janjī*	bechāra ber-janjī
Nest	*pūgad*	sarang
„ (of commerce)	*salang*	sarang būrong
Net, drag-	*pūkāt*	pūkat
Never	*wāi tūd, di tūd*	ta' pernah
„ mind	*di mŭg-āno, s'ārī na*	tīdah meng-apa
Nevertheless	*dien pa na maien*	welakin, semāja
New	*bāgū*	bhārū
New-moon	*būlan bāgū*	būlan bhārū
News	*gāwi*	khabar
Newspaper	*katas gāwi*	kartās khabar
Nib (bill)	*tuka*	pāroh
Nich (notch)	*sumbīng*	sumbīng
Niece	*anak-an babai*	anak sānak
Night	*dūm*	mālam

ENGLISH.	SULU.	MALAY.
Night, mid-	*tingah dūm*	tengah mālam
,, , to	*dūm īni*	mālam īni
,, , last	*k'ābi*	sa' mālam
Nightmare	*mang-logau*	mimpī ada hantū
Nine	*sīam*	simbīlan
Nineteen	*angpoh-tūg-sīam*	simbīlan blas
Ninety	*ka-siām-an*	simbīlan pūloh
Nip (pinch)	*gipit*	chūbit
,, (with the fingers)	*kiubut*	pījit
Nippers	*hi gipit*	sepit
Nipple	*pungau duruh*	māta sūsū
Nit	*lessah*	telor kūtū
No	*wāi, di*	tiāda, tīdah
No matter	*di mug-ūno, s'ārī na*	tidak meng-apa
No use (effectless)	*lio-og-an*	per-chuma
Noble (by birth)	*bangsāwan*	bangsāwan
Nobleman	*ōlang kāya baginda*	ōrang kāya
Nod, to	*tūmangoh, tangoh*	unggul
Nodes (of cane etc.)	*būkā*	būkū
Noise, a	*tūngog*	būnyi
,, , to make a	*kāloh*	gādoh
None	*wāi rūn (dūn)*	tiāda
Nonsense	*bechāla babal*	sīa-sīa
Noon	*ogtoh in sūga*	tengah hārī
Noose	*hīkog, jalat*	jerat
North	*ūtāla*	ūtāra
Nose	*ilong*	hīdong
,, , projecting	*panshong ilong*	hīdong munchong
Nosegay	*sāmping sa pūtus*	s'ikat būnga

ENGLISH.	SULU.	MALAY.
Nostalgia	*na bimbaug in hātai ha hūlah*	
Nostrils	*lāngag ilong*	lōbang hīdong
Not	*di*	tīdah
Not, is	*wāi*	tiāda, ta'da
,, , do	*āiau*	jāngan
,, , it is	*būkūn*	būkan
,, yet	*wala*	balúm
,, at all	*wāi rān tūd, di tūd*	tiāda s'kāli
Notch	*sumbīng*	sumbīng
Nothing	*wāi rūn ūno-ūno*	sātu apa tīdah
,, , good for	*wāi gūna-gūna*	tiāda ber-gūna
,, , for	*lio-ōg-an*	per-chūma
Notice (to heed)	*jāga*	ingat
Notwithstanding	*mīsan, minsan*	welakin, maskī
Nourish	*īpat, palihala*	pīāra, paliara
Now	*bī h'aun, bihaiaun*	s'kārang
,, (this moment)	*hēn dūn, sin-īni-īni*	s'kārang īni
,, (the expletive)	*maka*	maka
Nudge, to	*man-āntok**	kuet *
Number	*numbul†*	numbur †
Nuptials	*tīaun*	nīkāh
Nurse	*tūmanūd*	īnang, peng-āsoh
,, , wet	*dūrū-an*	pen-iūsū
Nurture	*īpad*	pīāra
Nymph (celestial)	*bidādāli*	bidādarī

Oar, an	*dāyōng*	dāyōng
,, (a paddle)	*būgsai*	peng-āyūh

* To dig in the ribs.   † Adopted from English and used in classifying.

J

ENGLISH.	SULU.	MALAY.
Oath	*sāpah*	sūmpah
„ , to take an	*múg-sāpah*	ber-sūmpah
Obeisance	*hūmūboh, hūboh*	tunduk
Obey	*agad, sālāt*	tūrut
Object (of sight)	*ka-kīta-an*	ka-līāt-an
„ (of pursuit)	*pa-lawag-an*	pen-charī-an
Obscure (dark)	*tigidlam, malindom*	klam, glap
Obstinate	*ma-tras in hātāi*	hāti kras
Obstruct	*múg-sasat, ma-sasat*	menyasak
Obstruction	*sankūt-an*	sankūt-an
Obvious	*ma-lehau, ma-sawa*	trang, niāta
Occidental	*bāgat, sedlūpan,*	bārat,
	hatās hangin	di-ātas angin
Occupation	*pūg-hīnang-an*	pe-karjā-an
Occupied	*aun hīnang-an*	ada karja
„ (busy)	*wāi sanang*	ta' senang
„ (as a house)	*tūga tāu*	ada ōrang
Occupier	*tūg bāi*	tūan rūmah
Ocean	*lāūd*	lāūt
„ (the deep)	*tawīd*	lāūt besár
Odour	*bahū, bāū*	bāū
„ (of perfume)	*mamūd*	wangī
Of (belonging to)	*kan, sin*	ampūnia, pūnya
„ (from)	*dien ha*	deri pada
Off, from	*dien ha-tās*	deri ātas
„ , to break	*baleh*	pātah
„ , to cast	*biugit*	būang
„ , to fall	*tanak*	tanggal
„ , to leave	*dumuhong*	ber-hentī

ENGLISH.	SULU.	MALAY.
Offer homage, to	sūmūmbah	sembah
,, , to (a price)	tāwal	tāwar
Often	maka matāud	ter kādang
,, , how	maka pela	brāpa kāli
Offence (fault)	sāh, dōsa	sālah, dōsa
Office	gēdong,* ofis †	gēdong,* ōfis †
,, (employment)	āsāh-an	pegāng-an
Oh !	arōhi !	adōhī !
Oil	lanah	mīnyak
,, , earth	lanah lopa ‡	mīnyak tānah ‡
Oily	ma-lanah	ber-mīnyak
Old (aged)	mās, malas	tūah
,, (decayed by time)	logai	lāma
Omit (forget)	lūpa	lūpa
On (upon)	ha-tās, ha	di-ātas, di
Once	maka mīsan	sa'kāli
On dit	kuno, sui-sui	kata ōrang
One	īsa, sa, hambok	suatu, sātu, sa
,, , it is all	sari na	sāma jūga
,, eyed	tunggal māta	māta sa'blah
,, at a time	īsa angka mīsan	sātu sa'kāli
Onion	bāwang	bāwang
Only	sāja, sagūah, lūal	sāja, hānia
,, (sole)	tunggal	tūnggal
Opal, the	biduri	biduri
Opaque	būkin ma-lehāu	tiāda trang
Open	ākab	būka

* Literally, Store-house.   † Adopted from English.

‡ Such as Kerosene.   § In Malay, malas lazy.

ENGLISH.	SULU.	MALAY.
Open, to	*ūkāi*	būka
,, (untie)	*ābad*	meng-ūrei-kan
,, (as an umbrella)	*tūkag*	būka, kumbang
,, (as a flower)	*muskag*	kumbang
Opinion	*agī, sāmbat*	fikīr-an, sangka
Opium	*apīun*	afyūn
,, (prepared)	*marat*	madat, chandū
,, , to smoke	*mūg-hanggop marat*	īsap chandū
Oppose	*meng-ātu*	me-lawan
Oppress, to	*mang-anīaya*	anīaya-kan
Opulent	*dāya-han, langke*	kaya
Or	*atawa*	atau
Orange	*sūah*	līmau mānis
Order (command)	*dāk*	sūruh
,, (to commission)	*tārūn, tūgūn*	pāsan
Ordnance	*espil*	marīam
Organ, an	*olgano**	organo *
Oriental	*tīmol, shūbangan*	di-bāwah angin
Origin	*asal*	asal
Ordure	*tāi, tāhī*	tāi, chīrit
Oriole, golden-	*tehelau*	kūtilang
Ornament, to	*pūg-daiau*	hias-kan
Ornaments	*pūg-daiau-an*	per-hias-an
Orphan	*īlo,† yātīm‡*	piātū, yātīm
Other	*dōāin, dōwāin*	lāin
Otherwise	*ma-lain-kan*	ma-lain-kan
Ought	*sobai*	pātut, hārus
Our	*ka-atū, ka-amu, k'ātu*	kīta pūnya

*Spanish, "organo."   † Motherless.   ‡ Fatherless.

ENGLISH.	SULU.	MALAY.
Ourselves	*baran namu*	kāmī sindīrī
Out	*gūah*	lūar
Outcast	*panama, abu*	bangsat
Outcry (clamour)	*latah, bākag*	gampar
Outrigger	*kātig*	chādī, rūbīng
Outside	*ha-gūah*	di-lūar
Over (in position)	*ha-tās*	di-ātas
,, (excess)	*lebih*	lebih
,, (in degree)	*pakaraian*	amat
,, (across)	*ha-ang-sipak*	di-sabrang
,, (behind)	*ha-lio*	di-bālik
,, (finished)	*hobus*	habis
Overcome	*riang, tīwas*	alah, tīwas
,, , to	*gimaug, sumauk*	menang
Overflow	*lasai*	limpah, lampar
Overladen	*tugub*	sārat amat
Overplus	*ka-lebih-an*	ka-lebih-an
Overseer	*mandōl*	maudōr
Overset (capsize)	*rāub*	jūkang
Overtake	*sambat*	ambat
Over, more-	*sahadān, īsab na*	lāgī-pun, sahadān
Owe	*mūg-ūtang*	ber-ūtang
Owl	*lok-lok*	būrong hantu
Own (possessive)	*sin-baran*	ampūuya
,, (belong to)	*kan*	pūnya
,, (acknowledge)	*atās*	aku
Owner	*in tūg*	īang ampūnya
Oxen	*sāpī*	lembū
,, , wild	*līsang*	silādang

ENGLISH.	SULU.	MALAY.
Oyster	*tuba*	tīram

Pace, to (as horses)	*pāso* (Spanish)	līgas
,, , a	*tĭkang*	langkah
Pacer, a (horse)	*kŭda pāso*	kŭda līgas
Pack up	*potūs-a*	bŭngkus-i
Package	*pūtūs, potūs*	bŭngkus
Paddle, a	*bŭgsai*	pengāyŭh
,, , to	*mŭg-sai*	ber-kāyŭh
Paddy	*pai*	padi
Padlock	*kandaru*	candado (Sp.)
Pail (bucket)	*baldī, gāyong*	baldī, timbā
Painful	*ma-sākit*	sākit, pĕdih
Paint	*sāt, atal*	chat
,, , to	*mŭg-sāt, mŭg-atal*	sāpū chat
Painting	*pāta*	gambar
Pair (couple)	*angka pāsang*	sa'pāsang
Palace	*astāna, mālegai*	astāna, mālegei
Pale (wan)	*pīrang, pūchat*	pūchat
Paling	*sasak, ād*	pāgar
Palm (of the hand)	*pād*	tāpak
,, (as a measure)	*ang pād*	sa'tāpak
Palpitate	*nŭg-badlak*	ber-dabar
Pan (of iron)	*kuāli*	kuāli
Pant, to	*tānga, tumānga*	mangah
Pap (dug)	*pungau dūrāh*	māta sūsū
Papa	*amah*	bāpa
Papaya fruit, the	*kapāya*	papāya
Paper	*kātās*	kartas

ENGLISH.	SULU.	MALAY.
Paps (dugs)	*pungau dūrāh*	māta sūsū
Paragraph	*pāsal*	per-kara, fasal
Paradise	*firdās*	firdūs
,, (heaven)	*sōrga*	shorga
,, , bird of	*manok dēwātu*	būrong sūpan
Parasol	*pāyong*	pāyong
Parcel	*potūs*	būngkus
Pardon	*ampūn, màāp*	ampūn, màāf
,, , to beg	*mīki ampun or màāp*	minta ampūn
Parrot (green)	*kanyay, hāyap*	nōrī, angak
,, (white)	*bukai*	kakatūa
Paroquet	*kobisī*	kēkek
Parsimonious	*ma-ītong*	kīkir
Parry, to	*tangkis, man-angkis*	tangkis
Part, a	*ang-ūtād*	sa'potong
,, , to (as a rope)	*mogtoh, bogtoh*	pūtūs
Partition	*ka-bahāgi-an*	ka-bhagī-an
,, (of a building)	*dinding*	dinding
Partnership	*kongsi*	kongsi
Pass by, to	*lūbai, lāmūbai*	lālū
Passage (channel)	*taus-an*	trūs-an
Passenger	*tāu tūmpang, numpāng-an*	ōrang numpang, tūmpāng-an
Passion (anger)	*dūgal, ka-paso-an*	mārah, hangat
,, (affection)	*ma-lōi*	ber-āhī
Passionate	*ma-pāso in hātāi*	hāti pānas
Passport	*sāp bības*	chāp bībās
Past	*bakas*	telah, sudah
Patch, to	*tupak-an*	tāmpal

ENGLISH.	SULU.	MALAY.
Path	*dān*	jūlan, lūrong
Patient	*sabal*	sabar, derīta,
Pattern	*lajawan*	chontoh
Paunch	*tian, kamamāw*	prut
Pause (to stop)	*dumuhong*	ber-hentī
Paw	*sīkī*	kāki
Pawn (pledge)	*sēnda, sānda*	gādei
Pay	*bāyad, ōngsud*	bāyer
,, (wages)	*tangdan-an*	gāgī
,, cash, to	*mag-sambat*	bāyer tūnei
Pea	*bātong*	kāchang
Peace	*dumahong, duhong*	dīam
Peak (of a hill)	*puntuk*	ponchak
Pearl	*mūchia*	mutīa, mutīāra
Peasant	*gimba-han-an*	ōrang dūsun
Peck, to	*tūk-tūk, ma-nuktuk*	pāgut
Peel, to	*lanit-an*	kūpas, kalūpas
,, (rind)	*pāis*	kūlit
Peep, to	*simib-sib, sib-sib*	tĕngok, intei
Pen	*kalam*	kalam
,, (for cattle)	*pagal sāpī*	kandang
Penalty	*sāh-an*	denda
Pencil	*pensīl*	pensīl, patlut
Penetrate, to	*limagbus*	tembus
Penis	*utin*	būtū, peler
Penitence	*simanggop, sianggop*	taubat, sasal
Penman	*jūlo tūlis*	jūro tūlis
Penurious	*paisī*	kīkir
People	*tāu*	ōrang

ENGLISH.	SULU.	MALAY.
People, common	*layat*	rayat
Pepper	*lāra, maīsa*	lāda, marīcha*
,, (chilli)	*lāra pūla*	lāda mērah
,, plantation	*ka-lāra-han*	kabūn lāda
Perambulate	*lonsol-lonsol*	men-jalān-i
Perch (as a bird)	*timapoh, tāmapoh*	hinggap, angkap
Perdition	*jehannam* (Heb.)	jehannam
Perform (do)	*hīnang*	būat
Performance	*piey-hīnang-an*	būat-an
Perfume	*laksī*	raksī
Perfumed	*mamūd*	wangī
Perhaps	*kālō-kālō*	bārang-kāli
Peril	*bāhia*	bāhia
Period (of time)	*waktu, māsa*	waktu, māsa
,, (conclusion)	*akhil*	ākhir
Permission	*bības, tūgūt, maiad*	idzin, mōhon
Permit, a	*sāp bības*	chāp bības
Perplexity	*sukāl-an*	sukār-an
Perspiration	*hulas-an, hulas*	peluh
Pester, to	*lutah, sasat*	bīsing, ūsik
Pestle, a (wooden)	*alū, halō*	alū, halū
Petition, to(ask for)	*mīki, pangaioh*	minta, pōhon
Phlegm	*gudhad, pughad*	dāhak, hingus
Pick (chose)	*peh-peh*	pīlih
,, up	*ka-pūt*	pūngut
Picul (133⅓lbs.)	*pikul*	pikul
Pickles	*gīamūs bawang †*	āchār
Picture	*pāta*	gambar

* Javanese. † Literally, pickled onions.

ENGLISH.	SULU.	MALAY.
Piebald	*kabang**	baláng
Piece	*angka tioh tioh*	sa'krat
,, of cloth	*ang-bus*	sa'kāyū
Piece-work	*hīnang-an tughan*	karja bōrong
Pier (wharf)	*pantān, pantālan*	jambatan, tītī
Pierce	*tugsuk, limagbas*	jerek, tembus
Pig	*baboi*	bābi
Pig-tail (queue)	*punjong*	thāu chang
Pig-trap	*litag baboi*	per-angkap-an bābi
Pigeon (tame)	*achang*	merapāti
,, (small)	*bānd*	dawa
,, (large)	*kamasoh*	pergam
Pile (a heap)	*na bād*	tambun
,, up, to (in order)	*sūsun*	sūsun
Pilfer	*tiakan, takau*	chūrī
Pilgrim	*hāji*	hāji
Pilgrimage, to go on a	*mag-hājī*	nāīk hāji
Pillage, to	*lampas*	rampas
Pillar, (post)	*hāg*	tīang
Pillow, a	*ō-an*	bantal
,, , end of a	*sampong-an*	tampok bantal
,, case	*pūtūs ō-an*	sārong bantal
Pilot, a (guide)	*malim*	malim
Pimp, a	*sulu-han*	berwah, barot
Pimple (on the face)	*ampūgud*	jerāwat bātu
,, (boil)	*bahū ūtūt*	bīsul, bāra
Pinchers	*gipit*	sepit, penyepit
Pinch, to	*gipit-an, hubut-an*	chūbit, pīchit

* *Anak kabang*—half-cast.

ENGLISH.	SULU.	MALAY.
Pine apple	*pīsang, pitukal*	nānas
„ , screw-	*pangdan*	pandan
Pipe (for smoking)	*hōng-soi*	hūnchui
„ (conduit)	*selūran*	selūran
Pipkin	*kopsio*	kipsiau
Pirate, a	*salusu, panalusu*	p'rompak
„ , to	*mang-alusu*	meng-rompak
Pirating, to go	*mang-angaiau* *	meng-ayūh *
Piss	*mīhī, īhī*	kinching
Pit	*lüngag*	lōbang, serbong
Pitch	*gāgāh*	gala-gala
„ (resin)	*būletek*	dāmar, salang
Pitcher	*pāga*	būyong
Pith	*ēsok*	pūlor
Place, a	*tungud*	tāmpat
„ , to	*bātang*	taroh, būboh
Placid	*lenau*	tedoh
Plain (flat)	*dātag*	rāta
„ (glade)	*pantai*	pādang
Plait (to twist)	*sūbir-an, sābid*	pintal
„ (as rotan &c.)	*anyam*	anyam
Plane, a (tool)	*katam*	katām
„ , to	*katam-i*	ber-katām
Plank, a	*digpi*	pāpan
Plant, to	*tīanam, tānam*	ber-tānam
Plantain (musa)	*sāin, sāing*	pīsang
Plantation	*jambangan, hacienda* †	kabūn
„ (of sugar cane)	*ka-tūbū-han*	„ tabū

* To go on a piratical expedition.   † Spanish.

ENGLISH.	SULU.	MALAY.
Plate (dish)	*lāi*	pinggan
Play	*nāīm, naiam*	māīn
Plaything	*pāg-nāīm-an*	ber-māīn-an
Pleasant	*ma-tanam*	sedap
Please	*māg-yen*	brī sūka
,, , if you	*ka-lela-han*	līla
Plenty	*ma-tānd, ma-selūg, sakian*	banyak
Pliant (flexible)	*lūmit, lunuk*	lambēk, līat
Plough, to	*māg-'aru*	men-anggāla
Plough, a	*araru* *	tanggāla
,, (also dredge)	*bājā* +	bāja
Plough-share	*sulab*	nāyam
Pluck	*larut, kawa*	chābut
,, (as fruit)	*ma-pāt, pāt-an*	pūngut
,, or draw out, to	*hūblūt-an*	chābut
Plug (stopper)	*hūlat, dabus-an*	sumbat
Plunder, to (on land)	*liog-an*	rampas, sāmun
,, , to (at sea)	*mang-salusu*	meng-rompak
Plunge (dive)	*lerop*	selam
,, in, to	*togpa*	terjun
Pocket, a	*būsa*	sāku, kandōng
Podicem detergere	*mamaupoh*	istinjā
Poem	*ka-lang-an*	pantun
Point (extremity)	*dohol*	ūjong
,, (cape)	*tandoh, tandok*	tanjong
,, (to indicate)	*tūjū-han*	tūjū-kan
,, (to aim at)	*kītal-an, tūjū*	tūjū
,, (of a weapon)	*puchuk*	tuntung

* Spanish, "arado."   † *Mug-baja*—to dredge for pearl-shell.

ENGLISH.	SULU.	MALAY.
Poison	*lachūn*	rachūn
Poison (venom)	*bīsa*	bīsa
Poke, to	*mang-ēke, ēke*	men-inunkil
Pole, a	*tārok, tūkū*	tīang, bātang
Polecat	*mūsang*	mūsang
Polish, to (brighten)	*sāia-han*	chāia-kan
,, (to make smooth)	*pa-lanoh*	lichen-kan
Polite	*ma-arab*	adab, sūpan
Pollute	*ūmēh-an*	chumar-kan
Polluted	*ūmēh*	chumar, nejis
Pony	*kāra, kūdu*	kūda kechil
Pool	*lublub-an*	kūbang
Poor	*miskin*	meskin
,, (lean)	*kāiṅg*	kūrus
Populous	*ma-lamai*	rāmeī
,, (crowded)	*ma-sumbūl, ma-lau-jiet**	punnuh sasat
Porcupine	*landak*	landak
Pork	*ūnūd baboi*	daging bābi
Porpoise	*lumba-lumba*	lumba-lumba
Portion (share)	*bahagi-an*	bhāgī-an
Portrait	*pāta*	gambar
Positive (certain)	*tantū*	tantū
Possess	*īpat, tīau*	simpan, taroh
,, (to have)	*aun, tūga*	ada
Possibly	*kālō-kālō*	kālō-kālō
Post, a	*pangtūd, hāg*	tīang
Posterior	*ha-likūd, ha-lio*	di-blākang
Posteriors	*būlī, tāikud*	pantat, blākang

* Chinese.

ENGLISH.	SULU.	MALAY.
Pot	*anglit, bānga*	priok, blānga
Pot, iron	*kwāli*	kwāli
,, (of salt)	*sukul*	
Potherbs	*sāyol*	sāyor
Potlid	*tūtūp-an*	tūdong
Potatoe (tuber)	*pānggi*	ūbī
,, , sweet-	,, *bagūn*	ūbī kantang
Pound, to *	*bāioh-an*	tumbok
Poulet (poult)	*pa-panggang-an*	anak āyam
Pour out, to	*mūg-hain, tūang*	chūchur, tūang
Power	*ka-gaus-an, kuāsa*	ka-kuasā-an
Powerful	*ma-kūsog, gaus*	kuāsa, kūat
Pox, small-	*pangkūt*	chāchar
Practice (custom)	*hadat*	ādat
Prau (Malay)	*sakaian*	praū
Prawns	*ūlang, ārang*	ūdang
Pray	*sambayang*	sambayang
Preacher	*hātib*	khatīb
Precede, to	*pa una-han*	daūlū-kan
Preceptor	*gūlā*	gūrū
Precinct	*halam-an*	alam-an
Precious	*mahal*	indah-indah
,, (dear)	*mahonet*	mahal
Precipice	*titab, pang-pang*	tarjal, dalang
Precipitate	*tomegpa*	terjūn-kan
,, (headlong)	*tīmōngke*	pūkang
Precise (certain)	*tantā*	tantu
,, (exact)	*sa ūt †*	tertib ‡

* As rice in a mortar.　† Time.　‡ Manner.

ENGLISH.	SULU.	MALAY.
Prefect, a	*panglīma*	panglīma
Pregnant	*būrus*	bunting, hamil
Prepare	*paniāp, chakap*	sediā-kan
Prepuce	*mūmād*	kŭlop
Presence	*harap-an, hawarat*	adāp-an
Present	*bī h'āun*	s'kārang
,, (a gift)	*būdi, sampang*	per-sambāh-an
Presently	*dai-dai dakoman*	sa'buntar lāgi
Press, to	*ragan-an*	tekan
Pretend	*āla-āla*	pūra-pūra
Pretty	*maraiau, bisai*	bāgus, mūlek
Prevent	*hawid, hawir-an*	tegah, larang
Previous	*in nakauna*	iang daūlu
Price	*hāga, halga*	harga
,, , to offer a	*tāwal, māg-halga*	tāwar
,, , to (by the lot)	*tāghan*	bōrong
Prick (to pierce)	*tugsuk*	chūchuk
Prickle	*tūnok-an*	dūrī
Prickley heat	*habas*	
Pride (proud)	*takabūl*	sombong
Priest (Christian)	*padri*	padri
,, (Mahomedan)	*pakil, hatib, biral*	imām, khatib
Prime cost	*pāhūn*	pōkok
Prince	*anak datoh*	anak rāja
,, (heir apparent)	*rāja mūra*	rāja mūda
Princess	*dāyang pātlī*	tūan pūtrī
Private	*lahsia*	rahsia
Probably	*kalō-kalō*	bārang kāli
Probe, to	*īke, mang-īke*	chungkil

ENGLISH.	SULU.	MALAY.
Proboscis	*mayong, kalolai*	bulälei
Proceed (advance)	*song, lamanjal*	pergi, jälan
,, (with a crowd)	*luruk, lumuruk*	per-arak
Prodigious	*ajaib*	ajeb
Professor (learned)	*pandīta*	pandīta
Profit	*untong, lāba-lāba*	untong, lāba
Prohibit	*lāng*	lārang
Prolix	*ma-tāud bechāla*	panjang bechāra
Prolong	*laus*	lanjut
Promise	*janjī*	janjī
Promontory	*tandok*	tanjong
Prompt	*sāmāt, chapat*	chepat
Prone (on the face)	*domaub*	tiārap
Prong	*gangat*	tārang
Prop, a	*tongkud*	tongkat, sōkong
,, , to	*tongkas-an*	ber-sōkong
Proper	*pātut*	pātut
Property	*ata, alta*	harta
,,	*wakap**	wakaf*
Prophet	*nabī*	nābī
Prostitute	*ka-bīga, ka-bais*	sūndal
Prostitution	*ka-biga-an*	pe-sundal-an
Protection	*selong* (shelter)	lindong
Protract	*laus*	lanjut
Provisions	*lutoh-an*	bakal, bakas
Proud	*takabāl*	sombong, kāchak
Provided that	*asal*	asal
Prow (a vessel)	*sakaian*	praū

* Property given up for the good of a community.

ENGLISH.	SULU.	MALAY.
Proxy (agent)	*wakīl*	wakīl
Puberty	*bālig*	bālig
Pudendum muliebre	*bīlat*	pūki
Puddle (pool)	*lub-lub-an*	kūbang
Pull	*ūtng, ūtăng, hēlā*	tārek, hēlā
,, out	*larut*	chābut
,, down	*lābūh*	rōboh
Pulley	*timun-timun*	kapi, lorah
Pulp	*ānūd*	isī
Pulse (arterial)	*badlak*	nādī
,, (beans)	*bātong*	kāchang
Pump	*ombak-ombak*	bomba
Pumpkin	*kabasi*	lābū mērah
Puncture	*tugsuk*	chāchat
Pungent	*ma-lara, mala*	pedas
Punish	*picg-hukum-an*	meng-hukum-kan
Punishment	*hukum*	hukum
Puppy	*anak crok*	anak anjing
Purchase	*bī, mī (haidah*)*	bilī
Pure	*ma-lanoh*	brīsih
Purple	*ūngū*	ūngū
Purpose	*sangāja*	sangāja
Pursue	*hapas, urol, turol*	kejar, ūsir
Pus (matter)	*nānah*	nānah
Push	*tōlak, tomōlak*	tōlak, sōrong
Put	*tāu, bātang*	tāroh, boboh
,, by	*tāu, itau, tiau*	tāroh, simpan
,, on	*ma-makai, sāng-an*	pākai, pāsang

* To purchase charms or holy books.

K

ENGLISH.	SULU.	MALAY.
Put out (extinguish)	*pohng-an, pong*	pādam
,, out of joint	*na-miula*	
,, between, to	*sip-sip*	sisip
,, down, to	*bātang*	latak
Putrid	*hāloh*	būsuk
Python, a	*hās sawa*	ūlar sawah

Quadruped	*opat sīkī*	ampat kāki
Quadruple	*maka opat*	ampat kālī
Quake	*na midpid*	gomitar
Quantity	*ka-taur-an*	ka-banyāk-an
Quarrel (fight)	*mŭg-lorai*	ber-klāhī
,, (contention)	*bantah*	bantah
,, , to	*nug-kāloh*	ber-gādoh
Quarter, a	*ang ūtād*	sa'sūkū
Query (expression of doubt)	*indai*	antah
Question, to	*mŭg-sual* *	sual *
Quick (quickly)	*ŭs-ŭs, sāmŭt, segla*	lekas, pantas
Quick-sand	*hi ad-ad*	lāniū
Quid (of betel)	*apil*	sapah
Quiet (tranquil)	*sanang, tanam*	senang
,, (motionless)	*dumahong*	dīam
Quit (let go)	*ŭg-i, butan-i*	lepas
,, (leave)	*maka-bīn*	tinggal
Quite (entirely)	*ka-tan-tan, lūn-lūn*	sakāli
Quite right	*āmū-bah, ma-tūd*	betul sakāli

Race, a	*lomba*	lomba

* On Scientific or Religious subjects.

ENGLISH.	SULU.	MALAY.
Race course	*lomba-an*	lomba-an
,, , to	*mŭg-lomba*	ber-lomba
,, (generation)	*bangsa*	bangsa
Radish, a	*lebanos*	lōbak
Raft (of rotan)	*lanting*	lantin
,, (of bamboo etc.)	*alūl*	rākit
,,	*giakit* *	rākit
Rafter	*kāsauh*	kāsau
Rag	*daymai, ragmai*	percha
Rage	*ma-gama, agama*	mārah, amārah
,,	*molka* †	morka †
Ragged (torn)	*na gisi-gisi*	robak-rabek
,, (tattered)	*daymai-ragmai*	kōyak-rabek
Rain	*ālan*	hūjan
,, , to	*mŭg-ālan*	ber-ūjan
Rainbow	*andāhu, bangau*	kūng palāngī
Raise (lift)	*bāhat*	angkat
,, (to erect)	*bangun*	bangun
,, (on end)	*tindog*	dīrī-kan
,, (at one end)	*jongkat*	jongkat
Rake, a	*bājā, kās*	peng-gāris
,, , to	*mŭg-bājā, mŭg-kās*	gāris
,, (like a mast)	*sondong*	chondong
Ram (male goat)	*kambing ūsog*	kambing jantan
,, , to	*mŭg-darasok*	lantak
Rambutan (fruit)	*ūsaā*	rambūtan
,, (another kind)	*tamāsān*	maritom

* Wood secured to a bangka (prau).

† Used when speaking of high personages.

ENGLISH.	SULU.	MALAY.
Rampart	*kūbū*	binting
Ram-rod	*darasok*	plantak
Rank (a row)	*balis-balis*	bāris, jājar
Ransom	*bayad*	tabus
Rap, to	*pok-pok, kāgūl*	katok
Rapid	*domāgan, tūgda*	dras
Rare (precious)	*mahal*	indah
Rarely (seldom)	*mahang-mahang*	kadang, jārang
Rash	*ūs-ūs*	dengan gopoh
Rat, a	*ambāu*	tīkus
Ratan-cane	*wāi*	rōtan
Rave	*man-jādi gīla*	menjādi gīla
Raw	*hīlau*	mantah
Ray, a (of light)	*sīlau*	sīnar
Razor, a	*laring pūg-bagong-an*	pīsau chūkor
Reach (attain to)	*abūt*	sampei
Read	*bāsha, bācha*	bācha
,, (a holy book)	*mang-āji*	meng-āji
Ready (prepared)	*peniap, chakap*	sedīa, sīap
Real	*amūna*	betul
Really	*būnal-būnal*	sunggoh-sunggoh
Reap, to	*mūg-ānī*	tuwei, katam
Rear (to bring up)	*īpat, paliala*	paīāra
Reason (cause)	*sabab-kālna*	kārna-sabab
,, (understanding)	*akal*	budī
Rebell	*daulaka*	durāka
Recall	*tawag pa balck-an*	panggil balck
Recede	*sībūg, simibūg*	undor
Receive (accept)	*tāīma*	terīma

ENGLISH.	SULU.	MALAY.
Recently	*bāgū-iaun*	bhārū tādī
Reckon (to count)	*ītong*	bīlang
,, (compute)	*kīla-kīla*	kīra-kīra
Recline (lean)	*sandig, samandig*	sandar, lungguh
,, (repose)	*kolang, komolang*	bāring, limpang
Recognise	*ingat, pāham, kakīla*	kenal, cham
Recollect	*tŭm-tŭm*	īngat
Record, to	*maniālat, peniñlat*	meniũrat
Recover (from sickness)	*hiāuli-an*	sumboh
Recreation	*pŭg-naiam-naiam-an*	ka-maīn-an
Rectitude	*ka-tulir-an (tālid)*	ka-lurūs-an
Red	*pūla, lāg*	mērah
Reed (in weaving)	*bailah*	balera
Redeem (from pawn)	*lukat*	tabus, tebus
Reduce (lessen)	*kōlang-an*	kōrang-kan
Reef (of rocks)	*tākut*	kārang
Refuse, to	*hawid, hawir-an*	anggan
Regent	*giba-han sin sultan*	ganti rāja
Region	*benña*	dāīrah
Reign	*pŭg-palentah-an*	pegang parentah
Rein (bridle)	*kakang*	kakang, dras, ras
Reiterate	*ūlang-ūlang*	ber-ūlang
Reject, to	*biugit*	būang
Relapse (in sickness)	*bīūghat*	balik sākit
Relate	*baita*	bīlang, cherīta
Related, to be	*mŭg-pŭg-tungud*	ber-sanak
Relation, a	*tāu tāi anak*	dūsānak
Release, to	*ēg-i, pa-butun-an*	lepas
Relief (assistance)	*tābang*	tōlong

ENGLISH.	SULU.	MALAY.
Relieve*	*gomanti*	gantī
Religion	*agama*	agama
Relish (taste)	*anam*	rāsa
Reluctant	*hūkaw*	ta māū, segan
Rely	*andal, māndal*	hārap
Remain here, to	*domī, dimī*	tinggal sīni
,, there, to	*dūmūn, pa-rūn-an*	tinggal sana
,, (wait)	*tagad, tomagad*	nanti
Remedy	*tāmbal*	penāwar
Remember	*tŭm-tŭm*	īngat
Remind	*pa-tŭm-tŭm-i*	meng-īngat-kan
Remnant	*kāpin*	sīsa
Remote (distant)	*māioh*	jāūh
,, (in time)	*mōgai*	lāma
Remove	*pindah*	pindah
,, (take away)	*dān matoh*	bāwa perji
Rend (split)	*sīpak, pītas*	blāh
,, (tear)	*gisi*	kōyak
Renegade	*multad†*	murtadd †
Rent	*sūkai, chukai*	sēwa
,, (to farm)	*pājak, tūghan*	pājak
Repair (mend)	*daiau-i*	bāīk-i
Repast	*santap-an*	santap-an
Repay	*bayad ūtang*	bayer ūtang
Repayment, to ask	*samūkut ūtang*	men-āgi ūtang
Repel	*dui-a, bogau-a*	hālau
,, (push away)	*tōlak*	tōlak
,, (ward off)	*tangkis, tomangkis*	tangkis

* By taking the place of.　　† From the Mahomedan religion.

ENGLISH.	SULU.	MALAY.
Repent	*taubat*	sesal
Replace	*ganti, gomanti*	ganti
Replete (full)	*hīpo*	punoh
,, (satiated)	*kiensūbahan*	kenniang
Reply	*sambag, sābūt, asip*	sāhut, jawāb
Report (rumour)	*sui-sui, kuno*	brīta, kunan
Repose (rest))	*kolang, balaro*	baring, beradu
Reprehensible	*sāh*	sālah
Representative	*wakīl, wali*	wakīl, wali
,,	*wakīl mutalak**	wakīl mutalak *
Repudiate	*talak*	telāk, sārak
Repulse	*tōlak, dui-a*	tōlak, hālau
Request	*mīki*	minta
Resemblance	*sali-sali*	sa'rūpa
Reside	*hūlah*	dīam
Resin	*buletek*	dāmar, salang
Resist	*atu, mam-abag*	lāwan, menāhan
Resource (expedient)	*akal*	akal, dāya
Respect	*holmat*	hormat
Respectful	*sūpan, arab*	adab, sūpan
Rest (tranquility)	*sanang*	senang
,, (remainder)	*na kāpin*	peninggal
Restless	*ma-linsah*	lasah, līsah
Restore	*ūlih, hiūlih-an*	pūlang-kan
Restrain	*mang-hawid*	men-āhan
Result	*ka-putus-an*	ka-sudah-an
Resurrection	*kīāmat*	kīāmat
Resurrection-day	*adlau kīāmat*	hāri kīāmat

* Plenipotentiary.

ENGLISH.	SULU.	MALAY.
Retain (hold on)	*bŭg-bŭg*	tāhan
,, (keep)	*itāu*	simpan
Retaliate	*baus*	bālas
Retch, to	*lio-duk-an*	muntah-muntah
Retinue	*ka-bunyog-an*	peng-ikut
Retreat	*sibŭg*	undor
Retribute	*būsong*	tŭlah
Retribution	*kia-busong-an*	ka-tulah-an
Return, to	*nŭg-bālek, bieng, mūi, minŭi*	balik-kombali, pūlang
Reveal	*baītu-i*	brī tāhu
Revenge	*baus-an*	pem-balās-an
Revenue	*hāsil*	hāsil
Reverse	*dowain*	lāīn
,, (quite different)	*doain-doain*	liān sakāli
Revive	*sadar*	sadar
Revolt	*dāulaka*	durāka
Revolve	*bĕng*	pūsing, kītar
Reward	*tangdan*	ūpah
Rheumatism	*sangal*	sangal
Rhinoceros	*bādak*	bādak
Ribs	*gūsuk*	rūsuk
Rice	*bras, bugas*	bras
,, (in the husk)	*pāi*	pādī
,, (boiled)	*k'aun-an, ūmai*	nāsī, īnei
Rice-flour	*tapong*	tepong
Rice, to sift	*mŭg-ayag*	tinting
Rich	*dayahan, kauasa*	kāya
Riches	*ka-kuāsa-han*	ka-kāyā-an

ENGLISH.	SULU.	MALAY.
Riddle (sieve)	*legoh, ayag-an*	ūyak, nyīrū
,, (conundrum)	*ka-tukud-an*	tuka-tuki
Ride	*peng'ūra*	tunggang kūda
Ridge (of a roof)	*biūbōng-an*	per-ūbong-an
,, (of a hill)	*puntuk*	ponchak
Right (truly)	*bunal-bunal*	benar-benar
,, (proper)	*amūna, ma-tùd*	betul, pātut
,, (opposed to left)	*tō*	kānan
,, (straight)	*tūlid, bùntul*	lūrus
Rigging (shrouds)	*tambilang*	tambirang
Rigid	*ma-tras, ma-tugas*	kras
Rigorous	*anyāya*	anyāya
Rim (edge)	*hēgad, biring*	pinggīr, tepi
Rind	*pāis*	kūlit
Ring (finger)	*sing-sing*	chin-chin
,, (for the wrist)	*galang*	galang
,, , ear	*bāng*	krābū, sūbang
Ringleader	*mās-mās*	kapāla
Ringlet	*kulong*	chechintong
Ringworm (tetter)	*kūlap*	kūrap
Rinse (cleanse)	*tīmud*	chūchi
,, (the mouth)	*mamai mùg-mùg*	kūmur
,, (dip in water)	*randam*	rendam
Riot (uproar)	*hīlo-hālo, būkag*	hīru-bīrū
Ripe	*hīnog*	māsak
,, , half	*mangkol, mùngkol*	mangkol
,, , over	*liasau-an*	ranūm
,, , un-	*helau, būlak*	mantah, mūda
Rise (ascend)	*samakat, sakat*	nāīk

ENGLISH.	SULU.	MALAY
Rise, to (sit up)	*bangun*	bangun
,, up, to (stand)	*tindog, mindog*	ber-dīrī
,, (to the surface)	*lantop*	timbul
Rite (ceremony)	*hādat*	adat
River	*sōbah*	sūngei
,, , up the	*sūmūd ha sōbah*	mūdik
,, , down the	*lūmaras*	hīlir
River's mouth	*sīmud sōbah*	kuāla, mūāra
Road (path)	*dān*	lūrong, jālan
,, (highway)	*dan dākolah*	jālan rāya
Roar (bellow)	*sūaluk*	terīak
Roast, to	*panggang-an*	panggang
Rob	*tīakau, takau*	chūrī
,, and kill, to	*liāñg-an*	sāmun
,, (plunder)	*lampas-an*	rampas
Robber	*shugarol*	peniāmun
,, (thief)	*tāu tīakau*	penchūrī
Rock, a	*bātu*	bātu
Rocks (reef)	*kālang*	kārang
Rocky	*ma-bātu*	ber-bātu
Roe (small deer)	*kījang*	kījāng
Roll (as a cask)	*giling-an*	gōling
,, (as a mat)	*lūn-an*	gōlong
,, (as a ship)	*linggang*	lenggang
,, (as the hair)	*ma-māgos*	kūndei, sanggul
Roof	*atùp*	ātap
,, (of the mouth)	*delang-delang*	lāngit-lāngit mūlut
Rook	*wāk*	gāgak
Room (apartment)	*bīlik, tāmbok*	bilek

ENGLISH.	SULU.	MALAY.
Room (space)	*tungud*	tampat
Roomy (spacious)	*lūag, hāyang*	lūas, lāpang
Roost	*ma-tōg*	tīdor
,, (perch)	*timapok*	angkap
Root	*gāmut, akag*	akar
,, (origin)	*asal*	pūhn, asal
Rope	*lūbid*	tālī
Rotten	*goyah, gabok, tapok*	būrok
,, (putrid)	*hāloh*	būsok
Rough	*kāsap, dagmul*	kāsap
Round	*tībuk*	būlat
,, (plump)	*nŭg-lapinig*	bontar
,, about	*lībut*	koliling
,, , to go	*mŭg-lībut-lībut*	meng-olīling
Rouse, to (waken)	*bangun-i, pukau*	bangūn-kan
Rout (in battle)	*riaug, diaug*	meng-ālah
Row, to (with oars)	*mŭg-dāyōng*	ber-dāyōng
Royal	*ka-ratoh-an*	rāja ampūnia
Royalty	*ka-laja-an*	ka-rajā-an
Rub	*kŭs-kŭs*	gōsok
Rubbish	*sagbut*	sampah
Rudder	*bānsan*	kamūdi
Rude (unmannerly)	*hak, kōlang arab*	pangkoh
Ruffian	*tāu mang-i*	ōrang jāhat
Rugged	*kāsap*	kāsap
Ruin (to destroy)	*nŭg-larak-an*	mem-benasā-kan
,, (to spoil)	*nŭg-kangi*	rōsak
,, (demolish)	*nŭg-lūbuh*	rōboh, runtoh
Rule, to	*palentah*	parentah

ENGLISH.	SULU.	MALAY.
Ruminate	*mūg-sopah* *	mamah bīak *
Rumour	*gawi*	khabar, brīta
Rump	*ogpoh*	ponggong
Run	*dāg-an, domāg-an*	lārī
,, away, to	*pāgoi, māgoi*	lāuī
,, against	*dogtol, doktol*	sontoh
Runaway	*tāu māgoi, tāu pāgoi*	pe-lārī
Rupture (hernia)	*mustik*	būrut
Rusa (large deer)	*āsa*	rūsa
Rush (reed)	*rantek*	rantek, karchut
Rust (rusty)	*gāha*	kārat
Ruthless	*būngis*	bīngis
Sabre (sword)	*pădang, kaliawang*	pedang
Sack, a (bag)	*kārot, bāyot* †	kārong
Sacrifice, to	*sambāi* ‡	sambilih ‡
Sad	*sūsah*	duka chita
Sadness	*ka-susah-an*	ka-dukā-an
Saddle, a	*pakāl*	sela, palāna
,, cloth, a	*lāmpit, lampik*	lapis-an
Safety	*salāmat*	salāmat
Saffron	*dūlau*	kūnyet
Sage (wise)	*budīmān*	budīmān
,, , a	*pandīta*	ōrong budīmān
Sago palm	*sāni*	rumbīa, sāgū
,, flour	*lūmbīa*	sāgū, rumbīa
Sail (of a vessel)	*lāyag*	lāyer

* To chew the cud.   † Native rice bag.

‡ To kill animals, with religious ceremony.

ENGLISH.	SULU.	MALAY.
Sail, to	*mūg-lāyag*	ber-lāyer
,, , a (jib)	*pūk*	jib
Sailor	*kalāsī* *	kalāsī *
,, (of a praŭ)	*sakai*	anak praŭ
Sake of	*sabab-kālna*	kārna-sabab
Salary (wages)	*tangdan-an*	gājī
Salacious	*gilok-an*	gātal, kanjī
Saline (brackish)	*ma-bāngog*	māsin
Saliva	*lūrah*	lūdah
Salt	*āsin*	gāram
,, , to make	*pūg-asin-an*	bŭat gāram
,, (briny)	*ma-āsin*	māsin
Saltpetre	*sindāwa*	chendāwan
Salute	*man-agina* †	meng-alu
,, , to	*mŭg-sālam*	ber-sālam
Salver (of metal)	*tālam*	tālam
Same, the	*sali*	sāma
,, (not different)	*būkūn doāin*	būkan lāin
,, (one kind)	*angka gīnīs*	sātu macham
Sample	*lajawan, sontoh*	chontoh
Sand	*buhangin*	pāsīr
,, bank	*hūnas-an, gōsong*	gōsong, beting
Sandals (slippers)	*taompa*	tarompa
Sandal-wood	*sāndana*	chendāna
Sap	*tāgok*	getah
Sarcasm	*ūjā-ājā*	per-katā-an sindīr
Sargasso ‡	*dampal*	dampar (Brunei)

* Of a European vessel. † To salute a visitor approaching.

‡ Drifting sea-weed.

ENGLISH.	SULU.	MALAY.
Sash *	*salendang, saul*	salendang
Satan	*sāitan, shaitan*	shēitan
Satiate	*kien-subāh-an*	mengenniang
Satiated	*puas, timus*	jūmū, kenniang
Satisfied	*puas in hatai*	puas hāti
Saturday	*adlau sabtu*	hārī sabtu
Sauce	*sābau*	kūah
Saucer	*tapak*	pīring
Savage, a	*tau kātian*	ōrang ūtan
,, (ferocious)	*tālon*	gārang
Saw (small)	*gangari*	gargājī
,, (large)	*kat-kat*	gargājī besar
Say, to	*kūno, pāmong, lōng*	kāta
,, , to (address)	*mñg-sagda*	ber-sabda
Scab	*āgūd*	kūdis
,, (of a sore)	*kūgang*	krūping, salaput
Scabbard, a	*tagōban*	sārong pedang
Scald	*hanglus, busogan*	lechor-kan
Scales (of a fish)	*hoināp-an, sīsik*	sīsik
,, (for weighing)	*timbang-an*	dāching
Scandal	*fitnah, ompat*	ūpāt, fitnah
Scanty	*kōlang*	kōrang
Scapula	*kūka*	balīkat
Scar	*bakās pali*	pārut
Scarce	*mahang*	jārang
,,	*mahonet ka-bāk-an †*	sūsah dapat
Scare (frighten)	*kieblah-an*	meng-ajut
Scatter	*sabād*	hambur, tabor

* Worn over the shoulders.   † Literally, difficult to get.

ENGLISH.	SULU.	MALAY.
Scent (perfume)	*laksi*	raksī, ayer wangi
Scent (odour)	*bāhu, bau*	bāū, bāhu
Scented	*mamud*	wangī
Scholar	*pandita*	pandita
Schoolmaster	*gūlū*	gūrū
Schooner, a	*goleta* *	skunyir
Science	*ilmu*	ilmu
Scissors	*gunting*	gunting
,, (for betel-nut)	*ka-kati*	klati, kachit
Scoop (ladle)	*sūrūh, ogab*	sūduk, gāyōng
Scope (space)	*tungud*	tampat
Scorch	*sūnog*	bākar, lāyur
Score, a (twenty)	*sa-kōri*	sa'kōdī
Scour	*hūgas*	ūpam
,, (cleanse)	*tīmūr*	chūchi
Scorpion	*kāla jangking*	kāla chingking
Scrape. to	*kagis-an*	kīkis-kan
Scratch, to	*kamas, kas-kas*	chākar, garu
Scream, to	*nūg-kāiba, hibok*	ber-trīak, tampik
,, (as a child)	*jalat*	menjerit
Screw, cork-	*buli itek* †	peler itek
Screw-pine	*pangdan*	pandan
Screw-nail	*lansang sīput*	pākū skruf
,, -propeller	*kapai*	kīpas
Scribe	*jālo tūlis, katib*	jūro tūlis
Scripture	*kītāb* ‡	kītāb ‡
,, (the koran)	*kōlān*	korān
Scrotum	*lūyong*	tampat būah peler

* Spanish, "galeta." † Or: *ta tabid hulat kacha.* ‡ Sacred writings.

ENGLISH.	SULU.	MALAY.
Scrub, to	*măg-nis-nis*	gōsok
Scrutinise	*paleksa*	preksa, sīdik
Scum (froth)	*būkal*	būhī
Scurf	*lōbag*	dakī
Scurrilous	*mangi sīmud, tākbūh*	mūlut jāhat
Sea, the	*dāgat*	lāūt
,, , at	*ha lāñd*	di lāūt
,, faring people	*bājau, samul lāñd*	ōrang lāūt
,, -shore	*hĩgad dāgat*	pantei, tepī lāūt
,, -sick	*hĩlo-alun, hĩlo*	mābok lāūt
,, -slug	*bāt* *	trīpang *
,, -water	*tūbig dāgat*	ñyer lāūt
,, -breeze	*hangin ha lāñd*	angin lāūt
,, -weed	*lāmūt dāgat* †	agar-agar ‡
Seal, a (signet)	*sāp*	chap
Seam, a	*tāi-an, tahi-an*	jāīt-an
Search, to	*lāg, lawag*	chārī
,, (investigate)	*paleksa*	preksa
,, diligently, to	*siasat*	siasat
Season	*mūsim*	mūsim
Seat, a	*ka-lingkūr-an*	tampat dūduk
,, (a chair)	*sīa*	krosī
Second	*ka-dña, ka-rūa*	ka-dūa
,, finger	*lasoh*	jārī hantū
Secret	*lahasia*	rahsia
Secretly	*tāpōk-tāpōk*	ber-sumbūnī
Security	*tanggong*	tanggong
Sediment	*lidang, ākal, tāi*	chīrit, tāhī

* Bêche-de-mer.   † Or: *agal-agal*.   ‡ Plocaria candida

ENGLISH.	SULU.	MALAY.
Seduce (lead astray)	*sasat*	men-yasat-kan
,, (deflower)	*iusibah, măg-oerg*	perūgal
See, to	*kīta*	lihat
Seed (of plants)	*bīgi*	bīgi
Seed-time	*picg-bakal-an*	māsa men-ābur
Seek, to	*lawag*	chārī
Segar	*dubla*	cherūt (cheroot)
Seize (catch)	*ma-pūt, ka-pūt*	tankap, pegang
,, (as a bird of prey)	*pang-dagīt*	sambar
Seldom	*māhang, najajang*	jārang
Select, to	*peh-peh, măg-pīpī*	pīlih
Self	*baran, badan*	sindīrī, dīrī
,, , my	*baran-ku, īsa-isa-ku*	dīrī-ku
,, , him or her	*baran-nia*	dīrī-nia
Selfish	*tamah-an*	lōba
Sell, to	*păg-bī*	jūal
Selvage (border)	*jāmbu*	tepī kāīn
Senate (council)	*maupakat*	himpūn-an mantri
Send (order)	*dāk*	sūruh
,,	*palā, parā*	kīrim *
,,	*hiatud, atud†*	hantar †
,, for (call)	*tāwag, tāg*	panggil
Senior (elder)	*magolang*	ābang
Sense (meaning)	*māna, hatī*	ma'ana
,, (of feeling)	*lāsa*	rāsa
Sensible ‡	*saiomān, saioai*	siyūman
Sensual	*lasig*	ber-īngan
Sensuality	*hawā-napsu*	hawā nafsu

* Thing. † Person. ‡ Having feeling.

L

ENGLISH.	SULU.	MALAY.
Sentence (decision)	*hukum-an*	hukum-an
Separate, to	*būtas, chelai*	cherai
Sepulchre	*kūbūl*	kubūr
Serpent (snake)	*hās*	ūlar
Servant	*batah, īpūn*	būdak, hamba
Serve (wait upon)	*suapan*	layānī
Set, a	*sūsun*	sūsun
Sets, to lay in	*mūg-sūsun*	ber-sūsun
Set up (erect)	*pīcg-bangun*	men-dīrī-kan
,, , sun-	*samadlūp in sūga*	māta hārī māsok
Settle (adjust)	*salasai, pūtus*	selesei, pūtus
Seven	*pēto*	tūjuh
Seventh	*ka-pēto*	ka-tūjuh
Seventy	*ka-peto-an*	tūguh pūloh
Seven-fold	*pēto angka lāpis*	tūjuh lāpis
,, (seven times)	*maka pēto*	tūjuh kālī
Several	*ma-tāud*	bānyak
Severe (cruel)	*būngis, bīngis*	bīngis
Sew, to	*tāi, tāhi, man-āhi*	jāīt, jāhit
Shackles (fetters)	*ikang-ikang*	kang-kang
,, (chains)	*billanggok*	rantei
Shade	*selong*	lindong
Shadow	*lambong*	bāyang
Shaft (of a weapon)	*tāngkai*	ūlū
,, (of a spear)	*ālisi*	ūlū
,, (of a fish spear)	*tutah-an*	ūlū
,, (of a pātōk *)	*palih-an*	ūlū
Shake, to (as a leaf)	*jag-jag, unsang*	gōyang

* Patok:— native axe.

ENGLISH.	SULU.	MALAY.
Shake, to (shog)	*hibal, kimibal*	kiber
Shake, to	*tangkog, pak-pak*	gonchang
,, the head, to	*lingat-lingat*	
Shaky (loose)	*mŭg-hakul*	lūngar
Shall	*mau-bayah*	handak
Shallow	*bābau, chētek*	tōhor, dangkal
Sham (to feign)	*āla-āla*	pūra-pūra
Shame	*sīpŭg, ma-sipŭg*	mālū
Shameless	*wāi rūn sīpŭg, ma-bias, wāi āib*	kōrang mālū, tiāda tāu mālū
Shampoo	*pījī, pīsol**	pīchit*
Shape (form)	*rŭgbus, dŭgbus*	rūpa, sīkap
Share (portion)	*bahagi-an*	bhāgī-an
,, , half-	*ang-sīpak*	sapārō
,, , to	*mŭg-bahagi*	bhāgi
Shark	*kāītan*	īkan īyū
Shark's fins	*sik kāītan*	sisik īyū
Sharp	*ma-hāīt*	tājam
,, (cunning)	*pandai*	cherdēk
Sharpen, to	*mŭg-hāīt*	tājam-kan
,, (to whet)	*mŭg-āsah*	meng-āsah
Shave, to	*bagŭng (sūsoh +)*	chūkur
She	*sia, nia, sila, nila*	dia, ia, nya
Sheath, a	*tagōban*	sārong
Sheathe, to ‡	*sūlog-an, manggābok*	tāroh dālam sārong

* To pinch the limbs; to massage.

† To shave the eyebrows or temples.

‡ To sheathe a sword—*sul in takus halam tagoban.*

ENGLISH.	SULU.	MALAY.
Sheathe, un-	*larut*	ūnus
Shed, a	*kamalig*	pondok
Sheep	*bīlī-bīlī*	bīrī-bīrī
Sheet (covering)	*sīob*	salimut
,, (of a sail)	*jampang*	daman
Shelf, a	*paga*	para
Shell (mollusc)	*bubu, panagat-an*	sīput, bīa
,, (of a cocoa-nut)	*ogab, hungut*	tempūrong
,, , tortoise-	*sīsik*	sīsik
,, , seed pearl	*salisip*	salisip
,, , M.O.P.	*pāis tīpai*	kūlut mutiāra
Shelter	*selong*	lindong
Sherbet	*salbat*	sarbat
Shew (point out)	*hindoh*	unjuk, tunjuk
Shield	*tāmīng*	tāmīn, prīsei
Shift (to change)	*sālin*	ganti
,, (to move)	*pindah*	pindah
Shine (shining)	*selau, sāia*	gīlang, kīlau
Shingle (gravel)	*karsik, pāsil*	bātu klikir
Ship, a	*kapal*	kapal
,, , a sailing	,, *lāyag*	kapal lāyer
,, , a steam-	,, *kāyu or aso*	kapal āpī
,, (gunboat)	,, *jāga-jāga*	kapal p'rang
,, , to	*lūan*	mūat
,, , to un-	*hāwas, hāas*	ponggah
,, , master of a	*kapitan, nakora*	kapitan, nakoda
,, -wreck	*na bag-bag in kapal*	pechah-an kapal
Shirt, a	*kamisa*	kamēja
Shiver (shake)	*ma-milik-pilik*	galīgī

ENGLISH.	SULU.	MALAY.
Shiver (quake)	*ma-mid-pid*	gomitar
Shoal (rocks)	*tākut*	kārang
,, (sandbank)	*hūnas-an*	gōsong
Shock (fright)	*kieblah-an*	kajūt-an
,, , a (concussion)	*hantak*	gegak
Shoes, boots and	*sapatos, kapatos*	kāsut, sapato
Shoot at, to	*tembak*	tembak, pāsang
,, (with a blow-pipe)	*sumpit*	sumpit
,, (as plants)	*tumūbuh, tūbuh*	tumbuh
Shop, a	*tīnda*	kadei
Shore (a prop)	*tūkū, tongkud*	sōkong, tongkat
,, (on shore)	*ha-lopa*	di-dārat
,, , sea	*hēgad dāgat*	tepī lāūt
Short	*haupoh*	pendek
,, (wanting)	*kōlang*	kōrang
,, -sighted	*ma-lamān*	
,, -cut	*tulibas*	pintas
,, time ago	*kaina*	tādī
Shot (bullet)	*pūngloh*	pelūrū
,, , small-	*hambūl*	penabūr, sambūr-an
Should (ought)	*sobai, pātut*	pātut, hārus
Shoulder	*abāga, agāba*	bāhū, bāūh
,, -blade	*kūka*	balikat
Shout, to	*sñalak, ālangī*	sūrak, laung
Shove	*tolak, sōng*	tolak, sōrong
Shovel	*sūrūh, susūrūh*	sūduk
Shower, a (rain)	*tūga ūlan*	hūjan
Shrewd	*pandai*	cherdĕk
Shriek	*tūlik, sñalak*	trīak

ENGLISH.	SULU.	MALAY.
Shrill	*lagting*	niāring, marsīk
Shrimp	*ālang manahut*	ūdang kechil
Shrink	*samigpid*	karūkut
,, (recede)	*sībŭg*	undor
Shut	*tambal, taplŭk* *	tūtup
,, , to (as the eyes)	*perong-an*	tūtup
Shuttle	*tōlak, anak-olak-an*	tōrak, bālēra
Shy (bashful)	*sīpŭg-sīpŭg*	mālū-mālū
,, (untamed)	*tālon*	liar
Sick (ill)	*sākit, mangi-lasa*	sākit
,, sea-	*hēlo-alun*	mābok lāut
Sickness	*ka-sakīt-an*	peniāket
Side, a	*sīpak, ūtūd, tampal*	blah, fihak
,, , other	*ang sīpak doain*	sa-blah lāin
,, (ribs, flank)	*gūsok, kēd*	rūsuk, lambong
,, (border)	*hēgad*	tepī
,, (of a square)	*sāgī*	sāgī
,, (of a house)	*dinding*	dinding
,, by side	*araig-daig*	ber-sīsī
,, (sidle)	*ma-tapil*	tampil, rāpat
Sieve, a	*legoh, ayag-an,*	nyīrū, āyak,
	jibul-an, bigul-an	tambus-an
Sift, to	*mng-ayag*	āyak, krasei
Sigh, to	*mŭg-napas*	kaloh
Sight (faculty of)	*pa-kīta*	peng-līhat
Sighted, dim	*mng-abun in māta*	māta kābur
Sign	*indah-an*	tanda
Signature	*tulis ingan*	tapak tāngan

* To shut as an umbrella.

ENGLISH.	SULU.	MALAY.
Signify	*aun ka-hatī-an nya,*	ada artī nya,
	aun mīna nya	ada ma'ana nya
Signification	*ka-māna-han*	ma'ana
Silent, be	*dūhong, dumahong*	dīam
Silk	*sūtla*	sūtra
Silly	*dōpang*	bōdoh
Silver	*pērak*	pērak
Similar	*sali-rūgbus*	sāma rūpa
,, (no difference)	*wāi na bīdah*	tiāda bīdah
Simpleton	*binggong*	bīngōng
Simulation	*ūla-ūla*	pūra-pūra
Sin	*dōsa*	dōsa
Sincere	*hātāi būnal*	tulus
Sincerity	*islas*	ekhlas
Sinew	*ūgat, ūrat*	ūrat
Sing, to	*mŭg-bāt, janjam*	ma-nīanyi
,,	*mŭg-dindang* *	ber-dindang *
,,	*mŭg-dōa* †	ber-dōa †
,, a lullaby, to	*langan-an*	meng-īdong
Single (sole)	*tunggal, īsa-īsa*	tunggal, asa
,, (unmarried)	*būjang,‡ sūbūl* §	būjang
Sink, to	*lūnūd*	tingglam
Sir	*tūan*	tūan
Sister	*taimanghūd babai*	sudāra perampūan
Sister-in-law	*īpag babai*	īpar perampūan
Sister, elder-	*kakah*	kakak
Sit	*lingkūd*	dūduk

* To sing jocundly.　† To sing from the koran in chorus.

‡ Female.　　§ Male.

ENGLISH.	SULU.	MALAY.
Sit, to cause to	pa-lingkūr-a	dūdok-kan
,, (cross-legged)	ma-mīlang	ber-sila
,, , to (as a hen)	mang-ām	meng-aram
Six	ûnom	anam
Sixteen	hangpoh-tñg-ûnom	anam blas
Sixty	ka-ûnom-an	anam pūloh
Size	lagkû	besár
Skate (fish)	istā palit	ikan pari
Skill	pandai, akal	pandei, akal
Skin	pāis	kūlit
,, , to	pāis-an	kūpas
Skip	na-gingki-inki	ber-jenke
,, -jack (fish)	tambilawang	ikan ber-jengke
Skirt (of a dress)	pemsha	pemcha
Skull	kulakub-ō	tingkōrak
Sky	lāngit	lāngit
Slack (loose)	mûg-hakul	lūngar
Slander, to	fitnah, ompat	fitenah, ūpât
Slap	sampak	tampar
Slave	īpun	hamba
,, (captive)	tawan	tawan
Slay	būnoh	būnoh
Sleep, to	ma-tōg, tōg	tīdor
,, , to (sound)	halok, kūkam	nīadar
,, (with mouth open)	nûg-kā-kūsai	
,, , to talk in	man-damat	ngīkū
,, (repose)	balaro	berādū
Sleepy	kierroh	antuk, kalat māta
Sleeping place	kolang-an	tampat tīdor

ENGLISH.	SULU.	MALAY.
Slender	*manahut*	ramping, nīpis
Slide (slip)	*limigdas, ligdas*	galinchir
Slime (mud)	*pīsak*	lumpur, lūluh
Slimy	*landag*	lindir
Slippers	*taompa, tompa*	sliper
Slippery	*lingahas, landog*	lichin, lindir
Sloth (slow-lori)	*kūkam, kūkang*	kūkang
Slough (miry pool)	*lublub-an*	kūbang
,, (of a snake)	*hīlūnā*	lamūs
Slow (indolent)	*ma-huskau*	mālás
,, (not prompt)	*lālai*	lālei
,, (leisurly)	*īnāt-īnāt, anai-anai*	perlāhan
Small	*asīvī, manahut*	kechil
,, -pox	*pangkūt*	chāchar
Smart, to (pain)	*hapdus*	pedih
Smash (to atoms)	*ma-tūmā*	hanchor
Smell (odour)	*bāhū, bāū*	bāū, bāhū
,, , to	*ma-mauhu auhu*	chiūm
,, (to scent)	*ma-nimut simut*	chiūm
Smelt, to	*tunau-an*	leborkan, anchor
Smile	*humaiam, homiām*	sinyum
Smith	*tūkang bāsī*	tūkang besī
,, , gold-	*pandai balāwan*	tūkang amas
Smoke	*aso*	asap
,, , to (as a pipe)	*hanggop*	īsap, mīsa
,, , to (cigarettes)	*mūg-sīgup*	minom rōkōk
,, , to (cigars)	*mūg-dūbla*	minom cherūt
Smooth	*lanoh*	lichin, lindir
,, , to make	*pa-lanoh*	lichin-kan

ENGLISH.	SULU.	MALAY.
Smother, to	siampong	lemas
Snake	hās	ūlar
Snap (break)	balch	pātah
,, (as a rope)	bogtoh	pūtus
Snare	jalat	jarat
Snatch	dagmit, dagtu-an	rabut, sintak
Sneeze, to	bāhānūm, bahan	bersin
Snivel	sihpun, sīpun	īngus, lisma
Snore	nūg-singok, hagong	rāban, dungkor
Snout	panshong īlong	īdong munchong
,, (trunk)	mayong, kalolai	bulālei
Snow	salju	salju
So	demikīan	demikīan
,, (in that manner)	bī-ha-ien	bagītū
,, (thus)	bī-ha-īni	bagīni
,, , just (exactly)	āmū-na	betul
So-and-so	kūan	ānō
So be it	amīn	amīn
Soak (steep)	randam	rendam
,, (absorb)	sūp-sūp, tūpūs-an	īsap
Soap	sābūn	sābūn (Port.)
Sociable	nūg-bagāi-bagāi	sohbat-ber-sohbat
Socks	mējis, tagoban sīki	sārong kāki
Sodomy	mūg-jūbūl	pālat
Soft	lūnuk, hablo, buyog	lunak, lumbūt
Soil (earth)	lopa	tānah
,, , to	mūg-lūmēh	kōtor-kan
Soldier	sondālō	soldādō (Sp.)
Sole (only)	tunggal	tunggal

ENGLISH.	SULU.	MALAY.
Sole (of the foot)	*pād sīki*	tāpak kāki
Solicit	*mīki, pangaioh*	minta, pohon
Solitary (sole)	*tunggal*	tunggal
Some	*ka-ibān-an, münga*	bārang
,, (a little)	*tīoh-tīoh*	sedīkit
Somebody	*hi-kñan*	si-ānō
Something	*münga-āno-ūno*	bārang apa
Son	*anak üsog*	anak lākī-lākī
Son-in-law	*anak-an*	menantū lākī-lākī
Song	*ka-bāt-an*	niānyī-an
Soon (presently)	*dai-dai dakoman*	sa'buntar lāgi
Soot	*būling anglit*	ārang pāra
Sore	*ma-sākit*	sākit
Sore-eyed	*māta bīlas*	māta bīlas
Sorrow	*sūsah hātāi*	sūsah hāti
Sort (kind)	*ginis*	jinis, macham
,, (to arrange)	*hatol, mūmūs*	meng-ātor
Sorcery	*pangūng ōbat*	hōbat-an
Sovereign	*junjongan*	yang-de-per-tuan
Soul (life)	*niāwa*	niāwa, jīwa
Sound (noise)	*tingāg, tüngog*	būnyi
,, (try depth)	*müg-dūga*	būang from, lūga
Soup	*sābau*	kñah
Sour	*maslüm, pukat*	māsam, peder
Source	*asal*	asal
,, (of a river)	*ō sin sōbah*	ūlū sūngei
South	*sātān, slātan*	slātan
Sow (female pig)	*baboi omagak*	bābī betīna
,, (as seed)	*müg-bākal*	tābūr

ENGLISH.	SULU.	MALAY.
Spacious	*ma-hāyang, līag*	lāpang, lūas
Spade	*susārāh*	peng-gālī
Spain	*Lopa-Kastela*	Tānah-Spaniol
Spaniard	*Tāu-Kastela*	Orang-Spaniol
Span	*dangau*	jangkal
Spare (lean)	*kāiūg*	kūrus
Sparrow	*paupit*	pīpit
Speak	*pāmong, kūno, lōng*	kāta, chākāp
,,	*na pānga, hamal :*	rāban :
Spear	*būjak, binangkau* *	tombak, limbing
,, , fish-	*sapang, manalioh*	sarampang
,, , to	*tigbak, tībak*	tīkam
Specimen	*sontoh*	chontoh
Speckled	*butikan*	ber-intik, sūpak
Spectacles	*sāmin māta*	chermin māta
Spectre	*lītau*	hantū
Speech (language)	*bahāsa*	bhāsa
Speed (velocity)	*dāgan, pa-rāg-an*	ka-lajū-an
Speedily	*segla*	segra
Spell (a charm)	*ajīmat, hajīmat*	azīmat
,, , to	*ēja, hēja*	ēja
Spend, to	*peg-balanja*	balanjā-kan
Spices	*lampah †*	rampah-rampah †
Spider, a	*lāwa-lāwa*	lāba-lāba
Spiders web	*lāwai lāwa-lāwa*	sarang lāba-lāba
Spill	*āsay*	tūmpah
Spin	*maningkal*	pintal, ganteh

* A spear with a short blade used in the chase. † Used as condiments.

‡ To speak through the nose.

ENGLISH.	SULU.	MALAY.
Spine	*bŭkoj sin taĭkūl*	tŭlang blākang
Spirit (soul)	*niāwa*	niāwa
,, (ghost)	*lūtau, gālāp* *	hantū
,, evil-	*jin*	jin
,, (arrack)	*ālak, pengasi*	arak
Spit (expectorate)	*mŭg-lūrah*	ber-lūdah
Spite	*na sākit hātāi*	sākit hāti
Spittle (saliva)	*lūrah*	lūdah
Spittoon	*bātil*	tampat lūdah
Spleen	*bagoh*	kurra
Splice	*supat-an, sugaya*	ūlas
,, (join on)	*sāmbong*	sāmbong, ūbong
Split	*sĭpak*	blah
,, , to	*mŭg-tad-tad* †	ber-palupah †
,, (rotans etc.)	*salik-an*	mem-arang
,, (in quantities)	*lepak*	ber-lepak-lepak
Splinter, to	*tñis-tñis*	ber-tatal, turis
,, (lath of bamboo)	*bulah*	tatal
,, (lath of nĭbong)	*banga*	blambang, tatal
Spoil	*na-kangi, na-larak*	rūsak, bināsa
Spoon, a	*sārūh*	sendok, sūduk
Sport (to play)	*naiam*	māin
Spot, a (place)	*tungud*	tāmpat
Spots (on the skin)	*ap-ap*	panau
Spotted	*butikan*	ber-intĕk, sūpak
Sprain	*piol*	sālah ūrat
Spray (foam)	*būkal*	ārū, būhī

* Spirit of the ocean.

† To split open bamboos used for the walls of houses.

ENGLISH.	SULU.	MALAY.
Spread out, to	*īklad, īklar-an*	ampur, kambang
Spring, to	*ma-ompat, laksù*	lompat
,, (fountain)	*bual, tubur-an*	māta āyer
Spring-tide	*dagat dākolah*	pāsang besár
Sprinkle	*sābūlak-an*	sīram
Spur (of a cock)	*tāhūd*	sūsoh āyam
,, (gaffle)	*būlang*	tāji
,, , to	*handuk, hondūk*	gārtak
Spy, a	*tāu seb*	peniūlu
,, , to	*seb*	sūlū
Spying-glass	*tolompong*	trōpong
Squall, a	*hānus*	bādong
Square, a	*pa-sāgī opat*	ampat per-sāgī .
Squeeze (press)	*kām-kām-i*	apīt, tākan
,, (pinch)	*gipit, hubut*	chūbit, pīchit
Squint-eyed	*lībat in māta*	māta-jūlīng
Squirrel, a	*basing*	tūpei
Squirt, to	*bustak*	lunchūr
Stab, to	*tigbak, tībak*	tīkam
Stable, a	*pagal*	kandang
,, (for horses)	*bāī kūra*	rūmah kūda
Staff, a	*tongkād*	tongkat
Stag, a	*ūsa ūsog*	rūsa jantan
Stain, a	*ka-ketamak-an*	mūting
,, (to colour)	*ketamak-an*	chalak, parut
,, , to(the teeth)	*pūnglas, latak*	chachat,chōring
Stairs	*hāg-dān*	tanggah
Stale, to	*mīhī, īhī*	ber-kinching
Stalk, a (stem)	*tangkai, bātang*	tangkei, bātang

ENGLISH.	SULU.	MALAY.
Stallion	*kūra mandangan*	kūda jantan
Stammer	*tāngah*	gāgap
,, (lisp)	*kātop*	gāgâp
Stamp, a (seal)	*sāp*	chap
Stand	*tindog, tumindog*	dīrī
Star, a	*bītin, bītūhun*	bintang
,, morning-	*maga*	bintang bābi
,, evening-	*hi-tong*	,, zaharat
,, -fish	*tangan-tangan*	
Starbord	*tō* *	kānan *
Starch	*kanjī*	kanjī
Stare, to	*nig-lēlīgat*	pandang
Start (alarmed)	*kieurgnāt*	kajut
Starved	*biūntas*	bulor-bulor
Stay	*tagad*	nanti
Stead, in-	*sābli*	ganti
Steal	*takau, tīakau*	chūrī
Steam	*wāp, aso*	awāp
Steed	*kūra pang-āra-an*	kūda tunggang
Steel	*balan*	bāja
Steep (to soak)	*randam, tāpūs-an*	rendam, chelop
,, (precipitous)	*mu-titab, pang-pang*	tega, tarjal
Steer, to	*ka-mapūt ha bānsan*	pegang kamūdi
Stem (stalk)	*tangkai, bātang*	tangkei, bātang
,, (of a tree)	*puhun, bātang*	puhun, bātang
Stench	*baū hāloh*	bāū būsuk
Step (a pace)	*tīkang*	langkah
Step-father	*bāpa tīrī*	bāpa tīrī

* Right-hand side.

ENGLISH.	SULU.	MALAY.
Step over, to	*lakad*	langkah
Steps	*hāg-dān*	tanggah
Stern (of a vessel)	*būlī*	burīt-an
Stew (to boil)	*tolah*	rebūs
Steward	*bandārī* *	bandhārī *
Stick (to pierce)	*tugsuk*	chūchuk
,, (be impeded)	*sagnat, sasat*	sangkūt
,, (to adhere)	*pīkit, mīkit*	lekat
Still (yet)	*maien, mayen*	jūga, lāgi, pūla
,, (calm)	*lēnau*	tedoh
,, (motionless)	*tūnah, tūmūnah*	kuchiba
Sting (of an insect)	*ka-bīsa-han*	sangat
Stink	*bāhū hāloh*	bāū būsok
,, , to	*ma-bāhū*	ber-bāhū
Stipulate, to	*mug-janjī*	ber-janjī
Stirrup	*ka-geīk-an, gigīkan*	tampat kāki
Stock (capital)	*mōdal, puhun*	mōdal, pōkok
,, (of a gun)	*tagōban*	bātang
Stockings	*mējis, tagōban sīki*	sārong kāki
Stomach	*babat*	ampadal
,, , pit of the	*ū hātāi*	ūlū hāti
Stone	*bātu*	bātu
,, , precious	*palmāta*	permāta
,, (of fruit)	*bīgi*	bīji
Stool (a chair)	*sīa*	krosī
,, (a seat)	*ka-linkūr-an*	tampat dūduk
,, , to (evacuate)	*mintāū*	bērak, būang āyer
Stoop	*humubuh*	tunduk, lāyah

* Also cook for the crew of a vessel.

ENGLISH.	SULU.	MALAY.
Stop (to cease)	*dumuhong, duhong*	ber-hentī
,, up	*hulat-an*	meniampal
Stopper	*hūlat*	sampal, sūmbat
Stork	*bangau*	bāngū
Storm	*hūnus*	rībut, tūfān
,, , to (assault)	*langgal*	langgar
Story (a floor)	*pangkat*	pangkat
,, , lower	*angkap ha-babah*	,, di-bāwah
,, , upper	*angkap ha-tās*	tingkat
,, (tradition)	*bechāla sin ka-mās-an*	hakāyat
Stout (corpulent)	*ma-tambŭk*	gumok
Straddle, to	*ma-bingkang*	kangkang, jūlang
Straight	*tūlid, buntol*	lūrus, betul
,, (towards)	*tūjū*	tūjū
Strain (to filter)	*sāh, mŭg-lchau*	tāpis
,, (to draw tight)	*nŭg-kansang*	kinchang-kan
Strainer	*sāh-an*	tapīs-an
Strait (narrow)	*sigpit, sigpid*	sumpit
,, (channel)	*tāns-an*	trūs-an, salát
Stranded	*sanglad*	ter-kāndas
Strange (foreign)	*dowain, dōāin*	asing
Stranger (trader)	*anak dagang*	ōrang-dāgang
,, (foreigner)	*tāw dōāin*	ōrang asing
,, (new comer)	*tāu bāgū*	ōrang bhārū
,, ,, ,,	*singke* *	singke *
Strangle	*pīkol*	kūjut, chekek
Straw (stubble)	*būnglai*	mārang
Streaked	*manas*	chūra-chūra

* Applied to Chinese only.

ENGLISH.	SULU.	MALAY.
Stream (river)	*sūbah*	sūngei
,, , to go down	*lūmaras*	hĭlir
,, , to go up	*sūd pa ō*	mŭdek
,, (current)	*hāus*	hărus
Street (road)	*dān*	jălan
Strength	*ka-gaus-an*	ka-tagōh-an
Stretch	*būntang*	bentang
,, out the hand, to	*ongsūd*	ŭnjuk-an
Strike, to	*lōbak, lagut*	pūkul
,, (to hammer)	*pŭk-pŭk*	timpa
,, (with the fist)	*sontok*	gōchoh
,, (to slap)	*sampak*	tampar
,, against, to	*dogtol*	injat, sontoh
Strip, to (unhusk)	*manilad*	kūbak
String (cord)	*lūbid*	tăli
,, , to file on a	*tūhog*	chūchuk
Strong (as the wind)	*kansang*	kinchang
,, (vigorous)	*ma-basag*	kŭat
,, (muscular)	*gaus, tagap*	tagap, tagoh
,, (powerful)	*kuasa, kŭsog, gaus*	kuāsa, kŭat
,, (vocally)	*gagah*	kŭat suāra
,, (as currents etc.)	*tŭgda*	drăs, kinchang
Struggle (contend)	*mang-ātu, lūmūn*	ber-lăwan
Strumpet	*ka-bīga, mapachik*	sundal
Strut, to	*ma-lingkat*	ber-gambīra
Stuff, to	*mŭg-durasok**	memumnŭ-ī sasak*
Stump (of a tree)	*tunggul*	tunggul
Stupid	*kangog*	kăguh, mŭrong

* To fill by thrusting.

ENGLISH.	SULU.	MALAY.
Stupid (foolish)	*dōpāng*	bōdoh, bingong
Stutter, to	*tangah*	gagap
Subsequently	*ulih-an*	kamadīan
Substitute	*sābli*	ganti
Subtle	*bījak*	bījak
Success	*untong*	untong
Succour	*tābang*	tōlong, bantū
Suck, to	*sûp-sûp*	īsap
Sue (solicit)	*mīki, pangaioh*	pohon, minta
,, (to prosecute)	*pūg-dāwa*	ber-dāwa
Suet	*dāging*	lemak
Suffer (to endure)	*sandal, andūl*	tāhan
,, (permit)	*bīa, bial*	bīar
Sufficient	*sarang, ganap*	chūkup, sedang
Suffocate	*siampong*	lemas
Sugar	*sākal*	gūla, sakar
Sugar-cane	*tubu, tabu*	tebu
,, -cake	*bināgol*	kuēh mānis
,, -candy	*sākal bātu*	gūla bātu
Suit (to fit)	*ma-tāp*	katūju
Sulky	*sākit hawatīl*	rājuk
Sulphur	*mailang*	balērang
Sultan	*Sūltan, Junjongan*	Sūltan
Sultana	*Pangīan*	Permisūri, Rāni
Sultry	*ma-pāso*	pānas-pānas
Sulu (the island)	*Pū-Sōg, Lopa-Sōg*	Pūlau-Suluk
Suluman, a	*Tāu-Sōg*	Orang-Suluk
Sum (amount)	*jŭmlah*	jumlah
Summit	*puntuk*	ponchak

ENGLISH.	SULU.	MALAY.
Summon	*tāwag, tāg*	panggil
Sun	*māta sūga, sūga*	māta hārī
Sun-dry, to	*buhad, buhar-i*	jemur
Sun-beam	*sinag sin sūga*	sīnar māta hārī
Sun-rise	*gimūah in sūga*	māta hārī terbit
Sun-set	*samadlŭp in sūga*	māta hārī māsok
Sunday	*adlau ahad*	hārī ahad
,,	*rominggo* *	hārī minggo *
Sunder	*būtas*	cherai
Sup (to spoon)	*mŭg-sūrāh*	ber-sendok, īrup
,, (to eat)	*ka-maun*	mākan
Superintendent	*mandol, nakora*	kapāla, mandor
Superior (greater)	*lebih dākolah*	lebih besár
,, (higher)	*matās*	lebih tinggi
Superlative (signs of)	*tŭd, pakariau*	ter, sakāli
Supple	*lumit*	lumbūt, lentok
Supplicate	*mīki*	pohon, minta
Support (sustain)	*tanggong, bŭgbŭg-an*	tanggong
,, (to prop)	*tongkas-an*	ber-sōkong
Suppose (imagine)	*āgī, sāmbat*	sangka
Suppurate	*mŭg-nānah*	ber-nānah
Supreme	*dākolah pakaraiau*	mahā besár
Sure	*tantu*	tantu
Surety (bail)	*ātas-an, tanggong-an*	akū-an
Surf	*ma-alun*	ombak, galōrō
Surface	*ha-gñah, ātas*	di-lūar, atas
,, (of water)	*babau tūbig*	di-ātas āyer
Surfeited	*kien-subāh-an*	kenniang

* Spanish, "domingo."

ENGLISH.	SULU.	MALAY.
Surgeon	*tabib, tabid*	dūkun, bōmo
Surly, to be	*mŭg-dub-dub*	kāser, māsam
Surplus	*ka-lebīh-an*	ka-lebīh-an
Surprised	*hāilan*	hēiran
Surround	*mŭg-lībut*	meng-apong
Sustain (support)	*tanggong*	tanggong
Sustenance	*ka-aun-an*	ka-īdūp-an
Swagger, to	*ma-lingkat*	ber-kāchak
Swallow (the bird)	*īd-īd*	lāyang-lāyang
,,	*kalam pisau* *	lāyang būhi*
,, (white headed)	*lingat-lingat*	
,, , to	*tūn, tūan*	talan
Swamp, a	*sāpa*	rāwah, pāya
Swathe, to	*lampik*	lampin
Swear at, to	*peninggad*	mākī
,, (take an oath)	*mŭg-sāpah*	ber-sumpah
Sweat	*hulas*	peluh
,, , to	*hulas-an*	ka-lūar peluh
Sweep, to	*mŭg-sāpū (maspas +)*	sāpū, meniāpu
Sweeper (a broom)	*sa-sāpū*	peniāpū
Sweepings	*sagbut*	sampah
Sweet	*maimoh*	mānis
,, scented	*mamūd*	wangī
,, in sound	*ma-lōi*	mardū
,, -heart	*tūnang*	kā-kāsih, tūnang
Sweetmeats	*maimōh-an*	manīs-an
Sweet-potatoe	*panggi bagūn*	ūbī kantang

* Hirundo esculenta; edible nest swallow. Javanese, "lawit."

† Maspas : to dust.

ENGLISH.	SULU.	MALAY.
Swell, to	*hūbag, bujol* *	bŭngkak
Swift	*ma-rāg-an, ma-buskai*	pantas, lājū
Swill (guzzle)	*la-lŭk-lŭk*	chăruk, īrup
Swim, to	*mŭg-langoi*	bernang
,, (to gloat)	*liantop, lantop*	timbul
Swine	*baboi*	bābi
Swollen	*hūbag, himūbag*	bŭngkak
,, (expanded)	*muskag*	kumbang
Swoon	*piūnong*	pangsan
Sword	*pudang*	pedang
,, , broad-	*kaliawang*	galiwang
Syrup	*tūbig sūkal*	āyer gūla

Table	*la-mīsa-han* †	mēja †
Tack, to (as a ship)	*pulta, bēlok* ‡	ber-pāl, bēlok ‡
Tail	*ēkog*	ēkor
,, (queue)	*punjong*	thāu chang
Take, to	*kawa, kā-ā*	ambil
,, away to	*kawa matoh*	bāwa pergi
,, in, to (cheat)	*lēgau, līgot*	kīchŭ, tipu
,, care	*kītu, saioi*	jāga
,, heed	*ingat*	īngat
Talisman (charm)	*ajimat*	azimat
Talk, to (speak)	*nŭg-pāmong*	ber-kāta
,, in sleep, to	*man-damat*	ngīkū

* Applied to animals.   † In Spanish, "la mesa" = the table.

‡ Pal = to tack; *belok*, — "to steer more to windward"-hence, the word of command used, in directing the helmsman of a vessel, to bring her round, during the operation of tacking. Ber-pal-pal = to beat to windward.

ENGLISH.	SULU.	MALAY.
Talkative	matāud beshāla	mūlut ganggū
Tall	ma-lanjang	panjang
,, (high)	ma-tās	tinggī
Tame	tūtūt, ka-pachut	jīnak
Tangle	na sagnat	mengūsut
Tap (to knock)	kagōl, pok-pok	tepok, ketok
Tapioca (plant)	pānggi kāhōi	ūbī kāyū
,, (flour)	lūmbīa pānggi kāhōi	tepong ūbī kāyū
Tar	aiketlan, aketlan	mīniak tar
Tarnished	wāi sāia	īlang chayā-nia
Tardy (slow)	ma-būskau, ma-lālai	lambat
Target, a	sasāl-an	sasār-an
,, (buckler)	iral-iral	prīsī, salūkong
Taro	haupe	kaladi
Tassel, a	jambu	jambul
Taste (flavour)	anam	rāsa
Tatters (rags)	ragmai, dagmai	percha
Tax	sākai	chūkei
Tea (infusion)	tūbig piaso (pāso)	tēh, cha
Tea-leaf	dāhūn tē	dāūn tēh
Tea-pot	pate-kūan	tēh-kūan (Ch.)
Teach, to	hindoh, mūg-gūlū	meng-ājar
Teacher	gūlū	gūrū
Teak	kāhōi jātī, jāti	kāyū jātī, jāti
Tear, to	gisi	kōyak
Tears	lūha, tūbig māta	āyer māta
,, , to shed	tomāngis, man-āngis	men-āngis
Tease	mūg-kakat, ūsik	sākat, ūsik
Teat	pungan dūrūh	ūjong sūsū

ENGLISH.	SULU.	MALAY.
Teeth	*īpūn*	gīgī
Telescope	*talompong*	tropong
Tell, to (count)	*ītong*	bilang
,, , to (relate)	*baita*	brī tāu, bilang
Temper (disposition)	*palangai*	parangi
Temple (church)	*bāi langgal*	rūmah sambayang
,, (mosque)	*mesgid*	mesjid
,, (at Mecca)	*kābah*	kābah
,, (of the head)	*pa badlak-an in ū*	palīpis
Ten	*hangpoh*	sa'pūloh
,, thousand	*sa'laksa*	sa'laksa
Tend, to	*jāga, tāmūnggū*	tunggū, jāga
Tent, a	*haima*	kheimah
Tepid	*sarang in pāso*	sūam
Terrified	*kiang-kang-an*	māngū
Testicles	*bīgī būyong*	būah peler
Tetter (ringworm)	*kālap, ugihap*	kūrap
Than	*dien-ha, dien*	deri-pada
Thank (thanks)	*taimahan ku*	tarīma kāsih
That	*ien, ietu, iaun*	ītu
,, , in order	*sobai*	sopāya, maka
,, will do	*s'ārī na*	sūdah la
Thatch	*atùp*	ātap
The	*ien, ietu, iaun, in*	ītu, īang
Theft	*ka-tīakau-an*	ka-chūrī-an
Their	*kan-nya*	dia pūnya
Them	*nila, sila, sia, nia*	dia, iya
Then (at that time)	*pa-bīla, sa-kāli*	pada katīka ītu
Thence, from	*dien dān, dien ha ietu*	deri sāna

ENGLISH.	SULU.	MALAY.
There	*ha ietu, dūn*	di-sītu, di-sāna
There !	*na !*	nah !
Therefore	*sabab iaun, būt kalna*	sabab ītu
These	*īni*	īni
They	*nila, sila, nia, sia*	dia ōrang, dia
Thick	*dŭkmal, ma-rŭkmal*	tabal
,, set (close)	*ma-sagbut, ragnut*	karáp, kadāp
Thief, a	*tāu takau, shugarol*	pen-chūri
Thigh	*pāhā, paā*	pāhā
Thimble	*sūploh*	didal, sūrong jārī
Thin (not thick)	*ma-nīpis*	nīpis
,, (lean)	*ma-kaing*	kūrus
Things (effects)	*ata, ka-kana, alta*	arta
,, (baggage)	*pūtūs-pūtūs*	bārang-bārang
Think	*pīkil, jangka*	fikir, sangka
Third	*ka-tō*	ka-tīga
Thirsty	*īūhāu, āhāu*	hāus, dhāga
Thirty	*katlūan, ka-tulu-an*	tīga-pūloh
This	*īni*	īni
Thorn, a	*tūnok, pohong*	dūri, unak
Thorough	*tāi*	trūs
Those	*icn, ietu, iaun*	ītu
Thou	*ĕkau*	angkau, mu
Though	*mīsan, minsan*	wolo, maski
Thought	*āgī, anām, jangka, ka-pikīl-an*	sangka, ka-fikīr-an
Thousand	*ību*	rību
,, , a	*ang-ību*	sa'rību
,, , ten	*sa'laksa*	sa'laksa

ENGLISH.	SULU.	MALAY.
Thread	*sāban, salban*	benang
Three	*tō*	tīga
,, quarters	*tō ang-ātād*	tīga sūkū
,, times	*maka tō*	tīga kālī
Thresh (as padi)	*gcīk-an*	lubor
Threshold	*langkah-an*	ambang, chupu
Throat (gullet)	*tūn-tūn-an*	kūngan
,, (windpipe)	*gùng-gùng-an*	rungkong
,, (exterior)	*lrùg, lŏhcy*	lĕher
Throb	*badlak*	ber-dabar
Through	*lagbas, limagbas*	trūs, lantas
Throw	*tēlo, lapud*	lempar, champak
,, (cast)	*biugit, sīapud*	bñang
Thrust (push)	*tōlak*	tōlak, sōrong
,, (push in)	*hitād, samād*	chabur
,, (stab)	*tigbak, tībak*	tīkam
,, (insert between)	*sip-sip*	sīsip
Thumb	*bakal, bakūl*	ībū jārī
Thunder	*dùg-dùg*	gūrub, gūntur
,, bolt	*lintch, litih*	hali-lintar
Thursday	*adlau hāmīs*	hārī khamīs
Thus	*bi-ha-īni*	bagīni
Thwart	*babag*	lintang
Thy	*kan ĕkau*	angkau pūnya
Thyself	*kan baran mu*	angkau sīndīrī
Tick (insect)	*kūtū bībang*	kūtū sāpī
Tickle, to	*gilok-an*	gilī-kan
Ticklish	*gilok, gitok*	gīlī, gillī
Tide, flood-	*taub, sùg*	āyer pāsang

ENGLISH.	SULU.	MALAY.
Tide, ebb-	*hūnas, lāng*	āyer sūrut
,, , spring-	*dagat dākolah*	pāsang besár
,, , neap-	*dagat-an, tubig-an*	āyer purbani
,, (current)	*hāus*	hārus
,, ripple	*abal, habal*	ombak-ombak
Tides, the	*sûg-lāng*	pāsang-sūrut
Tidings	*gawi*	khabar, brīta
Tie, to	*hīukit, bagkut*	īkat, tambat
,, (to knot)	*bākā-han*	simpūl-kan
Tier (a row)	*sūsun, pangkat*	sūsun, pangkat
Tiger, a	*halīmau*	harīmau
Tight	*kansang, sigpit*	ketat, trek
Tiles	*tīsa (Sp. teja)*	ginting
Till	*ampa*	hingga
,, (to plough)	*mug-araru*	men-anggāla
,, (to cultivate)	*mug-āma*	per-ūsah tānah
Timber	*kahōi*	kāyū
,, , to fell	*ma-mēla*	men-ābang
Time	*ganta, māsa*	waktu, tempo
,, (a date)	*tugun*	waktu, tempo
,,	*tumanggoh* *	tanggoh *
Times	*mīsan*	kāli
Timid	*ma-bōga*	tākut
Tin (the metal)	*mītal*	tīmah-pūteh
,, (a canister)	*mītal-mītal*	tin, bājan
Tinfoil	*pedlas*	kartas tīmah
Tip	*pūnshak*	pūnchak
Tiptoe, on	*ingki*	ber-jengke

* To grant time to pay a debt.

ENGLISH.	SULU.	MALAY.
Tipsy	*hīlo*	mābok
Tired	*hiapus*	panat, punat
Title	*gālal, gālal*	gālar
To	*kan, ha*	akan, semā, pada
,, (noting motion)	*pa*	ka
,, -day	*adlau īni*	hārī īni
,, -day	*adlau iaun**	hārī īni tādī *
,, -night	*dūm īni*	mālam īni
,, -morrow	*kin-shūm*	ēsok, besok
,, ,, morning	*kin-shūm mainat*	besok pāgi
,, ,, evening	*kin-shūm mahapun*	besok petang
Toast	*panggang*	panggang
Tobacco	*tabākū*	tambākū
,, , chinese	*hān, ang-hūn (Ch.)*	tambākū-chīna
,, (cigars)	*dābla*	cherūt
Toe	*gulamai sīkī*	jārī kākī
,, , great	*bakūl sīkī*	ībū kākī
Together	*dūngan-dūngan*	sāma-sāma
Toil (labour)	*pieg-ūsāh-an*	ūsāh-an
,, (to labour)	*māg-hīnang*	ber-ūsah, karja
Toils (snare)	*jalat*	jarat
Token	*indahan, īndān*	tanda
,, (keepsake)	*chela*	chendor
Tolerate	*sandal*	tāhan
Tomatoes	*tālong-iulopa*	trōng-iuropa
Tomb	*kūbāl*	kubūr
Tone	*tūngog, tingūg*	būnyi
Tongs	*hi-gipit, gipit*	sepit, penyepit

* The day that has just past.

ENGLISH.	SULU.	MALAY.
Tongue	*dīlah*	lidah
Too (in excess)	*lando, pakaraiau*	amat
,, (likewise)	*dākoman*	pūla
Tools	*ka-pāniap-an*	pagāwei, ālat
Tooth	*īpūn*	gīgī
,, eye-	*tāling*	gīgī tāring
,, (grinder)	*būgang*	garham
,, (to file)	*lagnas in īpūn*	merepang gīgī
,, (to brush)	*mūg-kūs-kūs*	sūgī
Toothache	*mang-ilu*	sākit gīgī
Toothpick	*tīnga, kūs-kūs*	chunkil gīgī
Top (summit)	*puntuk, punshak*	ponchak
,, (ridge of roof)	*biūbōng-an*	per-ūbong-an
,, (upper part)	*ha-tās*	di-ātas
,, (cover)	*saub, lohor*	sāū
Torch	*sōh*	sūloh
Torpid	*kūpong*	kāgoh
Tortoise	*paiokan*	pūnyū
,, , land-	*bāūh-o, kūla*	kurra-kurra
,, -shell	*sīsik*	sīsik
Total (amount)	*jūmlah*	jumlah
,, (all)	*ka-tān, ka-tan-tan*	samūa
Totter	*hoyoy, dūndang*	gōyang, tanggoi
Touch	*dimūpūn*	jāmah, jābat
,, (reach)	*ābūt, sampiy*	sampei
,, at	*hāpit, rāmānggo*	singgah
,, (close)	*rāig, dāig, lapat*	rāpat
,, (hit)	*kiēgdan*	kena
Tow, to	*guiud, tūnda*	tūnda, hīrit

ENGLISH.	SULU.	MALAY.
Towards	*man-ūjū, tūjū*	men-ūjū
Towel	*jimpau*	tūāla
Town	*banūa*	bendar, negrī
,, (village)	*lōng-an, ka-bāi-an*	kampong
Toy	*pŭg-nāīm-an*	per-māīn-an
Track (a path)	*dān, rān*	jālan, lūrong
,, (footmark)	*limpa sīkī*	bakas kākī
Trade (to traffic)	*mŭg-dāgang*	ber-nīāga
Trader (merchant)	*saudāgāl*	sudāgar
Trail (to drag)	*guiud, yuiur-an*	hīrit, tārek
Train (retinue)	*ka-agar-an,*	peng-īkot,
	ka-bunyog-an	peng-īring
,, (instruct)	*anad*	ajar
Trample	*mug-geīk, ka-geīk*	īrik, injak
Transcribe, to	*sālin, hālin*	sālin
Transgress to	*hīnang sāh*	ber-dōsa
Transgression	*ka-sāh-an, dōsa*	ka-salāh-an
Translate	*sālin bahāsa*	sālin bhāsa
Transplant	*pindah-an*	pindah-kan
Trap (snare)	*jalat*	jarat
,, , pig-	*lītag baboi*	per-ankap-an bābi
Trash (rubbish)	*sagbut*	sampah
,, (idle talk)	*kongkan, bāla-ūla*	sīa-sīa
Travail (child birth)	*picg-anāk-an*	per-anāk-an
Travel, to	*panau, manau*	ber-jālan
Tray (metal)	*tālam, suntai**	tālam
,, (wood)	*dulang, bintang†*	dulang
Tread (to step)	*nŭg-tīkang*	me-langkah

* Square.   † Round.

ENGLISH.	SULU.	MALAY.
Tread upon	*mūg-geīk, na ka-geīk*	īrek, injak
Treason	*daulaka*	durāka
Treasure (money)	*pēlak*	wāng
Treasurer, a	*bandāra*	bandahāra
Treasure-trove	*gadong sin ka-mās-an*	
Treat (entertain)	*pieg-oira-han*	men-jāmu
Treaty	*kapetorasion**	trīti (Eng.)
,, (agreement)	*pūg-janjī-an*	per-janjī-an
Tree	*kāhōi, bātang kāhōi*	pūhn, pōko kāyū
Tremble	*ma-mūd-pīd*	gomitar
Trench	*gāta*	pārit
Trial (judicial)	*bechāla, bīchala*	bechāra
,, (experiment)	*ka-solai-an*	ka-chobā-an
Triangle	*tō pu sāgī*	tīga sāgī
Tribe	*bangsa*	sūkū, lūrah
,, (race)	,,	bangsa
Tribulation	*ka-sukāl-an*	ka-sukār-an
Trick, to	*mūg-akal, akāl-an*	būat akal
Trickle, to	*mūg-tō*	ber-tītek
Trifle (to idle)	*lālai*	lālei
,, (play tricks)	*ūla-ūla*	gūrau
Trim, to (a boat)	*timbang-i*	timbang-kan
,, , (a wick)	*sugi-han*	gunting sumbū
Trip (to stumble)	*hantak*	hantok
Trot, to	*tūtūk*	lārī
Troubled (in mind)	*ma-sūsah hātai*	sūsah hāti
,, (afflicted)	*ka-susāh-an*	ka-susāh-an
Trousers	*sawal*	saluar

* Spanish, "Capitulacion."

ENGLISH.	SULU.	MALAY.
True	*bānal, angkan asa*	benar, sūnggoh
,, (exact)	*āmū, āmūna*	betul
,, (certain)	*tantū*	tantu
Truly	*hù, bānal-bānal*	iya, benar-benar
Trumpet	*tiŭp-tiŭp*	nafirī, sarunei
Trunk (of a tree)	*bātang*	bātang
,, (a chest)	*baul, bilolang*	petī
,, , elephant's	*kalolai, mayong*	bulālei
Trust (credit)	*pelchāya*	perchāya
,, (confide in)	*hālap, andal*	hārap
Truth	*ka-bunāl-an*	ka-benār-an
Try, to (attempt)	*sōlai*	chōba
,, (judicially)	*mag-hukum*	meng-hukum
Trysail, a	*lāyag kīpas*	bara gūsi, gūsi
Tub	*tong*	tong
Tuba *	*tūbli*	tūba
Tuber	*pānggi*	ūbī
Tuck up	*laisah, lais*	sing-sing
,, ,up (the trousers)	*kīn-kīn-an*	sing-sing
Tuesday	*adlau sālasa*	hārī salāsa
Tuft (of feathers)	*tarong*	jambūl
Tug (pull)	*hēlā, ātăng*	hēlā, tārek
Tugboat	*kapal tūnda*	kapal tūnda
Tumble	*holog, hōg*	jātoh, róntoh
,, (as trees)	*hoyog*	tumbang
,, (stumble)	*hantak*	sontoh
Tumour, a	*opāng*	karūpang, būsong

*The Malay name of a plant the root of which has a stupifying
effect upon fish. Tuba-fishing is an exciting pastime.

ENGLISH.	SULU.	MALAY.
Tumour (a boil)	*bahū ūtūt*	bīsol, bāra
Tumult	*hīlo-hāla*	hīrū-hāra
Turban	*pīs*	destar, serbān
Turbid	*lūbog*	kruh
Turk	*Tāu-Istambul*	Orang-Rōm
Turkey *	*Rōm, Stambul*	Rōm
Turmeric	*dālau*	kūnyit
Turn over, to	*bēng, bieng*	bālik
,, horizontally, to	*pūsal +*	pūsar +
,, , to (twist)	*sūbid, sūbir-an*	pintal
,, round, to	*līgut*	pūsing, kītar
,, the head, to	*limingi, lingit*	pāling
,, , to re-	*nūg-balck, minūi, bieng, mūi*	bālik kombāli, pūlang
,, back, to (repel)	*dui-a*	hālau
,, out, to (eject)	*biugit ha-gñah*	k'lūar-kan
,, toward, to	*mŭg-hārap*	meng-ādap
,, from, to	*mŭg-taikūr-an*	pūsing bālik
,, (by turns)	*nŭg-sūbli-sūbli*	ber-ganti-ganti
Turquoise	*pīlās*	firūz
Turtle, a	*paiokan*	penyū, kātōng
Tusk, boar's	*taling*	siyūng, taring
,, , elephant's	*gāring*	gāding
Tutor	*gūlū*	gūrū
Twelve	*hangpoh-tŭg-dūa*	dūa-blas
,, o'clock	*lesag hangpoh-tŭg-dūa*	pūkol dūa-blas
Twenty	*kaūhan (ka-rūa-an)*	dūa-pūloh
Twice	*maka-rūa (dūa)*	dūa kālī

* Ottoman Empire.   † As a mill-stone, or whirlpool.

N

ENGLISH.	SULU.	MALAY.
Twig, a	*tangkai*	ranting
Twilight	*lūgūb-lūgūb-māgālib*	suwāng
,, (nearly night)	*mārī na dūm*	hampir mālam
,, (dark)	*tigidlam*	gālāp
Twine, to	*sūbid, pinsal*	pintar
,, (string)	*lūbid*	tālī
Twinkle (sparkle)	*pelau-pelau*	gamīlang
,, (as the eyes)	*kalap*	kechap, kajap
Twins	*kambal*	kambar
Twirl	*giling*	lingar
Twist	*pinsal, sūbid*	pintal
Two	*rūa, dūa*	dūa
,, hundred	*dūa ang-gātus*	dūa rātus
,, or three	*dūa tū*	dūa tīga
,, -edged	*māta rūa*	māta dūa
Typhoon	*hūnus*	ribut, tūfān
Tyrannical	*anyāya*	anyāya

Udder	*dūrāh*	sūsū
Ugly	*mangi rūgbus, gābok in rūgbus*	rūpa jāhat, rūpa būruk, hūdoh
Ulcer	*peniākit pūlā*	pūrū, tōkak
Ultimate (finish)	*in ka-pūas-an*	īang ka-putūs-an
,, (last)	*ahil*	ākhir
Umbrage	*sākit hātāi*	sākit hāti
Umbrella	*pāyong*	pāyong
Unable	*di man-jāri*	tiāda būlih
,, (powerless)	*di maka gaus, di ka-kaya-han*	tiāda kūasa, tiāda būlih kūāt

ENGLISH.	SULU.	MALAY.
Unaccustomed	*būkùn bīaksa*	tiāda bīāsa
Unarmed	*wāi rūn takùs*	tiāda sinjāta
Unbecoming	*būkùn maraiau*	tiāda lāyik
Unbeliever, an	*kāpil,* tāu lanat*	kāfir *
Uncertain	*wāi pa tantū*	ta'tantu
Uncircumcised	*pūyos, pūgong*	ber-kūlop
Uncle	*amah-an*	bāpa sūdāra
Unctuous	*ma-raging*	ber-lemak
Undaunted	*maīsùg*	barānī
Under	*ha-babah, babah*	di-bāwah, bāwah
,, (less than)	*kōlang dien-pa*	kōrang deri-pada
,, (a house)	*ha-sùm*	di-bāwah rūmah
Undermost	*in ha-babah tùd*	īang dī-bāwah s'kāli
Understand	*maka-hāti, saioh*	meng-artī
Understanding	*budī, budīman*	budī
Undetermined	*bimbang*	bimbang
Undomesticated	*tālon*	jālang, liar
Undress, to	*hūkas*	būka kāin, tanggal
Uneasy	*sūkūl, muskil*	līsah, sughul
Unemployed	*wāi rūn hīnāng-an, wāi rūn peng-ūsāh-an*	tiāda ber-ūsah, tiāda karja
Unequal	*salisih*	selisih
Uneven (odd)	*gansal, gangsal*	ganjīl
,, (rugged)	*kāsap*	kāsap
,, (not level)	*lūbak buntud*	ta' rāta, lākok
Unexceptionable	*sempolna*	semporna
Unfasten	*ōbār-an, ūbad*	hūrei, būka
Unfathomable	*di matūngkad*	tūbir

* One who does not believe in the Mahomedan religion.

ENGLISH.	SULU.	MALAY.
Unfit	di maka-jādi	tiāda lāyik
Unfortunate	mangi sūkūd	nasib ta'bāīk
„ (wretched)	selāka	chelāka
Unfruitful	di mug-bānga	tiāda ber-būah
Unfurl	jag-jag-an in lāyag	būka lāyer
Unhappy	sūsah hātāi, nug-sūsah	sūsah hāti, ter-sūsah
Unite (connect)	sambong	ber-ūbong
„ (combine)	pākat	pakat
„ (adhere)	mīkit, pīkit	lekat
Unity	ka-īsā-an	ka-asā-an
Unlawful	halām	harām
Unless	ma-lain-kan, lñal	me-lain-kan
Unlike	dōāin-dōāin	tiāda sāma
Unload	hāwas	ponggah
Unlucky	mangi sūkūd	mālang
Unmarried	būjang, sābūl	būjang, gadīs
Unnecessary	wāi gūna	ta'ūsah, tiāda hārus
„ , it is	di mug-ūno, s'ārī na	tiāda mengapa
Unoffending	wāi rān sāh	tiāda ber-dōsa
Unpleasant	mangi in anam	īang tiāda sedap
Unpolished	kāsap, dagmul	kāsar, kāsap
Unrestrained	bības	bības
Unripe	helau, būlak, wala ma-hīnog	mantah, mūda, balūm māsak
Unseemly	sābul	chābul
Unsheath	lārut, hūblūt-an	ūnus, chābut
Unsuitable	di man-jāri	tā'jādi
Untie	ābad, ōbār-an	būka, hūrei

ENGLISH.	SULU.	MALAY.
Until	*ampa*	hingga, sampei
Unto	*kan, ha, pa-ka*	akan, ka-pada
Untrue	*pūting*	bōhong
,, (false)	*dusta*	dusta
Unusual	*māhang*	jārang
Unwilling	*ma-hñkau, di müg-ien*	tiāda māū
Unwise	*kōlang budīman*	kōrang budī
Up (above)	*ātas*	atas
,, to (as high as)	*abñt, tñb-tñb*	sampei, arah
,, , to go (ascend)	*samakat, sakat*	nāīk
,, , to go (climb)	*dāg, rāg, domag*	panjat
,, , to rise	*bangun*	bangun
,, , to set	*tindog-a*	men-dīrī
,, , to pull	*müg-sñat* *	men-chābut *
,, , to stand	*tindog*	ber-dīrī
Upland	*gimbah, ō*	būkit, pāsak
Upon	*ha-tās*	di-ātas
Upper, the	*in ha-tās*	īang di-ātas
Uppermost	*in ha-tās tñd*	īang di-ātas s'kāli
Upright	*tindog*	betul
,, (in morals)	*hākikahan, adil*	tūlus, simporna
Uproar	*kāloh, būkag*	gādoh, gampar
Upset	*rāub, domāub*	ter-balek
Upwards	*pa-tās*	ka-ātas
Urine	*pīeg-īhī-an*	āyer kinching
,, (to discharge)	*mīhī, mñg-īhī*	ber-kinching
Us	*kīta, kāmi, kāmu*	kīta, kāmi
Usage (custom)	*ādat, tabiat*	ādat, tabiat

* As weeds, etc.

ENGLISH.	SULU.	MALAY.
Use (utility)	*gūna, ka-guna-han*	gūna
,, , to	*pakai, mam-akai*	pakei, memakei
Useful	*in tūga gūna*	īang ber-gūna
Useless	*wāi rūn ka-gūna-han*	tiāda ber-gūna
Utterance	*túngog, tingūg*	būnyi
Uvula	*anak dīlah*	anak līdah

Vacant	*wāi lūan-an*	kōsong
Valiant	*ma-īsūg*	barānī
Valley	*lūbak*	lembah
,, (interstice)	*silut*	ka-selāng-an
Value (price)	*hāga, halga*	harga
,, , to	*mūg-halga, tāwal*	tāwar
Valve (a cover)	*saub*	sāū
Vampire, a	*balbal-an*	
Van, in the	*ha-ūna-han*	adāp-an
Variety	*ka-gīnīs indah lopa*	bagei-bāgei
Various	*ka-gīnīs ka-gīnīs-an*	jinis-jinis
Vast	*ma-lūag*	lūas
Veal	*ūnūd anak sāpī*	daging anak sāpī
Vegetables	*sāyol*	sāyor
Veil	*tābūn*	kāin salūbong
,, , to	*tirong*	tūdong
Vein	*ūgat, ūrat*	ūrat dārah
Venerate	*mūg-holmat*	brī hormat
Venereal	*sākit babai*	sākit perampūan
Venison	*ūnūd ūsa*	daging rūsa
Venom	*bīsa*	bīsa
Venomous	*ma-bīsa*	bīsa

ENGLISH.	SULU.	MALAY.
Venture (to try)	*sōlai*	chōba
Venus (the star)	*hi-tong*	zaharat
Verge	*hīgad*	tepī
,, (side)	*pigi*	pinggir
Verily	*bŭnal sa ma-tŭd*	se-sunggoh
Vermifuge	*ōbat kalŭg*	ōbat chāching
Vermin (in clothes)	*tūma*	tūma
Very	*tŭd, pakaraiau*	ter-lālū, amat
Veteran	*amās, mās*	ōrang tūah
Vex, to	*ñsih, mŭg-sasat*	ūsik, bīsing
Vicious	*mangi*	jāhat
Vie	*ātu, umātu*	lāwan
View (look at)	*hatud, pandang*	pandang
,, (object of)	*ka-kīta-an*	ka-līat-an
Vigorous	*ma-basag*	kūat
Village	*kampong, lōng-an*	kampong
Vinegar	*sñka*	chūka
Violin	*bīola*	bīola
Virgin, a	*dāgā, būjang*	anak dāra
Viscera	*lingan-lingan tīan*	īsī prot
Visible	*in ka-kita-han*	īang dapat di-liat
,, (evident)	*jumata, lumahil*	ka-nyatā-an
Vivid (bright)	*sāya*	chāya
Voice	*tŭngog, sñalak*	sūara, bhāna
Void (empty)	*wāi lŭan*	kōsong
,, , to	*mintāñ, intāhñ*	bĕrak
Vomit	*sūka*	muntah
Vow	*sāpah*	sumpah
Vowel-marks	*bālis*	bāris

ENGLISH.	SULU.	MALAY.
Voyage	*pieg-layag-an*	pel-layar-an

Wade	*ūbog*	merandau, arong
Wage war, to	*mūg-būnoh, parang*	ber-p'rang
Wager, to (stake)	*tāu-han, palis*	ber-tāroh
Wages	*tangdan-an*	gājī (Port.)
Waggon (cart)	*karosah*	krētā, pedāti
Wail, to	*langka*	ratap
Waist	*hawakan*	pinggang
,, -girdle	*kandit, jimpau*	tāli pending
Wait	*tūgad, tagad*	nanti
Wake	*bāte, jāga*	jāga, sadar
Walk	*panau*	jālan
Walking-stick	*tongkud*	tongkat
Wall	*dinding* *	dinding *
,, , stone-	*tambak*	tembok
Wallow	*lūb-lūb*	meng-glumang
Wan (pale)	*pūchat, p̄rang*	pūchat
Want (be deficient)	*kōlang*	kōrang
,, (desire)	*mau-bayah, miayah*	māū, handak
War	*pieg-būnoh-an*	p'rang, pāráng
Ward off, to	*tangkis*	tangkis
Wares	*dagāng-an*	dagāng-an
Warehouse	*tīnda, gēdong*	gudāng, gēdong
Warm	*pāso*	panas
Warp (in weaving)	*paindog*	langsin
Warped	*bengkok, kalok*	ber-langkok
Warrant	*tanggong*	tanggong

* Generally applied to walls made of light material.

ENGLISH.	SULU.	MALAY.
Wart	*tangkikil*	kakuwat
Was	*bakas*	telah, sūdah
Wash	*tīmud, tīmur-an*	chūchi, bāsoh
,, (scour)	*hūgas, mangumus*	ūpam, bāsoh
,, (as clothes)	*dak-dak*	sesah, bāsoh
Wasp	*lapinig*	tabūan
Watch, to	*jāga*	ūga
,, (timepiece)	*lelos (Sp. reloj)*	harlōji (Dutch)
Watchman	*jāga-jāga*	ōrang jāga
Watch-tower	*āngkup*	marchū
Water	*tūbig*	āyer
,, , salt-	,, *ma-āsin*	,, māsin
,, , sea-	,, *dāgat*	,, lāūt
,, , brackish-	,, *ma-bāngoy*	,, pāyau
,, , fresh-	,, *ma-tābang*	,, tāwar
,, -fall	*togpa tūbig*	,, terjun
,, -melon	*tīmun*	mandīkī
,, -pot	*kībūt*	kundī, taker
,, -spout	*būhawi*	pūting baliong
,, -worm (teredo)	*kāpang*	kāpang
Wattle (of a cock)	*pilih, pēh*	gūdābir
Wave	*alun*	ombak, alun
,, (billows)	*bombang*	galombang
,, (to beckon)	*kāmai (lajau*)*	lambei, limpei
,, to (brandish)	*sayang*	belāyam
Wax, bees-	*tālu*	lilin
,, , ear-	*atāli, ātil*	tāī telīnga
Way	*dān*	jālan

* To wave with a handkerchief etc.

ENGLISH.	SULU.	MALAY.
Way, in this	*bi-ha-īni*	bagīni
,, , in that	*bi-ha-ien*	bagītu
,, , get out of the	*shăma-i, hawa-i*	anniah
We	*kāmi, kīta, kātu*	kāmi, kīta
Weak (feeble)	*lema-lema*	lemah, letch
,, (silly)	*dōpang*	bōdoh
Wealth	*ka-daya-han*	ka-kayā-an
Wealthy	*dāya*	kāya
Weapon	*takŭs*	sinjātu
Wear, to	*ma-makai*	me-makai
Wearing apparel	*tāmŭngan*	pakāi-an
Weather (season)	*māsim*	mūsim
Weave	*mŭg-hablīn*	tanun, belut
Web, spider's-	*lāwai lāwa-lāwa*	sārang lāba-lāba
Wedding	*peng-asawa-han*	kāwin-an
Wedge	*kāhōi sīp-sīp-an*	bājī
Wednesday	*adlau alba*	hārī arba
Week, a	*angka pīto,*	tūjoh hārī,
	angka rominggo	sātu minggo
Weep	*tāngis, mŭg-tāngis*	menāngis
Weevil	*bōk-bōk*	bōbok
Weigh, to	*timbang*	timbang
Weights	*bātu timbāng-an*	bātu timbāng-an
Weighty	*ma-bōgat, bōgat*	brat
Welcome	*mang-alu-alu*	meng-alu-alu
Well (good)	*maraiau*	bāik
,, (convalescent)	*ka-ulih-an*	sumboh
,, (of water)	*kūpong*	prīgī, talāga
,, (in health)	*maraiau in anam*	bāik nyāman

ENGLISH.	SULU.	MALAY.
Well-bred	bangsa maraiau	bangsa bāik
Well-done!	maraiau bah!	bāik lah!
Wen	dūgal	kūtil
,, (on trees)	būtig	bungkol
West	bāgat, sedlūpan	bārat
Wet	pitak, bāsah	bāsah
,, -through	na lūmok	linchun
Whale, a	gājah mīna, ka-hūmbū	pāus
Wharf	pāntān, pantālan	jambatan
What	ūno	apa
Whatever	mūnga ūno	barāng apa
What's-his-name	hi-kūan	si-ānō
Wheel	silikan	rōda
When?	ka-ūno?	apa-bīla, bīla?
Whence?	dien-dien?	deri-māna?
Where	ha-dien	māna, di-māna
,, , any-	hadien-hadien	māna-māna
Wherefore?	mai, mai-ta,	meng-āpa,
	ūno in sabab?	apa sabab?
Whet, to	mūg-āsah, 'gīl	meng-āsah, kilīr
Whether (if)	bāng	kālau, jekalau
Whetstone	bātu asah-an	bātu peng-āsah
Which	in	īang, yang
Which?	in hadien, hadien?	īang māna?
Whip, a	la-lāgut, la-lōbak	chābok
,, , to	lagut-an	chābok-kan
Whirl (gyrate)	pūsal, līgot	pūsar, pūsing
Whirlpool	bulchok	pusār-an āyer
Whirlwind	hālimpūs	angin pūting balīong

ENGLISH.	SULU.	MALAY.
Whiskers	*bongus*	tāli tūdong
Whisper, to	*hi-gong*	bīsik
Whistle, to	*taghoi*	sīol
,, , a	*suling*	sūling
White	*ma-pūtih, pūtih*	pūtih
Whither	*pa-ka-ien*	ka-māna
Who?	*sīo! hi-sīo!*	siāpa?
,,	*in*	īang, yang
Whoever	*munga-sīo-sīo*	bārang siāpa
Whole (all)	*ka-tān, ka-tan-tan*	samña
Whoop	*gāsūd, ūlang*	tampik, sūrak
Whore	*sūndal, parunda*	sūndal, pandayang
Whose	*kan-sīo*	siāpa pūnya
Why?	*mai! mūg-ūno!*	meng-apa?
Wick, a	*sumbū, sumbūhan*	sumbū
Wicked	*mangi*	jāhat, fāsik
Wicker-ball	*sī-sīpah, sīpah*	rāga
Wide (broad)	*lūkbang*	lēbar
,, (spacious)	*lñag*	lūas
Widow, a	*baloh, bālū*	baloh, bālū
Wife	*asāwa*	bīni, istrī
Wild (as animals)	*ma-adla, tālon*	jālang, līar
,, -cattle	*līsang**	siladang †
Wild-hog	*baboi kātian*	bābi ūtan
Will (shall)	*mau-bayah, mūg-ien*	māū, handak
,, (pleasure)	*ka-bayah-an*	ka-handak
,, (testament)	*wasāyat*	wasāyat
Win	*gimāñg, dimang*	menang

* Bos banteng.   † Bos sondaicus.

ENGLISH.	SULU.	MALAY.
Wind	*hangin*	angin, hangin
„ , to (to reel)	*lebud*	lilit, likas
Winding	*sikā, malīkā*	balĭkū
Window	*panandawan*	jandělā, tingkap
Windpipe	*gŭng-gŭng-an*	rungkong
Windward	*ha-ātas hangin*	di-ātas angin
Wine	*anggōl*	anggōr
Wing	*pīk-pīk*	sāyap
Wink	*pirong, pe'oh*	kejap, lāwang
„ , to	*mŭg-pirong-pirong*	me-lāwang
„ (to twinkle)	*mŭg-kalap-kalap*	ter-k'lep-k'lep
Wipe	*sāpū, paihir-an*	sāpū, gōsok
Wire	*kāwat*	kāwat
Wisdom	*budīman, akal*	budī, akal
Wish (to desire)	*mŭg-ien, mau-bayah*	māŭ, sūka
Witchcraft	*hobāt-an, suānggī*	hobāt-an
With	*ĭban*	dengan, serta
„ , along	*dŭngan-dŭngan*	sāma-sāma
Withered	*līmanās*	lāyū
„ (prematurely)	*kimūlās, kūlās*	būrus
Within	*ha-lŭm*	di-dālam
Without	*ha-gñah*	di-lūar
Withstand	*ātu, sandal*	lāwan, tāhan
Witness, a	*saksi*	saksi
„ , to bear	*mŭg-saksi*	brī saksi
Wizard	*tāu suānggī*	ōrang pe-tanung
Woman	*babai*	perampūan
Womb	*kandāng*	kadōng, rahim
Wonder	*hāilan, kug-kug*	hēiran

ENGLISH.	SULU.	MALAY.
Won't (will not)	*di aku, di mäg-ien*	tīdah mäū
Wood (timber)	*kāhōi*	kāyū
,, , fire-	*kāhōi-dongol*	kāyū-āpi
Woof (in weaving)	*silag*	pākan
Wool	*bāl-bāl bīlī-bīlī*	būlū bīrī-bīrī
Word, a	*kabtang*	per-katā-an
Work	*hīnāng-an*	karja
,, , to	*mäg-hīnang*	ber-kraja
,, in iron, to	*mäg-sasal bāsī*	ber-kraja besī
Workman	*pandai, tūkang*	tūkang
World	*duniā, būmi*	duniā
,, to come, the	*ākhilat, āhirat*	ākhirat
Worm	*ūd*	ūlat
,, (of the intestines)	*kaliig*	chāching
,, (of a screw)	*buli itek*	peler itek
,, , water-	*kāpang*	kāpang
,, -tablet	*ōbat kaliig*	ōbat chāching
,, , wood-	*bōk-bōk*	bōbok
Worship	*sambayang*	sambayang
Worth (value)	*gūna*	gūna
,, (price)	*halga*	harga
Wound	*pāli*	lūka
Wrap	*potus-an*	bŭngkūs-kan
Wrapper, a	*potus-an*	bŭngkūs-an
Wrath	*molko, muka*	morka
,, (of God)	*ka-mukā-an sin tūhan*	morka allah
Wreck, a	*kapal na bāg-bāg*	pechahan kapal
Wrestle, to	*lumun, gumun*	ber-gōmul
Wretched	*selāka*	chelāka

ENGLISH.	SULU.	MALAY.
Wrinkled	*kimānūt, kūnūt*	krot
Wring (as linen)	*tābir-an*	pūlas
Wrist	*būkū-būkū tataklāīan*	būkū tāngan
Write	*mūg-sulat, tūlis*	tūlis, menūlis
Writer	*jūlo-tūlis*	jūro-tūlis
Writing	*kalāng-an*	karōng-an
Wrong	*sāh*	sālah
,, (sin, crime)	*dōsa*	dōsa
Yam (tuber)	*ūbī, pānggi*	ūbī
,, (taro)	*haupe*	kalādi
Yard, court-	*halāman*	alāman
,, (measure)	*bara, ēla*	tengah depa, ēla
,, (of a ship)	*bāhu tārok*	peru-an, pābuan
,, (member)	*ātin*	būtū, takoh
Yarn (thread)	*sārban, sālban*	benang
Yawn	*mang-iyaban*	men-gūap
Ye	*kāmu*	kāmu
Year	*tāhūn, mūsim*	tāhun, mūsim
Yell, to	*gāsūd, mūg-kāiba*	tampik, terīak
Yesterday	*ka-hāpun*	kalmārin
,, , day before	*takīsa, tūgīsa*	kalmārin daūlu
Yet (still)	*maien, mayen*	jūga, lāgi
,, , not	*wala*	balúm
Yoke (of bullocks)	*kokong*	kok
Yonder	*dūn-ha-iaun, ietu*	di-sāna, di-situ
You	*ēkau, kau*	angkau, kau
Young	*bata-bata, sūbūl*	mūda, anak
Young (of plants)	*anak*	anak

ENGLISH.	SULU.	MALAY.
Younger brother	*manghud*	adek
Your	*kaimu, kanio, kan ĕkau*	kāmū pūnya, angkau-pūnya
,,	*kan tŭan* *	tŭan pūnya *
Youth, a	*sūbūl, ka-bata-an*	ka-mudā-an
Zealous	*matŭgol*	rājin
Zigzag	*bikloh, mam-bikloh*	sīkū kluang
Zinc	*mītal*	tīmah sari

* Generally applied to Europeans.

PHRASES & SENTENCES.

ENGLISH.	SULU.
Do not abandon me on the road.	*Aiau mu aku biugitan di ha rān.*
Were you to stay at Pandāmi, you would obtain great gain from the pearl fisheries.	*Bāng kau nāg-hūlah ha Pandāmi, maka bāk kau ma-tāud untong dien ha pug-bājā-an.*
It is about two o'clock.	*Mārī na lesag dūa.*
Where is the owner of this house?	*Hāden in tug bāi sin bāi īni?*
He is absent.	*Wā'a dī (wala dī).*
Is your Master at home?	*Hi Tūan iaun ha bāi?*
No he is absent.	*Wala dūn.*
The Sultan pardoned that man for the crime he committed.	*Hi ampān sin Sāltan in tāu iaun, dien ha ka-sāh-an nia.*
Sūlūs are absolutely forbidden to eat pork.	*Halām mūtalak in Tāu-Sōg, bāng k'aun baboi.*
Do you know me.?	*Ka-ingat-an mu aku!*

o

ENGLISH.	SULU.
I will not have abuse from you.	*Di aku mau-bayah peninggar-an mu.*
They went in company to the Hill Tomantangis.	*Mŭg - dŭngan - dŭngan na sila pa Būd Tomantangis.*
Who was your accomplice in stealing the Chinaman's goods.	*Hi sīo in ïban mu nŭg-tiakau in āta indah Lanang.*
This man is very clever at examining accounts.	*Ma-pandai pakaraian in tău īni mŭg-paleksa ha kīla-kīla.*
Why do you accuse me of being an evil disposed person?	*Maita mu aku pāmong tŭgha tău mangi?*
People who are not accustomed to chew betel (on first trial) may feel giddy.	*In tău būkŭn bīaksa mŭg-māmah kalō-kalō ma hēlo sia.*
Go and acquaint him.	*Baita matoh kan nia.*
This mango is not yet ripe.	*In wāni īni wala-pa ma-hīnog.*
May he act instead of talk.	*Gām sia mŭg-hīnang dien-pa mŭg-pāmong.*
If three more be added this will make twenty.	*Bāng mŭg-dūang in tō man-jāri ganap kāūhan.*
The Island of Tulian is near Simogan Point.	*In Pō Tulian masŭk pa Tandok Simogan.*
I have made him my adopted child.	*Hīnāng-an ku sia anak pŭg-īpad.*

ENGLISH.	SULU.
Our vessel (prañ) is adrift.	*Hiānūd na in sakai-an tah.*
There is no advantage in being employed like this.	*Wāi na pāidah sin mŭg-āsah bi-ha-īni.*
It brings adversity only.	*Maka bāk sangsāh sāja.*
His adze very nearly hit his foot.	*In bansing nia mārĕ na kĭrgdān ha sīki nia*
We espied him from afar.	*Bakas kāmi nŭg-kita kan nia dien-ha māioh.*
Bring your buffalo to the stairs that I may mount it.	*Pa tapil-a in kābau mu pa hāg-dān samakat aku.*
Behold his affection for his children.	*Kīta bah in ka-lasa-han nia ha anak nia.*
This maiden has been betrothed to the son of a Datoh.	*Bakas in bājang īni nŭg-tānang īban sin anak sin Datoh.*
What use is this letter to me if the Sultan does not affix his seal (chop) to it.	*Bāng in Sūltan di maka būtang sāp nia ha sūlat ini, āno hun ka aku.*
Wood that does not float is no use for this work.	*Kāhōi di maka lantop wāi ka-guna-han ha pŭg-hīnāng-an īni.*
Be not afraid, for I am not a foreigner.	*Aiau na kau ma-bōga, bākŭn na kāmi tāu dōāin.*
You keep a look out ahead, I shall aft.	*Ekau in mŭg-jāga ha dong, aku ha-būli.*

ENGLISH.	SULU.
When your Sultan died, how old was he?	*Abila* in Junjongan nio malohom, pila in ūmol nia?*
I do not know, Sir, for we Sūlūs are not clever at reckoning our ages.	*Indai,† Tūan, sagñah kāmi Tāu-Sog, di maka pandai mug-ītong in ūmol nāmu.*
He has agreed with me.	*Nūg-jangī na sila ka aku.*
Ah! you also.	*Arī! īkau īsab īni.*
Oh! you buffoon! to give you a name, even your shadow would not care to do so.	*Arūi! tinggah dawa kau! bāng pug-ingan-an īkau, mīsan lambong mu ma-hūkau.*
Albinos cannot see during the day time, but only at night.	*In ūgis di maka kīta bāng adlau, sobai dūm āmpa maka kīta.*
Buy up the whole lot.	*Tughan na kāmu ka-tān.*
All the people of Pārang are bad.	*Tāu Pārang mangī lūn-lūn.*
On the top of Panamu Hill there is a lake; and in it are piebald crocodiles.	*Ha-tās Būd Panamu tūga lānau; in halim nya tūga būaya kābang.*
Who will defray the expenses?	*Hi sīo in ongsūd sin balanja?*
The Sūlū people have allied themselves with the sea-rovers.	*In tāu Sōg bakas nūg-bagāi ĭban samal lāñd.*

* *Abila* or *fa-bila* = at the time.   † *Indai* I do not know.

ENGLISH.	SULU.
Do not go alone.	Aiau kau mūg-panau isa-isa mu.
How many are there in your house?	Pīla in tāud nio dān ha bāi mu?
I am all alone.	Aku angka tāu sāja.
Although he were in stature like yonder hill, I should not be afraid of him.	Mīsan in lagkū nia bīa munga lagkū sin būd iaun, di aku ma-bōga kan nia.
I who am the Sultan's Ambassador, bring his compliments to you.	Aku in Dāk-an sin Sūltan, doma mārī kāimu selam-dōa.
Do you know how to mend a gun?	Maka-ingat kau mūg-daiau sin snāpang?
In mid ocean, they threw his body overboard.	Na biugit na nila in baran nia, ha gītong tawīd
What have you done amiss?	Uno in sāh mu?
When believers and un-believers fight (fanatically) that is called 'to sabil.'	Bāng islām iban kāpil nūg-būnoh āmū na ien mūg-sabil.
Heave up the anchor and let us sail.	Bongkal-a in bāogi lumāyag na kīta.
God's holy war.	Prang sabil Allah.
We are afraid of incurr-ing the Datoh's anger.	Ma-bōga kāmi pa mol-ka-han indah Datoh.
During my stay in Sūlū, I did not observe the anibong palm.	Sa lōgai ku ha Sōg, di na aku komītu anībong.

ENGLISH.	SULU.
He has sprained his ankle.	Na piol in bākā-bākā sīki nia.
Bring me another one.	Dahan mārī hambok dōāin.
Why don't you answer me?	Mai-ta kan di na mūg-asip ka aku?
If you do not reply, I shall not be responsible.	Bāng kau di samambag, di aku maka tāngoh.*
That man has most funny antics.	Tinggah dawa paka-riau in tāu iaun.
A closet is smaller than a room.	In tamboh asīrī dien ha bīlik.
What is the name of that person? I don't know.	Sīo īngan sin tāu iaun? Indai su aku.
What is your name?	Hi sīo ingan mu?
What do the Sūlūs call this?	Uno in pāg-tāg-an sin Tāu-Sūg ha īni?
Knock at the door.	Tupok † in lawang.
If you take away my arms, you may as well take my life.	Bāng kau nūg-komawa in takūs ku, gām bāng na lāwa in napas ku.
It is forbidden to drink arrak; besides, it inebriates.	Ma-halām in nūg-inom alak; malainkan, maka hēloh.
His stick does not reach his hat.	In tongkud nia di maka ābūt ha sārōk nia.
The vessel has not yet arrived.	In kapal walapa maka ābūt.

* *Tangoh* - responsible.   † *Mug-tupok* - to knock.

ENGLISH.	SULU.
When the vessel arrives I will go with her to Sandakan Bay.	*Bāng sum-ampai in kapal, magad aku pa Lōk Sandakan.*
I am too old to climb a tree.	*Mās na aku di na aku maka rāg ha kāhōi.*
It is difficult to ascend the stairs of this house.	*Mahonet pakaraiau mūg-gāban ha hāgdān sin bāi īni.*
We are out of breath climbing this hill.	*Hiapus na kīta tumukad ha būd īni.*
This youth has no shame.	*In bata-bata ini di masīpūg.*
Let us go to the other side of the river.	*Song na kīta matoh pa ang-sīpak sin sōbah.*
What is the use of your asking me.	*Nūg-āno kau mang-āsūbū ka aku.*
I am going to bed as I am sleepy.	*Matōg na aku bāt kierroh na aku.*
They were attacked by the pirates, at sea.	*Maka langgal na sila ha lāūd, ïban sin tāu samal lāūd.*
Heave up the anchor.	*Otong-an bāoji.*
If you do not attempt it how do you know you are unable.	*Bāng kau wā' maka sōlai bīadien in ka-ingat mu sin di kau kaya-han.*
I am unwilling to go to Tianggi.	*Ma-hūkau aku matoh pa Tianggi.*
Wait here until I return.	*Tūgad na kau rī mūg-balek dah aku.*

ENGLISH.

SULU.

ENGLISH.	SULU.
Who is that man?	Hi sīo in tāu iaun?
Is the Sultan awake?	In Sūltan jāga kah?
This awning is too short; it should be lengthened a little.	Ma-haupoh tūd in haima īni; gām dah bāng pa hābā-hābā tīoh-tīoh.
That man is brave; for see how awry he wears his head-dress.	Maīsig in tāu iaun; but kītu bah nug-kaking in pīs nia.
My axe is sharper than his.	In kapah ku ma-haīt dien-ha kan nia.
The bag is torn and the paddy is running out.	Na gisi in karot na hād-hād in pāi.
Who is surety for you?	Hi sīo in ātas-an mu?
The datching* of that Chinaman weighs very heavy.	In timbang-an sin Lanang iaun, ma-bōgat tūd.
If you do not bail the water out we shall sink.	Ma-lānūd na kītu bāng kan di māg-lelemas sin tūbig.
What is the price of a ball of your tabacco?	Pēla in hāga sin tabākā mu angka būngkal?
In one chest of opium there are forty balls.	Halium angka pāk marat tūga ka-opat-an angka limping.
There are many kinds of bananas in Sūlū.	Matāud ka-gīnīs-an in sāing ha Sūg.
This flag will not unfurl.	In pangi īni di ma-jag-jag.

* Chinese scale for weighing.

ENGLISH.	SULU.
Many people from the country are to banquet with the Sultan.	Mag-ñida (ñira) iban Sūltan matāud tāu dien ha gimbah.
Go and call a barber.	Tāwag-a matoh in tūkang baging mārī.
Let us barter our arms.	Mag-sīmbi na kīta takūs.
Twenty baskets mother-of-pearl shells, ten baskets cotton, and five baskets of lanzats.*	Kāñhan angka ambong tīpai, hangpoh angka salingkat kāpok, ībau līmā sñgūb bāahan.*
Klings,† are exceedingly fond of fruit.	In Kālīng, lando pakar-aiau kamaun būnga kāhōi.
People from 'Lōk‡' are not good.	Tāu dien ha Lok būkūn maraiau.
Let us go to the market.	Song kīta matoh pa pārian.
There is no market at Būalo now.	Wāi rūn tāboh ha Būalo bīhaun.
Let us bathe in the stream.	Maigoh na kīta halam sūbah.
The Sūlūs seldom wear beads	Māhang in Tāu-Sōg ma-makai manik.
Put on your arms for they are going.	Mag-takūs na bah kau būt manau na sila.
Why do you beat your horse so?	Maita mu liobakan in kūra mu?

* *Sulu* is famed for this fruit. † A people of India.

‡ *Lok* - bay of the sea. It is also the name of a district in *Sulu*.

ENGLISH.	SULU.
They are beating musical gongs.	*Nag-līsag na sila in ka-lintang-an.*
Go and wash your clothes.	*Dak-dak-i matoh in habūl tamāngan mu.*
That woman has a beautiful figure.	*Maraiau in rugbus sin babai iaun.*
I had not yet become a Mahomedan.	*Wā'pa aku ma Islām.*
Fetch me that sarong * that I may use it as a blanket.	*Da mārī in habūl† iaun, hīnāng-an ku siob.*
Many people were killed abreast of the fort.	*Ma-tāud tāu miatai ha ka-harop-an sin kōta.*
Begone.	*Song kāu.*
Lapidāwan is situated behind Zambongan.	*Lapidāwan ha-lio sin Zambongan.*
It is unmannerly to belch while eating.	*Mangi hadat bāng māg-sigūl ha pūg-k'aun-an.*
Don't be led away by what he says.	*Aiau kau māg-āgad sin sīmud nia.*
Whose house is this?	*Kan sīo in bāi īni!*
It belongs to us.	*Ka atu.*
I feel pleasure in having betel leaf.	*Mag-sūkūl na aku būt aun na būioh.*
His betel box was made of gold.	*In salapa nia balāwan.*
The fire is blazing.	*Ma-lāga na in kāyu.*

* The "sarong" is the national dress of the Malay.

† The *habul* is the national dress of the Sulu.

ENGLISH.	SULU.
I saw a large snake in the middle of the road.	*Bakas aku na kīta hās dākolah ha gītong sin rān.*
He crossed from beyond the river.	*Bakas sia lūmūbai dien ha ang-sīpak sōbah.*
Should it be ordered by the lady, it would even enter the cavity.	*Bāng dāk-an hi dāyang, mīsan sumud pa līang.*
Give me a jar of biscuits.	*Dihil-i mu akn angka pūgah bāng-bāng.*
Give him a quarter only.	*Damīhil kan sia āng-ūtūd sāja.*
If there be a heavy sea on am afraid I shall be sea-sick.	*Bāng tūga alūn dākolah ma-būga aku ma-hīlo.*
This Physician's medicine is very bitter.	*Ma-pait in ūbat sin Tabib īni.*
The Munari, may use a spear with two blades.	*In Munari, maka ma-makai būjak dūa sīlab nya.*
You should prescribe for the blemish on your horse's eye.	*Sobai ūbat-an in māta sin kūra mu būt ma-būlag.*
This barong* is blunt and will not cut.	*Barong īni na tūmpūl di tūd maka ūk.*
If that board breaks you will fall into the river.	*Bāng ma-buleh in digpi iaun, ma-holog sa kau ien halam sōbah.*
A 'sapit' has a bowsprit.	*In sapit tuga jūngal.*

* A short, broad, and thick sword, the edge of which is convex.

ENGLISH.	SULU.
My body feels as it were languid.	Bīa mŭnga ma-lema-lema in baran ku īni.
Take off the rind and then boil it.	Kawa-i in pāis-nya būt hi tognah-i pa kāyu.
How can we go not having cooked our rice.	Biardien in ka-toh-an namu sin wala kāmi maka pŭg-pangāiu.
Put in a little salt since the water is boiling.	Kauni tīoh-tīoh āsin būt miūkal* nu in tūbig.
Where were you born?	Hadien kan pŭg-anak?
I was born in Sūlū.	Pug-anak aku ha Sōg.
Lend us your boat to go to the shoal.	Būs-i kīta sakaian mu matoh pa hŭnus-an.
I cannot lend it as I wish to use it myself.	Di ku hi pŭg-bŭs aun ka-panau-an ku.
Do not borrow it there.	Aiau kau mŭg-bŭs matoh.
He won't lend it.	Di sa kīta ien bŭs-an.
Why don't you lend it to me?	Wāi mu aku di bŭs-an?
Go and borrow it from them.	Bŭs na kau matoh kan nila.
Bring them both.	Dah-a mārī in ka-rŭa-rŭa.
The Sultan has three designs of brands.	Tō angka gīnīs in sāp sin Sūltan.
The Spaniards, call the Sūlūs, Mūrūs.	Pŭg-tāg-an sin Kustela ha Tau-Sōg, Mārūs.

*Miukal or bukal   to be boiling.

ENGLISH.   SULU.

He says he shall lend it to you by-and-bye if you care to wait.

Hŭ long nia bŭs-an tah na kau bāng kau maka tugad dai-dai.

A 'sapit' has a bowsprit.

In sapit tāga jāngal.

'Bilolangs' and 'bauls' are made in China. In appearance they differ; the one being red, the other yellow.

Bilolang ïban baul ïni nug-hīnang ha Song-song. Dāäin in dugbus nya; in baul ma-biening,* in bilolang ma-pūla.

Behold the laziness of of this woman in pounding paddy.

Kīta bah in ka-buskau--an sin babai ïni pa pug-bāioh-an pāi.

Broken beyond repair.

Ma-bay-bay di na malap.†

Parted that it cannot be re-united.

Maytoh di na ma-supat.‡

Bring me my pistol.

Dah-i nio mārī pistol ku.

He has not brought it yet.

Wala sia mug-da mārī.

Bring it here, I say.

Dah-a na mārī, long ku.

Take it away.

Pa-rā-a na matoh.

Bring that child here.

Pakaria in bata-bata ien.

Bring it at once.

Pakaria-an bah ien.

Its breadth was twenty fathoms and its length a little more.

In lŭk-bang nya kāñhan ang rupa, in hābā nya kāñhan lebih-lebih.

* *Biening* – yellow.   † *Malap* – repair.   ‡ *Supat* – re-unite, splice.

ENGLISH.	SULU.
His younger brother was killed.	*In manghud nia mi-atai būnoh.*
Brush the table (cloth).	*Sāpū-a in lamīsahan īni.*
This bull is fat.	*Sāpī mandangan īni ma-tambuk.*
He has bought twenty bundles of Chinese tobacco.	*Bakas sia na ka bī kāūhan putus hūn.*
He has brought from the Kinabatangan River, one thousand bundles of ratan.	*Na ka rā sia wāi dien ha Sābah Kinabatangan, ang ību 'ka gālong.*
The City is on fire.	*Na sūnog in Banūa.*
A wicked man has burned up my paddy.	*In pāi ku sunog sin tāu mangi.*
Here is a field of dry lalang grass which will burn well.	*Aī-ya-rī (dī) pantai ma-takai in parang, maraiau in pāg-lāb-an.*
It is not I but you whom he abuses.	*Būkān aku but īkau in peninggar-an nia.*
May I ask what your business is here?	*Uno na maien in ka-hīnāng-an mu dī ha īni?*
He has bought this pony.	*Bakas sia na ka bī sin kūra īni.*
He stabbed the pig with a spear.	*Nag tigbak sia ha baboi ban būjak.*
Put the butter by.	*Tāu-an matoh in man-tagelia.*

ENGLISH.	SULU.
Wait till the afternoon and we can go to Tianggi.	*Gana-gana * mahapun manau na kita pa Tianggi.*
Go and call him.	*Tawag-a matoh kan nia.*
I have never called at your house.	*Wala aku maka hapit pa bai mu.*
Candles like these are worthless as they do not give a good light.	*Wai rūn ka-sūdah-an sin lansok bihaini but di maka ma-laga.*
I cannot.	*Di aku maka-jādi.*
This room is capacious.	*Ma-hāyang in bilik ini.*
There are two houses beyond that cape.	*Aun dūa angka bai halio sin tandok iaun.*
It is not as much as I gave for it.	*Wala-pa abūt in puhun.*
There are no capons in Sūlū	*Wai rūn manok kabili ha Sūg.*
Convey me to the palace.	*Hiatud aku pa astāna.*
The cart is destroyed and the wheels are broken.	*Nug-kāngi in karosah, ma-bag-bag in silik-an nya.*
Pray, what is the case at issue between you?	*Uno na maien in dawa mu kan nia?*
The cat and dog are fighting.	*In kūting ibun crok mug-lurai.*
I cannot catch his horse.	*Di aku maka sagau in kūra nia.*

* Gana-gana wait.

ENGLISH.	SULU.
At the fresh water cave there is a striped tiger.	*Tūbig liang ma-tābang tūga halīmau kābang.*
The cable has parted and we are adrift.	*Na mogtoh in gand-āwalī, liad* na kīta.*
It is not yet certain.	*Wala-pa tantu.*
This horse is so very fleet that it can overtake deer.	*In kūra īni ma-buskai pakaraiau maka hiapus ūsa.*
Let us go to the hunt.	*Song kīta matoh pa panhūt-an.*
What are they chasing?	*Uno na maien in hiapus nia?*
It is not dear but cheap.	*Mohai sa īni būkun ma-honet.*
That man is a cheat.	*Tau panīpu sa ien.*
Do not go with him. He will cheat you.	*Aiau kau āgad kan nia. Pieg-akal-an nia kāimu.*
When do you wish to return to China?	*Ka-āno kau mau-bayah mūi pa Song-song?*
This is a clever China-man.	*Ma-pandai pakaraiau Lanang īni.*
Choose those which are good.	*Peh-a matoh sin mar-aiau.*
When he left, the Capital (Benūa) had not yet been burned.	*Abila ka tolak nia, wa pa ma-sūnog in Banūa.*
It is not clean but dirty.	*Būkun ma-lanoh ma-ūmēh.*

* *Liad* adrift.

ENGLISH.	SULU.
He has not yet come.	*Walapa sia maka rātang.*
Who were your companions in the affray?	*Hi sīo in īban mu ha pug-būnoh-an?*
There is no completion to this work.	*Wāi ka-sudah-an in hīnang īni.*
Bad end.	*Mangi ka-sudah-an.*
Convey my compliments to the Sultan.	*Timugun selam dūa ku matoh pa Sūltan.*
If I am not guilty you cannot condemn me.	*Bāng wāi rān dōsa ku di kāmu maka hukum ka-aku.*
Conduct me to the boat.	*Hiatud-i nio aku pa sakaian.*
Let me lead you by the hand for the road is very rugged here.	*Ambit-an tah kau būt ma-bātu tiid di ha rān īni.*
Consider I say.	*Pikil-pīkil-a kūno.*
What are you constructing there?	*Uno in hīnang mu dūn ha ien?*
His conversation was very pleasant.	*Maraiau in beshala nia.*
This beef is not yet cooked; cook it well.	*In ūnūd sāpī īni walapa ma-lutoh; pa lutoh-a tiid.*
This cord has been made from the hemp of the musa textilis.	*In lūbid īni in tagnah nya lānūt āmpa hīnang lūbid.*
Come here.	*Dī na kau.*

P

ENGLISH.	SULU.
The women are using cosmetics for their faces.	*Pa-burak-an in babai sin baihok nya.*
What is the price of this fowl?	*Pēla in hāga sin manok īni?*
Count them for I am afraid of deceiving you.	*Hītong-a matoh, āmūna ka-bōga-an ku ka-rapat-an mu.*
He has deceived you.	*Ka-rapat-an nia kāimu.*
He is abusing you.	*Peninggar-an nia kāimu.*
Don't you deceive me.	*Aiau mu aku pa-rapat-i.*
Her countenance was like the full moon.	*In baihok nia bīa ha mīnga būlan dāmlag.*
We are second cousins.	*Pūg-tungad na kīta maka rūa.*
Not having committed any crime, why should I be afraid?	*Wala-pa aku maka dōsa, ūno in ka-bōga-an ku?*
The crow flew up on a tree.	*In wāk mūg-lōpad pa tās kahōi.*
Don't cry for he will return by-and-bye.	*Aiau kau mūg-tangis, būt bālek sa ien gana-gana.*
I do not know how to cure your desease.	*Di aku maka-ingat mūg-ōbat sin sākit mu.*
Such is not the custom.	*Wāi adat bi ha ien.*
I do not comprehend.	*Di aku maka saioh.*

ENGLISH.	SULU.
Do not cut that tree.	Aiau kau mǎg-tigbas ha kāhŏi ien.
There is a market daily at Membong.	Adlau-adlau tǎga parian ha Membong.
There is not a man who dare forbid him.	Wāi rūn tāu maka aisŭg mang-lāng kan nia.
It is nearly mid-day; so, let us go home.	Mārē na ogtoh; mŭi na kīta.
All the people were grieved when the Sultan died.	Abila in Sūltan malohom, ma-sǎsah in hatāi sin tāu katān.
Are you deaf? Can't you reply?	Bīsu tuh kau! Di kau maka asip!
Deduct a little.	Kŏlang-kŏlang-i tīoh-tīoh.
There are spotted deer in Sūlū.	Aun ūsa ha Sŏg nŭg-ka butikan.
There was not a house left by the flood last night.	Wāi na kapin in bāi na ra sin dunuk k'ābi.
Try your barong on his bones to see if it will become dented.	Solai na kau in barong mu ien bāng maka sǎmbing ha bǔkog ien.
He has gone.	Ictu na manau.
Go to the market.	Katoh na kau pa parian.
Depart from thence.	Eg na kau dien dūn.
They have departed.	Bakas na sila maka 'āi.
How deep is the water in this river? — Up to here.	Biardien in hālum sin sŏbah īni! — Na dūn ha īni.

212

ENGLISH.	SULU.
Get down to the ground and do not come up here again.	Ma-nōg na kau pa lōpa, aiau na kau īsab gomāban māri.
Why do you desert me?	Maita mu aku bugitan?
When I heard of his child's death I was in despair.	Abila aku na ka-rūngog in anak nia miatai masūsah tūd in hatāi ku.
You shall not detain me. I am not your slave.	Di kau maka hawid* ka aku. Būkūn mu aku īpun.
So and so is dead; the Datoh is deceased; the Sultan is demised; alas! they are all dead.	Na matāi indah kūan; na lindong indah Datoh; malohom in Sūltan; allahauala! matāi ka-tantan.
It is difficult to get.	Ma-honet ka-bak-an.
What are its dimensions?	Bīadien in laggū nya?
This woman is very diminutive.	Babai īni asīrī tūd.
Direct me to that which is good.	Hindoh-i aku sin maraiau.
Do not teach me that which is wrong.	Aiau mu aku hindoh-i sin mangi.
Point out to me the place where it is.	Pa tudloh-i aku sin tūngūd† nya.
This ship does not touch at Labuan but goes straight to Sandakan.	In kapal īni di na maka hāpit ha Labuan mūgtūi na pa Sandakan.

* Hawil or hawir-an = to detain. † Tungad or tungud = locality; place.

ENGLISH.	SULU.

This man's disposition is unequalled for goodness.

Wāi na sali sin palāngai sin tau īni but maraiau.

This boy is very disrespectful.

Wāi rūn adat sin bata-bata īni.

What this man says is quite different.

Dōāin-dōāin na īsab in pamong-an tau īni.

The ship at present is far distant at sea.

Māioh na in kapal bīh'āun ha lāūd.

If you speak ill of me I shall beat you.

Bāng mu aku pamong-an sin mangi lobak-an ta na kau.

Distribute it among the poor.

Nūg-bahagi bagi ha mūnga tau miskin.

The use of this is a toy for the children.

In ka-guna-han sin īni pūg-panaim-an sin bata-bata.

What is that you are doing?

Uno in ka-hīnāng-an mu ien?

Do not do so.

Aiau kau nūg-hīnang bī-ha-ien.

I am very ill. Run for the Doctor.

Ma-sākit na tūd in baran ku. Dāg-an na kau matoh pa Tabib.

He owes him a little over two hundred dollars.

In ūtang sia kan nia ien lebih-lebih dūn ha dūa ang-gātus pēlak.

What present have you brought for me, Sir?

Uno in sampang mu mārī ka aku, Tuan?

ENGLISH.	SULU.
Go and shut the door.	*Tambul-a nio matoh in lawang.*
If you will not go out of (down from) my house I will put you out (down).	*Bāng kau di maka nōg dien ha bāi ku īni, pa-nōg-an tah kau.*
I dreamt last night that the end of the world had come.	*Nūg-ka-inop na aku kaābi na raub in duniā.*
Please give me some milk of a young cocoa-nut to drink.	*Dihil-i mu aku ka-lelah-an tūbig bātng tīoh-tioh hinom-an ku.*
I am drowsy. Let us sleep.	*Kierroh na aku. Matōg kita.*
You beat the drum, I will beat the kalintangan, and they shall beat the gongs.	*Ekau in mūg-gāndang, aku in limīsag ka-lin-tang-an, sila ien in mang-agōng.*
I do not owe you any-thing.	*Wāi rūn ūtang ku kāimu.*
I have not paid the duty to the Sultan.	*Wala-pa aku maka bāyad sūkai ha Sūltan.*
Where do you dwell?	*Hadien kau nūg-hūlah?*
He asks where you dwell.	*Nūg-āsūbū hadien kau hūlah.*
By-and-bye, say to-morrow.	*Mohai na, mūnga kin-shūm.*
Eat this mango.	*Ka-aun na kau sin wāni īni.*
The sea is deep.	*Malūm in dagat.*

ENGLISH.	SULU.
I cannot eat that mango because it is sour.	*Di aku ma ka-aun wāni īni but ma-pukat.*
It is nearly low-water, so, let us go to the shoals and gather shells.	*Mārī na hūnas, song kīta managat* pa hūnas-an.*
If you don't make an effort you won't find it.	*Bāng kau di maka solai di kau maka bāk.*
What o'clock is it?—It is about eight o'clock.	*Lesag pīla?—Mārī na lesag wālū.*
Who is the elder?	*Hi sīo in magolang?*
Where is your elder brother?	*Hadien in magolang mu?*
I have never been on board an English ship.	*Wala-pa aku maka sakat ha kapal sin Anggalis.*
Have you not heard that the Sultan has gone on board Mr. Cowie's vessel?	*Wa' pa kau maka rūngog in Sūltan mūg-gāban ha-tās kapal sin Tūan Kāwī?*
If you have no employ-ment, come to me to-morrow, and I will employ you to make a fence round my plantation.	*Bāng wāi rūn ūsāh-an mu, mārī na ka aku kin-shūm māināt, pūg-tandan-an ta kau mūg-hīnang ād ka-lībut-an jambang-an ku.*
I knew from its sound that it was empty.	*Ka-ingat-an ku dien ha tinguy nya wāi lūan.*

* *Ma-nagat* = to gather shells; *pa-nagat-an* = mollusca. Both these words are derived from *dagat*, the sea.

ENGLISH.	SULU.
Work with more energy for it is getting dark.	*Kasai-kasai na kāmu mūg-hīnang būt dūm na.*
He is enraged.	*Ma-gama sa ien.*
Get under the awning as the sun is so hot.	*Sūd na bah kau palūm kājang būt ma-pāso in sūga.*
Your slave entreats forgiveness.	*Mīki ampūn in pātek.*
They are all equally foolish.	*Sali-sali na sila katan-tan dōpang.*
Go and erect the posts.	*Bangun-a nio na matoh in hāg.*
His slave escaped to Tianggi (Jolo).	*Nūg-pāgoi in īpun nia pa Tianggi.*
Who is to escort you?	*Hi sīo in maka hiatud kāimu?*
From morning till evening.	*Dien ha mahinat pa mahapun.*
From to-morrow till the next day.	*Dien ha kinshūm pa kunīsa.*
Wait till I bathe.	*Tugad-tugad na kau maigoh pa aku.*
All these durians are bad.	*In durian īni mangi lūn-lūn.*
That is not exact.	*Būkūn āmū ien.*
The flavour of this fish is very good.	*Maraiau pakaraiau in anam sin ista īni.*
No one knows except (you) yourself.	*Wai rān tāu maka ingat lual ēkau baran mu.*

ENGLISH.	SULU.
Who will bear the expense?	*Hi sīo in mag-ongsud balanja?*
I will expend whatever you want.	*Aku in pag-balanja-an sin pag-icn-an mu.*
I am inexperienced.	*Ma-kūlang aku bīaksa.*
Extinguish the candle.	*Pōng-a in lansok.*
Her complexion is fair, her tresses are luxuriant, her waist is slender, her feet are small, and her hands are elegant. Who can rival such a beauty?	*Ma-pūtch in baihok nia, ma-hābak in būhōk nia, ma-nahut in hawakan nia, asīrī in sīki nia, maraiau in līma nia. Hi sīo in maka ātū īban babai bīhaīni.*
Give me the fag end of your cigar, Sir.	*Dihil-i mu aku pupud dubla mu, Tūan.*
Dear me! my sīrīh has fallen on the road.	*Allah! na tanak in būioh ku dicn ha rān.*
We are all one family.	*Angka bāi sa kāmi īui.*
What is the fare from here to Sandakan?	*Pēla chukai dicn dī pa Sandakan?*
The manners of the Sūlūs are different from those of the Spaniards.	*Dōāin adat sin Tau-Sōg dicn ha Kastela.*
That 'dāpang' sails very fast.	*Ma-rāgan tūd in dāpang iaun.*
He is an orphan for he has neither father nor mother.	*Yatim īlo sa icn būt wāi rān īnah amah nia.*
Go in please.	*Sūd na bah palūm.*

ENGLISH.	SULU.
I saw a large number of birds feeding on his paddy.	*Bakas aku na kīta ma-tāud manok-manok kamaun ha pāi nia.*
After you have felled that tree, clear away the undergrowth at once.	*Hōbus kau mŭg-pēla sin kāhōi iaun, mŭg-tūi na kau mŭg-lāpa.*
Had I not fenced just now he would have hit me on the face with his spear.	*Bāng ku wa'pa tangkis-i h'ēn dūn, kīrgdān sin būjak nia ha baihok ku.*
Bring me a candle.	*Daha mārī lansok hambok.*
Last night I had fever (calentura) and to-day ague.	*K'ābi henglau aku, adlau iaun tiandŭg aku.*
Why do you not give your child a few bananas?	*Maita kau di domīhil ha anak mu munga tioh-tīoh sāing?*
Day and night they play the fiddle like so many buffoons.	*Dūm adlau mŭg-biola sila ka-tān bīa mŭnga tinggah dawa.*
There are not yet enough to make fifteen.	*Wa'pa gomanap† hangpok-tŭg-līma.*
If you would only file your teeth you would look a handsome man.	*Bāng kau mŭg-lagnas sin īpun mu ien domaiau‡ kau ūsog.*
This fish stinks.	*Na hāloh in istā īni.*

* *Tinggah dawah* =: buffoon.   † *Gomanap* or *ganap* -- enough, sufficient.

‡ *Domaiau* or *maraiau dugbus* -handsome, beautiful.

ENGLISH.	SULU.
My feet are sore so I cannot walk.	*Ma sākit in sīki ku di aku maka panau.*
Fill it full.	*Lñan-i na āmpa ma-hipoh.*
I fancy you have not filtered this water as it is still dirty.	*Hati ku* wa'pa sāh-a in tūbig īni ma-lōbag na īsab.*
Seek until you find.	*Lawag-a āmpa ka-bak-an.*
Kindle a fire for I am cold.	*Bōhe-a matoh in kāyu būt ma-hiaggut† na āku.*
He says you are to go first.	*Ekau na long nia mūna.*
Who is first?	*Hi sīo in ha ñnah-an?*
If the sea is rough we cannot dredge (for M.O.P. shells).	*Bāng ma-alun di kāmi maka bājah.‡*
Some men can dive a depth of fifteen fathoms.	*Aun tāu maka lerop§ līm hanpok-tūg-līma ang rupa (dupa).*
Hoist the flag for they are conquered.	*Hēlā in pānji but na raug na sila.*
The flavour of salt from China is not to be compared with the salt that is made in Sūlū.	*In āsin dien ha Song-song di maka ātū ha anam sin āsin in mūg-hinang ha Sōg.*

* *Hati ku* — I fancy or I suppose.　† *Hiaggut* or *haggut* — cold.

‡ *Mug-baja* or *bajah* — to dredge; to plough.

§ *Tau-fan-anaf* or *tau-fang-le-leref* — a diver.

ENGLISH.	SULU.
Do not destroy the floor of my house.	Aiau mu larak-a in lantai sin bāi ku īni.
He floated to the mouth of the river.	Hi anud sia na matoh pa babah sin sūbah.
The vampire can fly as it has wings.	Balbal-an īni maka lūpad būt tūga pīk-pīk.
Do not be fooling there.	Aiau kau nŭg-lāngog dūn ha īen.
Follow his foot-marks.	Urol-a in limpa sin sīki nia.
The way is narrow.	Ma-sigpit in dān.
I found him on the road.	Ka-bāk-an ku sila dūn ha rān.
He lost his chopper in the forest.	Na lāwa in ŭtak nia halam kātian.
I saw a large snake in the forest near Sandakan.	Bakas aku na ka kīta hās dākolah halam golan-gan ma-sŭk pa Sandakan.
Why did you forget? Have you no memory?	Maita kau na lūpa! Wāi tŭm-tum-an mu?
Yes, but I was in trouble and it slipped my memory.	Hŭ, bŭt in sūsah in hatāi ku di aku maka tŭm-tŭm.
Its form was like the appearance of a man.	In rŭgbus nya bīa bantok tāu
This youth is very fortunate.	Maraian in sūkŭd sin bata-bata īni.
They foundered among the islands of Tāwī-tāwī.	Na lūnŭd na sila ha ka-popō-an sin Tāwītāwī.

ENGLISH.	SULU.
Follow me.	*Agad na kau ka aku.*
I am a freeman and not a slave.	*Tau maraian pa aku mi, wāi tug īpun ka aku.*
If it is not fresh don't bring it.	*Bang būkun ma-tabang aian mug-dā.*
On Friday you should worship.	*Nag-sambayang na kāmu adlan Jamahat.**
It is proper to do so.	*Ma-tūlid in bi ha ictu.*
How far is it from here to there?	*Pēla māioh dien dī ha dūn?*
There it is in front of the house.	*Ai aun dūn ha harap-an sin bāi.*
Wait a while; I won't be long.	*Dai-dai dakoman; bū-kun dah mōgai aku.*
Split up the wood for fuel.	*Tūis-tūis in kāhōi pūg-dongol ta.*
The steamer is under weigh.	*Nā na mutput in kapal.*
This is a good place for a furnace.	*Ai-ya-rī maraiau hīn-ang-an dapol-an.*
There was not a tree left standing by the wind.	*Wāi na kapin sin kāhōi na rā sin hūnus.*
That man is a great gambler.	*Ma-kansang in tau iaun mug-gippo.*
I cannot shut the gate.	*Di aku maka tambal in lawang.*
Gather the mangoes that have fallen.	*Ma-pūt na matoh wāni ma-pak-pak.*

* *Jamahat* (Friday) is the Mahomedan Sunday.

ENGLISH.	SULU.
He is very generous to me.	*Maraian tŭd hatāi nia ka aku*
I have not found him yet.	*Walapa ku sila ka bāk-i.*
Get up for it is daylight.	*Bāte na kan bŭt adlau na.*
What is your gift to him?	*Uno in dihil-dihil mu kan nia?*
I love that child very much.	*Ma-kasih aku tŭd ha bata-bata ien.*
Give me just a little.	*Dihil-i mu aku angka tīoh-tīoh.*
Go away.	*Eg-i matoh.*
Let us go.	*Song na kita.*
Why don't you go?	*Maita kan di manau?*
Come up here.	*Gāban na kau mārī.*
Go down there.	*Ma-nōg na kau matoh.*
May you be accursed of the Lord.	*Intok-an kan sin Tūhan.*
Its price is one gold dollar.	*In halga nya hambok dūblān.*
He has not gone yet.	*Wa'pa sia maka 'ñi.*
Strike the gong as we are going to sail.	*Līsag-a in agōng bŭt măg-lāyag na kita.*
All right.	*Maraian na.*
Go and mend the sledge.	*Pug-daian-i matoh in bangun-bangun* īni.*

* A primitive vehicle moved on runners and very useful as a means of conveyance over swampy or friable soil.

ENGLISH.	SULU.
A good for nothing boy.	*Wāi gūna-gūna sin bata īni.*
Who governs Sūlū at present?	*Hi sīo in mamalentah bīh'āun hā Sōg?*
If the governor order you must obey.	*Bang dāk-an sin Gubir-narol sobai kan agar-an.*
Don't throw away the seed; give it to me to plant.	*Aiau mu biugit-an in bīgi nya ien; dihil-i aku hi tanam ku.*
What is your opinion?	*Biardien in āgī mu tah?*
If I have no knife how can I cut grass?	*Bāng wāi ûtak aku biadien aku ma-kā sagbut?*
Come and have something to eat.	*Dī na kau mug-kamaun.*
Thank you (I accept).	*Tāīmahan ku.*
It is not clean but dirty.	*Būkun ma-lanoh ma-ūmēh.*
This child is very clever.	*Ma-pandai tûd in bata-bata īni.*
I cannot climb that tree.	*Di aku maka pandai domāg hā kāhoi iaun.*
His clock is out of order; it does not strike.	*Nüg-kāngi in lelos nia; di maka tüngog.*
All his clothes were torn.	*Na gisi in tāmnngan nia ka-tantan.*
It is said that there is coal in Sūlū.	*Nüg-sui-sui* in tāu tüga būling-bātu hā Sōg.*

* Sui-sui = rumour; nug-sui-sui = it is said.

ENGLISH.	SULU.
You use very coarse language.	Ma-sāplah pakaraiau in pamong-an nia ien.
Cock fighting is held on Sunday only.	Sobai adlau rominggo āmpa mūg-būlang.
Transplant this young cocoa tree in the shade.	Pindah-i nio matoh in anak kākān īni pa selong.
Collect all the rubbish and burn it.	Tīpun-a in sagbut katān āmpa mu sūnog-a.
If the Sultan's commands are not followed it will be the worse for us.	Bāng di ma-āgad na tītah sin Junjongan kasakit-an na kita.
Go and let the horse loose to graze.	Pa bulvi-an na matoh in kūda āmpa mūg-kaaun sagbut.
This is greater than that.	Dākolah īni dien dūn.
Bring the grindstone to sharpen my barong.	Dahan nio mārī bātu-āsāh-an pa hāit-an in barong ku.
This is good soil for the cultivation of paddy.	Maraiau in lōpa īni pūg-bakal-an pāi.
Sugar-cane will not grow on land like this.	In tubu di tumūbūh ha lōpa bīhaīni.
Call the guard.	Tāwag-a in jāga-jāga.
Ho guard! come here.	Hua jāga-jāga! dī na kau.
Do not touch it.	Aiau mu ñsibah-i.
Come and cut my hair.	Kari mūg-ūtūd in buhok ku.

ENGLISH.	SULU.
Come and cut my hair.	*Utŭr-i mārī in bŭhŏk ku.*
Why does your horse limp?	*Maita in kŭda mu na tāngkah?*
You will break my arm.	*Ma-baleh in lima tuh.*
He grasped my hand in his.	*Ka put-an nia līma ku sin līma nia.*
Turn to the left a little so that I may pass.	*Bīeng-a nio pa lāwa tīoh-tīoh but lūmŭbai na kāmi.*
Where did this happen?	*Ka-āno man-jārī bi-ha-īni?*
This wood is very hard.	*Ma-lando ma-tras in kāhōi īni.*
This horse is a very fast runner.	*In kūra īni arohi ma lando tŭd domāgan.*
Make haste and gulp it down.	*Pa samut bah, tŭn-a tŭd.*
Make haste or I will overtake you.	*Us-ŭs na bah kan but mu ābŭt-an.*
Sūlŭs do not wear straw hats.	*Tāu-sōg di maka jārī ma-makai sapīno.*
Try to guess this: a tail-less bird pursues a tail-less bird?	*Tŭkŭd-tŭkŭd kāimu: manok tŭkong humapas tŭkong?* *
Have you a little (chinese) tobacco?	*Aun Kāimu munga tīoh-tīoh hun?*
I have.	*Aun pa.*
He says he has.	*Aun long nia.*

* Tukong = tail-less. Native conundrum.

ENGLISH.	SULU.
How can one who is ill go?	*Bāng tău tŭga săkit biardein maka katoh?*
Haul your prăŭ up on the beach.	*Hĩla mārī in sakaian mu pa-tās buhangin.*
I am afraid to go for people say it is haunted.	*Ma-bōga aku matoh but sui-sui sin tău tŭga saitan sa ien.*
Don't make a noise for I have a headache.	*Aiau kau mŭg-latah* dŭn ha ien but ma săkit in ũ ku.*
Do not walk in the heat of the sun.	*Aiau kau mŭg-panau ha ka-paso-an sŭga.*
How heavy is it?	*Biardien in bōgat nya?*
Last night the pigs destroyed the fence.	*Ka-ābi na larak in baboi sin ād.*
He is dead.	*Miatai na sia.*
Help me.	*Tābang-i nio aku.*
Put it down here.	*Bŭtang di ha ĩni.*
He is hiding in the forest.	*Na tăpōk na sila halam kătian.*
Let us take shelter under this tree for a moment.	*Pieg selong na kīta dī ha-babah sin kăhōi ĩni dai-dai.*
That hill is very high.	*Ma-tās tŭd in bŭd iaun.*
He has not hit.	*Wa' pa kĭ̄gdān-i.*
Stop up the hole to keep the water out.	*Hŭlat-a in lŭngag bŭt di pa sŭd-an in tŭbig.*
Come hither.	*Ka rĩ na kau.*

* Mug-latah = to chatter.

ENGLISH.	SULU.
I have one like that at our place (at home).	*Aun ka aku bī-ha-ien ha kāmoh.*
How much will you sell these deer horns for?	*Pēla hi păg-bī tandok ūsa īni?*
Let us go to the race course and see the races.	*Song kīta pa lomba-an kimīta kīta mug-pāso.*
An hour had not elapsed.	*Wa' pa maka kawa angka jām.*
How now?	*Būdien tah?*
How many dollars?	*Pēla pēlak?*
How much have you taken away?	*Pēla-pēla pa rā mu?*
Why have you not gone to hunt with the others?	*Maita kau walapa maka katoh mug-panhut ha múnga ka-īban-an mu?*
I am going.	*Matoh na kāmi.*
I can do it.	*Aku in pandai.*
He is an idle fellow.	*Ma-hūskau in tāu īni.*
Taken away by the spirits.	*Tōlak sin bāla.*
The Nakib is ill.	*Mangi lasa indah Nakib.*
I have no implements.	*Wāi rūn ka-pāniap-an ku.*
Your barong is in the house.	*In barong mu aun ha-lūm bāi.*
It is not in the house.	*Wāi rūn pa-lūm bāi.*
What is the price of your (indian) corn?	*Pēlā-pēla in gāndōm mu?*

ENGLISH.	SULU.
He found an infant dead on the river's bank.	Ka-bāk-an nia hambok bata-bata miatai ha hēgad sābah.
Inform me of what he said.	Baita-i nio aku sin pamong-an nia.
He has gone into the interior.	Na sṅd na sila pa ō.
He has gone into the country.	Matoh na sila pa gimbah.
Why do you not enquire of him?	Maita kau di āsābā kan nia?
Instruct me in your language.	Hindoh-a nio aku sin bahasa mu.
It is not enough.	Walapa ganap.
I have not received any intelligence.	Walapa aku maka rūngag sin gāwi.
Won't you give me interest for my money?	Di kau nūg-dihil anak sin pēlak ku?
I have never been round the island of Tāwī-tāwī.	Walapa aku maka lībut pō Tāwī-tāwī.
What is the price of ivory at Sandakan?	Pēla in hāga garing ha Sandakan?
Bring us a jar of biscuits.	Dā nio k'ātu angka pūgah bang-bāng.
Java is far from here.	Māioh in lōpa Jāwa dien dī.
Appeal to the judge.	Na rā in bechala pa hākim.

ENGLISH.	SULU.
I am afraid to go alone into the jungle.	*Ma bōga aku panau halam kātian īsa-īsa.*
He was here just now.	*Dī sila h'ēn dūn.*
Is it sharper than a needle?	*Hadien ma-hāīt ïban jāūm?*
Keep this till to-morrow.	*Tāu-an īni āmpa kin-shūm.*
They were killed on the way.	*Nüg-bānoh sila dūn ha rān.*
How many kinds of deer are there in Sūlū?	*Pīla angka gīnīs in āsa ha Sūg?*
I don't know.	*Di aku ma' ingat.*
Kiss your mother.	*Sium-i nio ha īnah mu.*
These kittens are fond of gamboling.	*Nüg-langog tüd in anak kūting īni aih.*
Go and kiss the Datoh's hand.	*Sium na kau matoh in līma hi Datoh.*
Lend me your knife.	*Būs-i nio aku in laring mu.*
He won't lend it to me.	*Di nia sa hāti aku būs-an.*
Go and borrow.	*Būs-i matoh.*
I don't know, do you?	*Indai sa kāimu?*
Why do you bring a spear into my house?	*Maita kau müg-dā būjak halüm bāi ku?*
Oh! The dog licks his hand.	*Are! Nüg-dīlah in eroh pa līma nia.*
There are none of these large, they are all small.	*Wāi rūn māslüg, mana-hut in ka-tantan.*

ENGLISH.	SULU.
Light the lamp.	*Sōh-a in palītahan.*
The last shall be first.	*In na ka-ulih maka āna.*
The first shall be last.	*In na-ka-ūna maka ulih.*
Why do you laugh at me?	*Maita mu aku pug-katāwahan.'*
Your buffaloes are all lean.	*Ma-kaiŋ in kābau mu ka-tantan.*
Don't lean against that post, it may fall.	*Aiau mu sāndig-an ha hāg ien, ma-ŋyog.*
I have left my umbrella in the house.	*Bakas naka bīn in payong ku ha bāi.*
This one won't do for it is too long.	*Ini di man-jādī but ma-hābah.*
Let it be like that.	*Pa bīa na ha ien.*
To morrow I will send a letter to my friend.	*Kinshūm mūg-parā aku sūlat pa taimanghūd ku.*
Don't be led away by that man for he is a liar.	*Aiau kau mūg ka-hagad but tau pūting-an sa ien.*
Where is the lid of this pot?	*Hadien in tūtōp-an sin anglit īni.'*
Why did you lie to me?	*Mai mu aku pūg-pūting-an.'*
I did not tell you a lie.	*Wala aku mūg-pūting kāimu.*
The pigeon has alighted on a teak tree.	*Timapoh in bāñd ha-tās kāhōi jāti*

ENGLISH.	SULU.
Bring me a small lemon.	Da-i aku hambok sūah manahut.
I think they have lingered on the way.	Pūg-halihan na sila hāti ku dān ha rān.
The fort of Singgah-māta is situated near fort Bākūd.	In kōta ha Singga-māta masůk pa kōta Bākūd.
Of what use is this small one to me?	Asīrī sa īni āno hun ka-aku?
I shall only be a short time away	Matoh aku dai-dai sāja.
Look, I say!	Kītu bah, kūno!
How fondly this woman loves her children.	Ma-kasih ma-lōi tůd babai īni ha anak nia.
The bamboos are all destroyed by the pigs.	Na hōbus in pātong kiaun sin baboi.
He has an idea that a bullet won't pierce a coat of mail.	Amā in āgī nia di limagbas īn pungloh ha lāmīna.
Do you know how to make a dapang?	Ma-ingat kau mug-hīnang dāpang?
I am just the one who knows.	Ma-ingat sa aku īni.
Twenty males and thirty females.	Kāūhan in ůsog, kat-lūan in babai.
Not even one of them could tell the truth.	Mīsan angka tāu di maka pāmong sin būnal.
He rushed in amongst the mangroves.	Nŭg-dāgan na sila halam bakau.

232

ENGLISH.	SULU.

Yes, I know.

There are few mango-steenes in Sūlū.

I will put a mark upon it so that I shall recognise it again if it be lost.

There is nothing here that I can recline on.

I have forgotten to bring matches.

What is the meaning of Siassi?—I don't know. I do not think it has a meaning, but is the name of an island only.

He has not yet set out for Mecca.

I met them in the country.

I do not know how to mend that.

A ship from China, has brought a large quantity of merchandise to the Chinese.

They foundered in mid ocean.

I have brought this milk a long way.

Amū, maka ingat aku.

Wāi ma-tāud manggis ha Sūg.

Gindah-an ku būt bāng ma-lāwa ka-kīla-han ku.

Wāi dūn ha īni pūg-haing-an ku.

Ka-lūpa-han ku wa' maka rā bāgid-bāgid.

Uno in māna sin Siassi?—Indai. Hāti ku wāi rūn māna nya lual ingan sin pō sāja.

Wa'pa sia maka tawap pa Makkah.

Bāk-an ku uila dūn ha gimbah.

Di aku ma-ingat mūg-daiau ha icn.

Domatang in kapal dicn ha Songsong, na rā ma-tāud dagang-an kan Lanang.

Na lūnūd na sila ha gītong tawīd.

Na rā aku in gatas dicn ha māioh.

ENGLISH.	SULU.
This mina-bird is most garrulous.	*Ma-latah pakaraiau tīong īni.*
This is mine.	*Ka-ku sa īni.*
His trousers were covered with mud.	*In sawal nia na hipoh sin pīsak.*
Do not make a mistake.	*Aiau kau mŭg-hīnang sāh.*
Mix with a little sugar to sweeten it.	*Lamūd-i īban tīoh-tīoh sūkal būt maka maimoh.*
The moat was full of the killed.	*Na hipoh na in gāta sin tāu nŭg-būnoh.*
What day is this? —Is it Monday?	*Adlau ūno ta īni? —Isnin ka?*
I have no money.	*Wāi rūn pĕlak ku.*
A monkey sat upon a tree.	*In amok nŭg-lingkūd ha-tās kāhōi.*
How many months will it be till he returns?	*Pīla-i būlan āmpa sia mūi mārī?*
Probably two months.	*Múnga dūai būlan.*
Many soldiers fell into the morass.	*Ma-tāud sondālo na legad halam sāpa.*
I have been seeking for him since morning.	*Nŭg-lāg aku kan nia dien sin mahinat.*
What is the price of a picul of pearl shells?	*Pīla in hāga sa pikul tīpai?*
Look out, or you will fall into the mud.	*Saio kau būt ma-hōg kau halam pīsak.*
He was murdered in the house.	*Būnoh-an sin tāu aŭn ha bāi.*

ENGLISH.	SULU.
Where was he killed?	*Hadien in ka-patai nia?*
In the house, I said.	*Halam bāi, long ku na.*
That is my house.	*Bāi ka-aku sa ien.*
Nail this plank.	*Lansang-a in digpi ini.*
What is your name?	*Hi sio ingan mu?*
What is his title?	*Uno in gālal nia?*
It will not touch you.	*Di sa ien mŭg-ūno.*
What do you want?	*Mug-āno tah kau?*
I declare I will strangle you.	*Pīkol-an ku na in lŏŭg mu.*
It is needless, never mind; it is of no use.	*S'ārī na, di na mŭg-āno; wāi ka-guna-han nyu.*
There are many nests (growing) at the Gomanton caves.	*Ma-tāud salang tumŭ-bŭh ha Gomanton.*
I never did.	*Wala aku tid nah.*
It must be night before they appear.	*Sobai dŭm āmpa nug-gomŭah.*
Don't come to-night.	*Aiau kau mārī dŭm īnī.*
They are making a noise.	*Nŭg-kāloh na sila.*
When the wind is from the north the current is excessively strong.	*Bāng hangin na ŭtāla ma-tŭgda na tid in sŭg.*
No, I won't.	*Di aku mau-bayah.*
I have brought nothing.	*Mīsan ang selag wala aku maka rā.*
When should it be?	*Sobai ka-āno?*

ENGLISH.	SULU.
When should it be?—It should be now.	Sobai ka-ūno?—Sobai bīh'aun.
He was here just now.	Aī-ya-rī h'ēn dūn.
He has gone. When?—Just now.	Ietu na. Ka-ūno?—Bāgū-bāgū iaun.
If you do not obey the Sultan's commands you will be punished.	Bāng kau di magad ha titah sin Junjongan ka-sākit-an sa kau ien.
What is your occupation?	Uno in hinang-an mu?
This house is occupied.	Tūgu tāu ha bāi ini.
There is the landlord coming.	Aī aun in tug bāi domatang na.
It grows not on the land, but only in the ocean.	Di tūmūbūh ha bed sobai ha gītong tawīd.
That man often comes here.	Tap-tap maka rī in tāu iaun.
This woman frequently comes here.	Abaran in babai ini maka rī.
Only, I am afraid of you.	Sagauh, ma-bōga aku kan nio.
One only.	Hambok buk sāja.
What is his opinion?	Bīadien in āgī nia?
I do not smoke opium.	Di aku mūg-murat.
Iron or wood will do.	Bāsī atawa kāhōi maka jārī.
I did not order him.	Walapa aku maka dāk kan nia.

ENGLISH.	SULU.
This is all that is over.	*Aī-ya-rī in lebih nia.*
Let us go outside.	*Song kīta matoh pa gñah.*
It is better to sit outside than inside.	*Maraiau mag-lingkūd ha-gñah dien ha-lūm.*
What do you owe me?	*Uno in pieg-ūtang-an mu ka aku?*
Where is the owner of the house?	*Hadien in tùg bāi?*
How many packages are there in one case?	*Pīla angka potūs ann halam angka tōng?*
How far is it from here to the palace?	*Biardien in lāioh nya dien dī pa astana?*
Lend me a little paper.	*Būs-i aku kātās tīoh-tīoh.*
I have forgotten to bring my umbrella.	*Ka-lūpa-han ku wa' ma-rā in pāyong.*
Leave it there.	*Bīn-an rūn ha ien.*
He has not yet come.	*Wa' pa sia maka ratūng.*
We wish to pass.	*Lūmubai na kāmi.*
I met her on the path that leads to the water.	*Pieg-bāk ku sila dūn ha rān pa tūbig.*
When will you pay your debt?	*Ka ūno kau mūg-bayad sin ūtang mu?*
In a short time.	*Būkūn dah mōgai.*
Bring me a pen that I may write.	*Daha na mārī in kalam, mam-iulat na aku.*
Be patient.	*Sabal na kau.*

ENGLISH.　　　　SULU.

Many people fled from the massacre.

Ma-tāud tāu nāg-pāgoi dien ha pāg-bānōh-an.

The Sultan will not grant his permission.

Di hi tāgāt sin Junjongan.

Pick out the good and throw away the bad.

Peh-peh-i sin maraian bugit-an sin mangi.

How many pieces of grey shirting are there in a bale?

Halam hambok bandala pēla ang bus gajaēlan?

There are one hundred.

Aun ang gātus.

The end of the wharf fell down.

Na holog in dōhol sin pantālan.

He has not yet become a pilgrim.

Walapa sia maka hājī.

He is on a pilgrimage to Mecca.

Mag-hājī sa ien pa Makkah.

Your debt to me you must pay.

Aun ūtang mū ka-āku sākāt-an ta na kau.

If a pilot cannot be got I shall not go.

Bāng wāi rān malim di aku maka katoh.

There are very few pine-apples in Sūlū.

Tīoh-tīoh dah in pīsang* ha Sōg.

Why are you afraid of pirates?

Mag-āno, kau ma-bōga salusu?

O dear me, Sir, you don't know their wickedness.

Allah, Tāan, wa' mu pa ka ingat-i in ngi nia.

* "Nanas" is the Malay name for pineapple; and *pisang* in Malay == banana or plantain.

ENGLISH.	SULU.
They have not planted coffee yet.	*Wala pa sila maka tānam kahāwa.*
It does not please me.	*Di aku mŭg-yen.*
Please give this to me.	*Dihili mu bah aku īni.*
Many people plunged into the sea.	*Ma-tāud tāu nŭg-lerop halam dāgat.*
Do not point your gun this way.	*Aiau mu pa tūjū-a in sanāpang mu mārī.*
I am poor.	*Miskin sa aku īni.*
Be very positive.	*Pa tantū-a tŭd.*
This country is possessed of devils.	*In hŭlah īni tŭga Sāitan.*
The posts have not been erected yet.	*Walapa maka bangun in hāg.*
Hitherto I have not seen potatoes like these.	*Wa'pa aku maka kīta pānggi bīhaīni āmpa bīh'aun.*
Night and day he does nothing but pray.	*Dŭm adlau mŭg-sambayang sāja.*
There is no profit in trading at present.	*Wāi untong mŭg-dāgang bīh'aun.*
He is coming presently.	*Mārī sa ien dai-dai dakoman.*
You need use no simulation; for, if it is really true, I will help you.	*Aiau kau mŭg-āla-ūla; but, bāng būnal, tabangan ta kau.*
That is not even what it cost me.	*Wa'pa ābāt in pūhūn ku.*
Let us proceed.	*Song na kīta.*

ENGLISH.	SULU.
The Princess Simīnal has sailed for Tāpol.	*Dāyang Pūtlī Simīnal bakas nug-tōluk pa Tāpol.*
That is proper.	*Pātut na īsab.*
Come under the shelter of this tree.	*Song kan mārī pa ka-selong-an sin kāhōi īni.*
What is to be done if you have not brought provisions?	*Bīadien in ka-āgī bang kan walapa maka rā lutoh-an?*
Pull till it breaks.	*Hēla āmpa bogtoh.*
Who purchased your Kris?	*Hi sīo in na mī sin kālis mu?*
The pony pursues the deer, and the dog the pig.	*Kūra nug-hapas ha ūsa, erok mig-turol ha baboi.*
What quantity is there?	*Bīadien in ka-tānd-an nya?*
Do not quarrel or fight.	*Aian na kāmu mug-bantah atawa mig-lorai.*
It is in the other quarter.	*Ien dān ha ang ūtūd.*
I shall not quit this spot if you do not pay your debt.	*Di aku m'ēg dien dī bang kan di maka bāyad sin ūtang mu.*
Any old rag will do.	*Munga ragmai ragmai maka jārī.*
You have bitten me.	*Man-utkut kan ka aku.*
A rat climbed up a post.	*Ambāu nug-dag ha hāg.*
There are no ratans here.	*Wāi rān wāi dī-ha-īni.*
If it be eaten raw it is intoxicating.	*Bang mig-ka-aun sin helau ma-hēloh sa ien.*

ENGLISH.	SULU.
I cannot reach it.	*Di aku maka ābūt.*
Read it, I say.	*Bacha-a, kāno.*
I received it from him.	*Bakas aku nūg-tāīma kan nia.*
They left quite recently.	*Bāgū-bāgū tūd ma-ūg na sila.*
Do you not recognise me?	*Di mu aku ka-kīla-han?*
They recollected simultaneously.	*Nūg-tūm-tūm na sila sāma-sāma.*
I prefer to use a Sūlū bridle.	*Maubayah aku makai kakang Sōg.*
I help him to carry fresh water.	*Tābang-i nio sila nūg-sauk tūbig tābang.*
If there is no one to relieve you, you cannot go.	*Bāng wāi rūn gomanti kāimu di kau maka ūg.*
Remain here until my return.	*Domī na kau āmpa aku mug-bālek.*
Don't bring it here; let it remain.	*Aiau mu pa ka rī; pa rūn-an na.*
Take away this child.	*Daha matoh in bata-bata īni.*
Lady, if you sail away, you repudiate me.	*Dāyang, bāng kau tōlak bīn-i aku mu talak.*
Where do you reside?	*Hadien kau nūg-hūlah?*
Restore his goods to him.	*Hi ālih in āta ma-aun kan nia.*
Are you not afraid of retribution following?	*Di kau ma-būga kia-busongan?*

ENGLISH.	SULU.
Think, I say.	*Pīkil bah, kūno.*
He says the very reverse.	*Dōāin-dōāin na īsab in pāmong niu.*
My mat is covered with rice.	*Na hīpoh in būras ku sin bugas*
Bring the rice and the dishes.	*Daha mārī in ka-aun-an ībun ka-k'aun-an.*
The Sultan lost a ring in Sandakan.	*Na lāwa in singsing sin Junjongan ha Sandakan.*
There is nothing but uproar in the market.	*Nug-hīlo-hāla sāja halam parian.*
It is unripe.	*Būlak pa walupa mahīnog.*
Who stole your horse?	*Hi sīo in tiakau sin kūra mu!*
Robbers are plentiful in Sūlū; but, the greatest thieves of all are Pārang people.	*Ma-tāud pakaraiau shugarol ha Sōg; but, in shugarol tūd āmū na tāu Pārang.*
The fish leapt on a rock.	*Mūg-luksū in istā patās bātū.*
The best leaves for making roofs of are sago palm leaves.	*Amū na maraiau mūg-hīnang atūp dāhūn sāni.*
They are making a moat round the fort.	*Nūg-hīnang na sila gāta ha lībut sin kōta.*
Rouse up so-and-so, for it is day.	*Bangun-i hi kūan but adlau na.*

ENGLISH.	SULU.
If it is not round it is square.	*Bang bukun tibuk pasagi.*
I cannot bear to live under Spanish rule.	*Di aku maka bug-bug ha palentah sin Kastela.*
All the children ran into their houses.	*Nug-dag in bata-bata ka-tan palam bai sila.*
It will not hold more than twenty sacks of paddy.	*Di maka luan lebih dun ha kaahan ka karot pai.*
What is the cause of your sadness, my lady?	*Uno in ka-susah-an mu, dayang ku?*
How much are you engaged at?	*Pela in hi tangdan mu?*
Work for me and I will pay you wages.	*Hinang-a bah ini ka aku tangdan-an tu kau.*
How many pots of salt have you brought?	*Pela angka sukul asin na ra nio?*
They are all the same.	*Sali sa ien ka-tantan.*
You should have brought a sample.	*Sobai nug-da ra sontoh.*
I saw a corpse on the sands.	*Na kita aku maiat ha buhangin.*
Let us go to the sand-bank to collect shells.	*Song kita pa hunas-an mug-panagat.*
These slippers, being too large, are no use.	*Wai guna-guna sin taompa ini, dakolah na.*
What does he say?	*Uno kuno?*
I will not have any of your impudence	*Di aku mau-bayah sin pamong-an nio ien.*

ENGLISH.	SULU.
What does he say?	*Uno lūng nia!*
A scorpion stung him on the hand.	*Kut-kut sin kāla jang-king ha līma nia.*
Scrutinize it well that you may know it again.	*Nŭg-paleksa mu tūd ampa kau maka kīla-i.*
I shall throw it into sea.	*Siapud ku sila palam dāgat.*
The Bajau and Sūlū dialects differ.	*Dūain in bahasa Bajau dien ha bahasa Sūg.*
Carry water from the sea.	*Sauk-i tūbig dāgat.*
I shall investigate the matter to-morrow.	*Mam-leksa na aku kin-shŭm.*
He has never sent it to me.	*Walupa sia mŭg-pa rā mārī.*
They are separated.	*Na būtas na sila.*
The meaning of the word "boy" is servant, but different from servant (slave) in Sūlū.	*In m'āna hi "boy" ipun, but maien būkŭn bīa īpun ha Sūg, dūain.*
What is the price of your pony?—Six dollars and a half.	*Pēla in hāga sin kūra mu īni!—Ka pēto ang sīpah pēlak.*
How often did you go? —Seven times.	*Maka pēla kau matoh? — Maka pēto.*
I shall not go.	*Di aku mau-bayah matoh.*
Should we near the shallows, steer for the sea.	*Bāng masŭk pa babau tūlak pa laūd.*

ENGLISH.	SULU.
How many piculs of sharks' fins did they bring from Umadal?	*Pīla pikol sik kaītan na rā sila dien ha Umaral?*
Are there any sheep in Sūlū?	*Aun kah bīlī-bīlī ha Sōg?*
There are no sheep in Sūlū.	*Wāi rān bīlī-bīlī ha Sōg.*
At present there are two or three.	*Bih'ann aun manga dūa tō.*
It is not forbidden to drink sherbet.	*Būkān halām mug-inom salbat.*
A Spanish ship has arrived.	*Dimatong na in kapal sin Kastela.*
The steamer is under weigh.	*Na mutput na in kapal aso.*
Look at the shape of that ship, its stem is formed like a shark's jaw.	*Kīta bah in rugbus sin kapal iaun, in dōhong nya bīu manga sīmud kaītan.*
Who is shooting in the forest?	*Hi sīo in nāg-tembak dān halūm golangan ien?*
Rain is indispensable before seeds will shoot.	*Sobai tūga ūlan āmpa bīgi tumūbuh.*
He is invulnerable, even the shot of a gun could not hit him.	*Panglias sa ien, mīsan pangloh sanāpang di kīrgdān-an.*
Shut the gate.	*Tambal-a in lāwang.*
On the other side.	*Ien dūn ha ang sīpak.*
It is on that side of the house.	*Ai aun dūn ha ang ātād sin bāi.*

ENGLISH.	SULU.
Of what are you to make the sides of your house?	*Uno in hīnang-an mu dinding sin bāi mu?*
Let us all join in a song.	*Mñy-bāt na kīta nio ka-tān.*
How much is this?—One for a cuarto.	*Pela - pela in īni?—Mag-tonggal kualto.*
How much is that one there?—Twenty-five cents.	*Pīla-pēla in hambok ien dūn'—Kāāhan-tug-līma cēn.*
Sister, dear, assist me to sew this head-dress.	*Kakah tābang-i nio aku man-āhi sin pīs īni.*
How long does a hen sit in hatching her eggs?—Fifteen days.	*Pēla in lōgai sin manok mang-ām āmpa ma-mūsah?—Hangpoh-tug-līma i rūm.*
He slapped me on the cheek.	*Sampak nia aku ha pisni.*
What can we do, Sir, being slaves only.	*Biardien tah kāmi īni, Tūan, īpun sāja?*
He had not gone to sleep.	*Wa'pa sia ma-tōg.*
How slowly you walk.	*Ma-huskau pakaraiau kau mūg-panau.*
I was very small at the time of the war in Sūlū.	*Asīrī pa aku abīla in ka pug-būnoh ha Sōg.*
Why do you smile at me?	*Maita mu aku pug-humaiam?*
Look, he is laughing.	*Kīta na bah, ka-tāwa sia.*

ENGLISH.	SULU.
Take it to the black-smith's to be mended.	*Parā-a na matoh pa tūkang-basī āmpa dumaiau.*
I do not smoke cigars.	*Di aku maka mūg-dābla.*
Give me a little soap.	*Dihili mu aku sābūn tīoh-tīoh.*
Some were armed and others were not.	*In ka-ībun-an mūg-takūs, in ka-ībun-an wala.*
How many kinds are there?	*Pīla angka gīnīs sin aun?*
Point towards the South.	*Tūjū-han pa Satān.*
They have not sown their paddy yet.	*Wa'pa sia maka bākal in pāi nia.*
I have been to Spain.	*Bakas aku maka katoh pa Lūpa-Kastela.*
I thought you were a Spaniard.	*Pīkil-an ku Tāu-Kastela sa kau ien.*
Why do you not speak?	*Maita kau di mūg-pāmong?*
For what purpose do you bring a spear? There are no evil disposed persons here.	*Mūg-ūno kau mūg-dā būjak? Wāi rūn tāu mangi dī ha ini.*
What is the name of that gentleman with the spectacles?	*Hi sīo ingan sin tūan iaun nūg-mamakai sāmin māta?*
Where is the spot?	*Hadien tungud?*

ENGLISH.	SULU.
There! you have spilt the water.	*Na! na āsag in tūbig.*
The spirit of the ocean dwells in the deep.	*In gālāp nāg-hūlah ha-lūm tawīd.*
This rope has parted. Do you know how to splice?	*Ma-bogtoh sin lūbid īni. Ma-ingat kau māg-supat?*
My gun is out of order.	*Ma kangi na in sanāpang ku īni.*
His house is destroyed.	*Na larak na in bāi nia*
My hand is sprained.	*Na piol in līma ku.*
I have never seen a squirrel in Sūlū.	*Wa'pa aku ma' kīta basing ha Sōg.*
They stabbed him in the breast.	*Tigbak na sia nila ha dagha nia.*
The robbers destroyed our stables.	*Na larak sin shugarol in pagal kūra nāmu.*
I cannot stay long.	*Di aku maka tagad mōgai.*
Do not steal; do not lie; do not swear; and don't kill or murder.	*Aiau ma-nakau; aiau ma-māting; aiau ma-ninggad; aiau ma-mānoh.*
I do not know how to steer.	*Di aku ma-ingat mapāt ha bānsan.*
How can we ever ascend these steps?—Easily, Sir, if you climb as I do.	*Biardien na kāmi īni samakat ha hāg-dān īni? —Mohai bah, Tūan, bāng kau sākat bīa aku.*

ENGLISH.	SULU.
Turn round the stern.	Bieng-i in būlī tah.
Go you aft.	Katoh kau pa būlī.
I have been pricked with a needle.	Na tuksuy aku sin jaūm.
A stork wades in the lake.	In bangau mug-ūbog halam lānau.
The roof was all blown away by the hurricane.	Wāi na kapin sin atūp na palid sin hūnus.
When you walk do not straddle.	Abila kau manau aiau ma-bingkang in sīki mu.
The vessel stranded on a sandbank.	Na sānglad in sakaian ha hūnās-an.
Do not strike me.	Aiau mu aku lōbak-an.
He struck me.	Lobak-an nia aku.
That lady struck me on the face with her slipper.	Siampak aku hi dāyang ien ha pisni sin taompa nia.
Do you know how to twist rope?	Ma-ingat kau mūg-pinsal lūbid ?
The wind is very strong.	Ma-tugda tūd in hangin tuh.
It is raining hard.	Ma-tugda in ūlan.
Where is your substitute?	Hadien in gomanti kāimu ?
Suffer it to be so.	Bīa na ha ien.
Make it sufficient.	Ganap-i nio bah.
They appealed to the Sultan.	Na rā na sila sin bechala pa Sūltan.
The day is very sultry.	Ma-pāso tūd adlau īni.

ENGLISH.	SULU.
Sum up the whole.	Jamlah-a na ka-tan-tan.
We have not yet reached the summit.	Wa' pa kami maka ābūt pa puntuk.
Put my coat out to dry, as it is wet.	Buhar-i in bājū ku bāt ma-bāsah.
The sun is about to set.	Mārī na samadlup in sūga.
A Datoh in Sūlū is superior to a Mahārāja.	In Datoh ha Sōg lebih dākolah dien ha Maha-lāja
What do you suppose?	Bīadien in nanam mu?
How does it taste?	Bīadien in nanam tah?
I am not certain.	Walapa aku ma-tantu.
Where is the surplus?	Hadien in ka-lebih-an nya?
That is swearing.	Peninggar-an sa ien.
Bring me a broom.	Daha nio mārī in sa-sāpū ka aku.
They are sweethearts.	Nūg-tūnang na sila.
I do not know how to swim.	Di aku maka ingat mūg-langoi.
Put the glass on the table.	Būtang in kāsa ien pa la-mīsa-han.
Do not take that.	Aiau kau mūg-kawa ha ien.
Why do you not plant tapioca on this land?	Maita kau di mūg-tanum pānggi kāhōi di ha lōpa ini?
He refreshed us with tea and biscuits.	Nug-labut nia aku tūbig piaso ībun bang-bāng.

ENGLISH.	SULU.
Teach me to speak your language.	Hindoh-i nio aku pamong sin bahasa mu.
Teak is good for making ribs of boats.	Maraiau in jāti mūg-hinang giak sin sakai-an.
I have teeth he has none.	Aku aun ipun sia wāi rūn.
He is good-tempered.	Maraiau in palangai nia.
This is better than that.	Maraiau in īni dien-ha ien.
Here is the best of all.	Ai-ya-rī maraiau tūd īni dien hu ka-tān.
Whose house is this?	Kan sīo in bāi īni?
Get away from there.	Eg na kan dien dūn.
This is very thick cloth.	Ma-rukmal tūd in kākāna īni.
He is a thief, do not let him enter.	Pa-nakau sa ien, aiau pa sūr-an.
If the cloth is thick the paper is very thin.	Bāng ma rūkmal in kākāna ma-nīpis tūd in katās.
Where can we place our things?	Hadien nāmu hi bātang mūnga pūtūs-pūtūs nāmu īni?
I am thirsty.	Ma-ūhau aku.
Though it were the Sultan, I would not be afraid.	Mīsan Junjongan, di aku ma-bōga.
It is short of a thousand.	Walapa ganap ang ību.

ENGLISH.	SULU.
Three men walked to the right, but those who went to the left were lost.	Tū anjka tāu nug-panau pa tō, na lāwa in tāu nug-panau pa lāwa.
Do you hear the thunder?	Maka rūngag na kau in dūg-dūg?
It is nearly flood-tide.	Mārī na taub.
What tidings have you brought?	Uno na maien in gāwi na rā nio?
His time has not yet come.	Walapa ābūt in ganta nia.
On what date did he promise to come?	Pila-i adlau in tugun nia āmpa domatang?
Give it to the gentleman.	Dihil-i kan tūan.
He has gone to Tianggi.	Bakas sia manau pa Tianggi.
He will come to-morrow.	Sobai kin-shūm āmpa domatang.
Give me a little tobacco.	Dihili mu aku tabāku tīoh-tīoh.
Let us go together into the country.	Mūg-dangan-dāngan na kīta manau pa gimbah.
Pull together.	Hīlā sāma-sāma.
Let us go and visit the Sultan's tomb.	Song kīta matoh komīta kīta ha kūbul sin Malo-hom.
What is the price of that tortoise-shell?	Pīla hāga sisik iaun?

ENGLISH.	SULU.
They went towards the country.	Nag-tūjū sila ma aun pa gimbah.
Bring towels and let us have a bath.	Ra-a in jimpan maigoh na kīta.
They followed the tracks of the robbers.	Nag-turol sila limpa siki sin shugarol.
Do not trample on my plants.	Aiau mu geik-i in tianam-an ku.
It is rumoured that the treaty is broken.	Na bogtoh in kapitora-sion kūno.
A new treaty had better be framed.	Sobai mug-hīnang pūg janji-an bāgū.
Why do you tremble so?	Maita kau ma-mīdpūd bi-ha-ien?
The rain dropped from the roof.	Mag-tō in ūlan dien ha atūp.
The water trickled from above.	Tumū in tūbig dien ha-tās.
Trim the boat or we shall capsize.	Timbang-i in sakai-an tah but ma-rāub na kīta.
It is perfectly true.	Būnal sa ma-tūd.
Were I a man I should transfix you with a spear.	Bāng aku ūsog tigbak-an tah kau sin būjak.
He would say nothing but the truth.	Di sa ien pāmong dōāin dūn ha ka-bunāl-an.
Try again.	Solai na īsab.
Tuck up your trousers lest they be soiled by the mud.	Kīnkīn-a in sawal mu but di ma-hipoh pīsak.

ENGLISH.	SULU.
Try once more.	*Solai maka minsan dakoman.*
The Sultan fell ill on Tuesday.	*Adlau sālasa in Sūltan mangi lasa.*
Put on your turban.	*Nūg-pīs na kau.*
What o'clock is it?—Twelve o'clock.	*Lesag pēla?—Lesag hangpoh-tug-dūa.*
He deceived me twice.	*Mag ka-rūa sila maka rūa ka aku.*
Twist the rope.	*Pinsal-a in lūbid.*
They are twins.	*Anak kambal sa ien.*
Bring two or three.	*Da mārī mūnga dūa tō.*
This kris is double-edged.	*Dūa māta in kālis īni.*
He has taken umbrage at what I have said.	*Mangi hatāi nia dien ha pāmong ku.*
This man is utterly unable.	*Di tiid man-jārī tau īni.*
It is not as though he were unaccustomed.	*Būkun bīa ha munga būkun bīaksa.*
He is unarmed.	*Wāi rūn takūs nia.*
He is my uncle.	*Amah-an ku sa ien.*
I shall marry him.	*Bana-han ku sa ien.*
I do not understand.	*Di aku maka hati.*
If you are unemployed seek employment.	*Bāng wāi rūn hīnang mu lāg kau hīnang-an.*
Why are all the trees in this place unfruitful?	*Maita in kāhōi ka-tantan ha hūlah īni di nug-būnga?*

ENGLISH.	SULU.
Unfasten the rope of my pony.	Ubār-i in lūbid sin kūra ku.
They have not begun to unload the cargo.	Wala-pa sila maka tagnah-i hāwas in lūan-an.
Why did you not bring it earlier? It is useless now.	Maita kau wa' mug-da mārī kaina? Wāi gūna bih'ann.
I shall not return until to-morrow.	Di aku mūi āmpa kinshūm.
It is unusual to do so.	Mahang nag-hinang bi-ha-ien.
The water was up to the knees.	In tūbig iaun tūb-tūb pa tūhud.
Put it on the chair.	Būtang ha-tās sīa.
What an uproar this is.	Nag-kāloh pakaraian sa īni.
That belongs to us.	Ka-atū sa ien.
Of what use is it?	Uno in ka-guna-han nya?
It is of no use.	Wāi rān ka-guna-han nya.
This is a most valiant man.	Ma-īsug pakaraiau tāu īni.
You can value it.	Ekau in mag-halga.
These ferns are used as vegetables.	In ka-guna-han sin pakis īni pŭg-sāyol-an.
I am afraid to venture.	Ma-būga aku mag-solai.
Ho! old man, whither goest thou?	Hua! mās, pakaien tah kau?

ENGLISH.	SULU.
There is no vinegar.	Wai rān sūka.
He answered in a feeble voice.	Samambay na sia asivī asīrī tungog nya.
They have cholera.	Sākit na sila intāhū sūka.
He has not paid my wages yet.	Wala-pa sia aku ongsur-i sin tangdan-an ku.
The waggon is upset on the road.	Na rānb in karosah dūn ha rān.
I cannot walk; my feet ache.	Di aku maka panau; ma-sākit sīki ku.
I do not want to go.	Di aku mau-bayah matoh.
Whom do you want?	Hi sīo in pāg-ien-an nio?
It is very warm to-day.	Ma-pāso tiud adlau īni.
He was here a while ago.	Bakas sia rī kaina.
If a wasp sting you it is poisonous.	Bāng lapiniy ien maka kut-kut kaimu ma-bīsa.
Give me a little water to drink.	Dihil-i mu aku tūbig tīoh-tīoh pa inom-a aku.
Is it fresh or salt water?	Tūbig ma-tābang tah atawa ma-āsin tah?
The sea is boisterous to-day.	Ma-alun adlau īni.
In this way, not that way.	Bīhaīni būkān bīhaietu.

ENGLISH.	SULU.
Get out of my way and let me pass.	Shimai kau lumūbai na aku.
I feel uneasy if I have no weapon.	Ma-sūsah aku bāng wāi rūn takās ku.
He sailed more than a week ago.	Bakas sia timōlak lebih angka pēto.
It is not heavy; it is very light.	Bukin ma-bōgat bah; ma-gāban tūd sa ien.
He has almost recovered from his illness.	Mārī na sila ka-ulih-an.
Let us walk to the end of the wharf.	Panau na kīta matoh pa dōhol sin pāntan.
What does he say?	Uno kūno?
Bring whatever you can get.	Daha mārī munga ūno-ūno in ka-bāk-an mu.
I have seen, what-do-you-call-him—I have forgotten his name.	Bakas ku kīta, hi-kūan, hi—ka-lupa-han ku na ingan nia.
When did he arrive?	Ka ūno sia sampai?
Where is my barong?	Hadien in barong ku?
Whether he permits it or not I will take it.	Bāng mau-buyah atawa būkin kā-an ku.
Which is the best?	Hadien in maraiau?
Your horse has been let loose.	Kāra mu bakas na biuloi.
Which one?	In hadien?
Who is there?	Hi sīo ien?
Whose land is this?	Kan-sīo lōpa īni?

* *Buloi-an* or *biuloi-an*   to loose.

SULU.

RANK.	FORMS OF ADDRESS.
Junjongan (sultan)	*Sin junjongan*
Sūltan	*Tūan sūltan*
Dātoh (chief)	*Dātoh*
Lāja (king)	*Lāja*
Selip	*Tūan selip*
Mantili (minister of state)	*Tūan mantili*
Hājī (pilgrim)	*Tūan hājī*
Panglīma (captain or prefect)	*Tūan panglīma*
Laxamana (com. in chief)	*Laxamana*
Mahālāja (prince)	*Mahālāja*
Nakib (religious title)	*Tūan nakib*
Katib ,, ,,	*Tūan katib*
Imam ,, ,,	*Imam*
Olang kaya baginda (nobleman)	*Olang kaya baginda*
Olang kaya (headman)	*Olang kaya*
Bāndari (steward)	*Bāndari*
Makahail (keeper of the markets)	*Makahail*
Sultana	*Dāyang-dāyang*
Pangian	*Dāyang pangīan*
Putli (princess)	*Dāyang putli*
Dāyang (lady)	*Dāyang*

When an inferior addresses the Sultan, a *Dātoh*, *Lāja*, or *Selip*, he speaks of himself as *patek*. There is no distinction made by an inferior when addressing persons of lower rank than these.

In addressing the Sultan the Sūlūs introduce the subject of discourse by the preliminary formula :—

258

Rank and Forms of Address
(Continued).

Ampūn barību ampūn ha tapak siki sin Junjongan sin patck, pardons, thousands of pardons (be extended) to this your slave; or *mīki ampūn in patck*. When addressing his Highness directly, they say *Junjongan* or *mūnga Junjongan*, may it be your Highness; Junjongan being the Sūlū title of the Sultan. Europeans in addressing the Sultan call him Tūan Sultan; this is not a Sūlū way of addressing him, but it is most common among foreigners. In speaking of the Sultan, his subjects never use Tūan before his title but say only Sultan or *Junjongan*, as: *kūra sin Junjongan*, the Sultan's pony; *astana sin Sultan*, the Sultan's palace.

The form so common among Malays of addressing persons of rank, and speaking of themselves to superiors in the third person is not so common among Sūlūs. There is a more independent tone about the people in this respect. With the exceptions already mentioned, *aku* and its abbreviation *ku*, I; *Kāmi*, we; *ckau* or *kau*, you; and *kāmu* with its abbreviation *mu* are used alike by superiors and inferiors in conversing with each other, but *ckau* should never be used in addressing the Sultan, although all below him may be addressed in the second person; e.g. :—

This (your) servant sues for pardon; where- | *Mīki ampūn in patck; but k'abi aun tau bakas*

RANK AND FORMS OF ADDRESS.
(Continued).

fore some one stole the pony of this (your) servant last night, and pray (your) servant has come to inform your Highness.

tiakan kūra sin pātek mārī na munga pātek mayen mŭg-baita na mŭnga Junjongan

When your Highness has returned from (your) pilgrimage to Mecca I intend paying a visit to Sūlū.

Bāng maka'ñi in Tuan* Sūltan dien ha mŭkkah matoh mayen aku pa Sōg mŭg-pang-īta-īta.

You cannot resist Dātoh.

Di kau maka atu Dātoh.

Had it not been for you, Sir, we should have died.

Bāng bākun ekau, Tūan, miatai na kāmi.

Where is your house panglīma?

Haden in bāi mu panglīma?

There it is on that hill; cannot you see it.

Iaun dūn ha-tās bŭd iaun; di kāmu maka īta

---

* Foreigners only use Tuan in addressing the Sultan.

POINTS OF THE COMPASS.

ENGLISH.	SULU.	MALAY.
North	ūtāla	ūtāra
South	sātan	slātan
East	tīmol	tīmor
West	bāgat	bārat
North-east	tīmol lāud	tīmor lāut
North-west	hilāgu	bārat lāut
South-east	tungāla	tunggāra
South-west	bāgat dāya	bārat dāya

In the Sulū, the following points of the compass, are formed from the cardinal points by the interpolation of *tuminga*, as—

N. N.E.	ūtāla	tuminga	timol
N. N.W.	bāgat	,,	ūtāla
E. N.E.	timol	,,	,,
W. N.W.	bāgat	,,	,,
E. S.E.	timol	,,	sātan
W. S.W.	bāgat	.,	,,
S. S.E.	sātan	,,	timol
S. S.W.	sātan	,,	bāgat

In the Malay they are as follows:—

N. N.E.	ūtāra sa-māta timor
N. N.W.	ūtāra bārat lāut
E. N.E.	tīmor sa-māta ūtāra
W. N.W.	bārat sa-māta ūtāra
E. S.E.	tīmor tunggāra
W. S.W.	bārat sa-māta slatan
S. S.E.	slātan menunggāra
S. S.W.	slātan dāya

PERIODS OF TIME.

ENGLISH.	SULU.	MALAY.
A day	*isai adlau*	sātu hāri
A week	*angka peto,*	tūjuh hāri,
	angka rominggo	sātu minggo
A month	*isai būlan*	sātu būlan
A year	*angka tāhān*	sātu tāhun
To-day	*adlau īni*	hāri īni
To-morrow	*kin-shām*	besok
Yesterday	*ka-hāpun*	kalmārin
„ , day before	*tak-īsa*	kalmārin dahūlu
„ afternoon	*ka-hapun*	kalmārin patang
	mahapun	
Day after to-morrow	*kun-īsa*	lūsa
Three days hence	*ha-tō*	tulat
Four days hence	*ha-ōpat*	tuban
Five days hence	*ha-līma*	jano
This month	*būlan īni*	būlan īni
Next month	*būlan hambok*	būlan dātang
	domatang	
Last month	*būlan miatai*	būlan lālū
Morning	*mahinat*	pāgi
Evening	*mahapun*	patang
Mid-day	*tengah adlau,*	tengah hāri
	ogtoh	
A night	*isai dūm*	sātu mālam
To-night	*dūm īni*	mālam īni
Midnight	*tengah dūm*	tengah mālam
An hour	*angka jām*	sātu jām
Moment	*angka sāat*	sa'sāat

HOURS OF PRAYER.

ENGLISH.	SULU.	MALAY.
3 a.m.	*lapit adlau*	sīang hārī
5 a.m.	*sūbūh-sūbūh adlau*	sūbūh
9 a.m.	*tengah naīk*	tengah naīk
12 noon	*ogtoh*	rambang
1.30 p.m.	*lohol*	lohor
3 p.m.	*asal*	asar
5 p.m.	*mahapun*	patang
6.50 p.m.	*magalib*	maghrib
9 p.m.	*aisa*	iasha

In Sūlū, the mode of dividing time is commonly by the hours of prayer. Those persons only who are accustomed to have intercourse with foreigners can divide the day into hours.

DAYS OF THE WEEK.

ENGLISH.	SULU.	MALAY.
Sunday	adlau ahad	hārī ahad
Monday	,, isnin	,, ithnain
Tuesday	,, salasa	,, salāsa
Wednesday	,, alba	,, arba
Thursday	,, hamis	,, khamīs
Friday	,, jamahat	,, jumāt
Saturday	,, sabtu	,, sabtu

MONTHS OF THE YEAR.*

Muharram	30 days.
Safer	29 ,,
Rabi alāwal	30 ,,
Rabi alākhir	29 ,,
Jemad alāwal	30 ,,
Jemad alākhir	29 ,,
Rajab	30 ,,
Shaban	29 ,,
Ramthan	30 ,,
Shawal	29 ,,
Zil kāadah	30 ,,
Zil hājah †	29 ,,
	354

* The Mahommedan year consisting of only 354 days, being fully 11 days short of the Solar year, the months do not recur at the same period in each year.   † Sometimes 30 days.

NAMES OF VARIOUS WEAPONS.

SWORDS.

Kampilan.
Eayan.
Kaliawang.
Utak angkñn.
Laring jambangan tuli.
Utak tira.
    ,, *lapokoh.*
    ,, *sa-suah.*
    ,, *la-lapah.*

KRISES.

Tūlid (straight) *samsil.*
    ,,   *būnga bung loi.*
    ,,   *balangkas.*
    ,,   *ka-kolang-an.*
    ,,   *dasag.*
    ,,   *dapau.*
    ,,   *panas.*
    ,,   *sabli.*
Lanteh (wavey) *bandos.*
    ,,   *panas.*
    ,,   *ga-gamutsun.*
    ,,   *liamai.*
    ,,   *malanau.*
    ,,   *janasuah.*
    ,,   *agau buku.*

NAMES OF VARIOUS WEAPONS.
(Continued).

Short Swords.

Bārong sāp* tunggal.

,, ,, *kamas.*

,, ,, *laipan.*

,, ,, *binlihan.*

,, ,, *angkūn.*

,, ,, *tō.*

Spears.

Būjak † awak-awak.

,, *bulanun.*

,, *sauh sok bulanun.*

,, *kalagan.*

,, *bangkau.*

,, *binangkau.*

,, *dahun bukau.*

,, *tiabulah.*

,, *kianus-kianus.*

,, *dūa sanga.*

,, *tunggal selab.*

,, *tungkud sin santilih.*

* Sap = Trade-mark.   † Bujak = Spear.

NAMES OF VARIOUS WEAPONS.
(Continued).

GUNS, ETC.

ENGLISH.	SULU.
Flint-gun	*Sanâpang bâtu âpi*
Enfield rifle	,, *kep*
,, ,,	,, *tō bûka*
,, carbine	,, *dûa bûka*
Fancy flint-gun	,, *turakol*
Remington rifle	,, *tud-tud*
Double-barrelled gun	,, *dûa selab*
Martini-Henry rifle	,, *jangat*
Snider rifle	,, *ukab-ukab*
Swiss repeater	,, *dûa balas*
Winchester rifle	,, *pa-junpang*
Ramrod	*darasok*
Cartridge	*kalachucho*
Shot	*hambul*
Bullet	*pungloh*
Cap	*batil-batil*
Cap	*kep*
Hammer of a gun	*punatok*
Trigger	*pachikan, pasikan*
Powder	*ōbat*
Flint	*bâtu âpi*
The strap	*saklaian, salaian*
Pouch	*aba-aba*
To pull the trigger	*pa-pasik*
Nipple	*butu-butu*

Guns, Etc.—(Continued).

Barrel	*bulu*
Stock	*tagōbahan*
Sight	*bijala*
Bayonet	*sangko*

NAMES OF VARIOUS GONGS.

Agōng bāah.

,,   *lūsong.*

,,   *bu-bundil.*

,,   *salbun.*

,,   *bolongan.*

,,   *samārang.*

,,   *kimānis.*

TERMS OF FRIENDSHIP.

Bagai

Agalap

Salanga

Indah

268

CURRENCY IN MEMBONG.*

Walū ang-gatus (800) *kus-*
hing ...*hambok* (1) *pelak* (dollar).
Ang-rātus (100) *sēn*
(cents) ... *hambok* (1) *pelak* (dollar).

The cash current in Membong is called by the Chinese "tang chi" (brass cash), and sometimes by the Sūlūs *tangsi*. Before the introduction of "tang chi," (brass cash), the currency was iron cash, 10,000 of which were equal to a dollar. The Chinese name for this kind of money is "thi chi," corrupted by the Sūlūs into *kūshing*, the name now applied to brass cash. A distinction is sometimes made by the addition of *tambāga*, as *kūshing tambāga* (brass cash), but *kūshing* alone is generally used.

CURRENCY IN SANDAKAN.

SULU.

Dūa (2) *dūit*	... *hambok* (1) *sēn* (one cent).
Ang-gātus (100) *sēn*	... *hambok* (1) *pelak* (one dollar).

MALAY.

Dūa (2) *dūit*	...sātu (1) sēnt (one cent).
Sa-rātus (100) sēnt	...sātu (1) ringgit (one dollar).

*In Membong and the Sulu Archipelago, excepting Spanish settlements, the currency is subject to change.

CURRENCY IN JOLO.*

Diez (10) cuartos†	... un (1) real, 12½ cents (old currency).
Dos (2) reales	... una (1) peseta, 25 cents (old currency).
Cuatro (4) pesetas	... un (1) peso, one dollar (old currency).
Ocho (8) cuartos	... un (1) real, 10 cents.
Dos (2) reales	... una (1) peseta, 20 cents.
Cinco (5) pesetas	... un (1) peso, one dollar.
Dos (2) medios pesos	... un (1) peso, one dollar.
Dos (2) pesos	... un (1) doblon de oro, two gold dollars.

PEARL WEIGHT.

Hangpoh (10) *angka chūchok* ... *ang* (1) *amas*

Hangpoh (10) *ang amas* ... *ang* (1) *basing*

A *chūchok* is equal to 6.24 grains (Troy).

Seven *amas* are generally reckoned equal to the weight of a Spanish dollar, although really a little heavier.

This table is also used in weighing opium and precious products, such as camphor, white bird's nests, &c.

* Spanish settlement in Sulu.　† 1 cuarto = 1¼ cents.

Avoirdupois Weight.

16 *basing* *	... *sa kati* (1⅓ lbs.)
100 *kati*	... *sa pikul* (133⅓ lbs.)
40 *pikul*	... *sa kōyan* (5333⅓ lbs.)

A *basing* is equal to 624 grains (Troy).

Measure of Capacity.—(Dry).

Opat (4) *angka pinggan*	... *angka* (1) *gantang* or 3⅓ *katies.*
Hangpoh (10) *angka gantang*	... *ang* (1) *kāga* or 33⅓ *katies.*
Tō (3) *ang kāga*	... *sa* (1) *pikul* or 100 *katies.*

These measures vary considerably, the *gantang* holding sometimes 2½, 3, 3½ and 4 *katies*; and the number of *pinggans* to a *gantang* depending on the size of the measure used. Reckoning the *pikul* at 100 *katies*, in measuring rice, the other measures would equal in *katies* what has been stated above. There is no standard *gantang* in Sūlū. The *pinggan* most frequently used is the common Chinese "mangkok." Rice, paddy, coffee and cocoa are bought and sold by this table.

* Basing = tahil = 1oz. 6½drs.

LONG OR CLOTH MEASURE.

Angka tūdloh ... breadth of a finger.

Dūa angka tūdloh ... breadth of two fingers.

Tō ,, ,, ... breadth of three fingers.

Opat ,, ,, ... breadth of four fingers.

Ang pad ... ... breadth of the hand.

Ang sāng ... ... the space from the end of the thumb to the end of the forefinger when the fingers are extended.

Ang dangau ... ... a span; the space from the end of the thumb to the end of the middle finger when the fingers are exended.

Lebih-lebih tingah or
tingah sin tingah ... a cubit; the length of the arm from the elbow to the tip of middle finger.

Angka bāra ... ... the length from the tip of the middle finger to the shoulder opposite an arm when extended.

Tingah dupa ... half-fathom; the distance between the tip of the middle finger and the middle of the breast when the arm is extended.

Ang dupa ... ... a fathom, generally of about 5 ft.; the distance between the extremities of both arms when extended.

Long or Cloth Measure.
(Continued).

Angka pis or *angka*
pēju   ... cloth measured by its width ; i.e., by folding over to form a square piece of cloth when cut.

Names of Various Bananas.

Sāing sābah

,,   *tajau*

,,   *hinogon*

,,   *bata-bata*

,,   *tindok*

,,   *amas*

,,   *timbokan*

,,   *panyiawar*

,,   *bātu*

,,   *tudloh*

,,   *tumbāga*

,,   *lanut* *

    * Musa textilis.

Treaty Between

ENGLAND AND BRUNEI

English - Malay.

TREATY BETWEEN ENGLAND & BRUNEI
(English).

TREATY OF FRIENDSHIP AND COMMERCE BETWEEN HER MAJESTY AND THE SULTAN OF BORNEO* :—

(Signed in the English and Malay Languages, May 27th, 1847).

Her Majesty the Queen of the United Kingdom of Great Britain and Ireland, being desirous to encourage commerce between Her Majesty's subjects and the subjects of the independent Princes of the Eastern Seas, and to put an end to piracies which have hitherto obstructed that commerce; and His Highness Omar Ali Saif Aludin, who sits upon the throne and rules the territories of Borneo, being animated by corresponding dispositions, and being desirous to co-operate in any measure which may be necessary for the attainment of the above mentioned objects, her said Britannic Majesty and the Sultan of Borneo have agreed to record their determination in these respects by a Convention containing the following Articles :—

ARTICLE I.

Peace, friendship and good understanding shall from henceforward and for ever subsist between Her Majesty the Queen of Great Britain and Ireland and His Highness Omar Ali Saif Aludin, Sultan of Borneo, and between their respective heirs and successors, and subjects.

* Brunei.

TREATY BETWEEN ENGLAND & BRUNEI
(Malay).

" Tarītī " Sahabat ber-sahabat dan per-nīāga-an antāra bāwa dūli " Queen " dengan bāwa dūli yang-di-per-tūan Sultan Brunei :—

(Sūdah di tāroh tanda tangan dālam bahāsa Anggaris dan bahāsa Malāyu, (dālam negri Brunei) kapada 27 hārī būlan " May," tāhun " 1847.")

Bāwa ada lah bāwa dūli " Queen " rājah yang mem-rentah-kan ka-rajā-an negri " Great Britain " dan " Ireland," ada sūka māū me-lūas-kan per-nīāga-an bāwa dūli " Queen " pūnya rāyat dan rāyat-rāyat rāja-rājah yang tiāda tālok di-lāūt-lāūt sa-blah tīmor, dan akan meng-hīlāng-kan pe-rompak yang sūdah men-ahan-kan per-nīāga-an ītu. Maka bāwa dūli yang-di-per-tūan Sultan Omar Ali Saif Aludin, yang semayam di-ātas takhta ka-rajā-na negri Brunei serta sakalīan tālok rantāu-nya, ada sāma-sāma būka nya akan maksud ītu; maka iya pūn sāma-sāma ber-ka-handak akan men-ōlong dālam sa-bārang jālan yang ber-patut-an akan men-dapat-kan hājat yang ter-sebut di-ātas ītu, maka bāwa dūli " Queen " dan Sultan Brunei sūdah sūka māū men-ulis-kan ka-putus-an maksud nya dālam per-kāra per-kāra dālam suāta per-janjī-an saperti yang ter-sebut dālam fasal-fasal yang ter-sebut di-bāwa īni.

FASAL YANG PERTAMA.

Maka handak lah ada per-damei-an, dan sahabat-ber-sahabat, dan mufākat yang bāīk deri sakārang īni sampei sa-lāma-lāma nya antāra bāwa dūli " Queen," rāja negri " Great Britain dan Ireland," dengan bāwa dūli yang-di-per-tūan Omar Ali Saif Aludin, Sultan negri Brunei, dan antāra ka-dūa nya pūn wāris-wāris dan peng-ganti-ganti, dan rayat-rayat.

ARTICLE II.

The subjects of Her Britannic Majesty shall have full liberty to enter into, reside in, trade with, and pass with their merchandise through all parts of the dominions of His Highness the Sultan of Borneo, and they shall enjoy therein all the privileges and advantages with respect to commerce, or otherwise, which are now, or which may hereafter be granted to the subjects or citizens of the most favoured nation ; and the subjects of His Highness the Sultan of Borneo, shall in like manner be at liberty to enter into, reside in, trade with, and pass with their merchandise through all parts of Her Britannic Majesty's dominions in Europe and Asia, as freely as the subjects of the most favoured nation, and they shall enjoy in those dominions all the privileges and advantages with respect to commerce or otherwise, which are now or which may hereafter be granted therein to the subjects or citizens of the most favoured nation.

ARTICLE III.

British subjects shall be permitted to purchase, rent, or occupy, or in any other legal way to acquire all kinds of property within the dominions of His Highness the Sultan of Borneo; and His Highness engages that such British subjects shall, as far as is in his power within his dominions, enjoy full and complete protection and security for themselves and for any property which they may so acquire in future, or which they may have acquired already, before the date of the present Convention.

Fasal Yang Kadua.

Ada pūn sakalīan rayat bāwa dūli "Queen" būlih men-dāpat sa-punoh-punoh ka-bibās-an akan masok, dan tinggal, dan ber-niāga, dan me-lālu dengan dagāng-an nya dālam sa-ganap tampat dālam ka-rajā-an bāwa dūli yang-di-per-tūan Sultan negri Brunei, maka iya sakalīan būlih men-dāpat samuā ka-bibās-an dan ka-untōng-an pada tampat-tampat ītu fasal per-niāga-an, atau lāin-lāin jālan, yang ada sakārang, atau yang akan di negrah-kan kapada rayat-rayat atau ōrang-ōrang negri deripada bangsa yang ter-pilih ītu ; maka rayat bāwa dūli yang-di-per-tūan Sultan Brunei, pūn bagītu jūga būlih men-dāpat ka-bibās-an akan masok, dan tinggal, dan ber-niāga, dan me-lalu-i dengan dagāng-an nya dālam sa-ganap tam-pat dālam ka-rajā-an bāwa dūli "Queen" dalām negri Europa dan Asīa, sāma biāsa saperti rayat-rayat deripada bangsa yang pilih-an, maka iya sakalīan būlih men-dāpat dālam ka-rajā-an ka-rajā-an ītu samuā ka-bibās-an dan ka-untōng-an fasal per-niāga-an, atau lāin jālan yang ada sakārang, atau yang akan di negrah-kan pada tāmpat-tāmpat ītu kapada rayat-rayat ōrang-ōrang negri derīpada bangsa yang pilih-an.

Fasal Yang Ka-tiga.

Maka rayat di-bāwa bandērā Anggaris būlih men-dāpat-i idzin akan mem-bāyar, dan sēwa, atau pakei, dengan lāin jālan yang ber-patut-an akan men-dāpat samuā macham bārang-bārang dālam ka-rajā-an bāwa dūli yang-di-per-tūan Sultan negi Brunei ; maka bāwa dūli yang-di-per-tūan ber-janjī ada pūn sakalīan rayat di-bāwa bandērā Anggaris ītu, dengan sa-būlih-būlih nya, di-dālam ka-rajā-an nya, men-dāpat sa-punoh sa-punoh dan ka-chū-kop ka-chūkop per-tulōng-an dan banter atas dīrī-nya sindīrī dan karna sa-bārang harta atau bārang-bārang yang akan di dāpat nya kamadīan hārī atau yang sūdah ter-lebih dahūlu di dāpat nya deri pada mem-būat sūrat per-janjī-an īni.

ARTICLE IV.

No article whatever shall be prohibited from being imported into or exported from the territories of His Highness the Sultan of Borneo; but the trade between the dominions of Her Britannic Majesty and the dominions of His Highness shall be perfectly free, and shall be subject only to the custom duties which may hereafter be in force in regard to such trade.

ARTICLE V.

No duty exceeding one dollar per registered ton shall be levied on British vessels entering the ports of His Highness the Sultan of Borneo, and this fixed duty of one dollar per ton to be levied on all British vessels shall be in lieu of all other charges or duties whatever. His Highness moreover engages that British trade and British goods shall be exempt from any internal duties, and also from any injurious regulations which may hereafter, from whatever causes, be adopted in the dominions of the Sultan of Borneo.

ARTICLE VI.

His Highness the Sultan of Borneo agrees that no duty whatever shall be levied on the exportation from His Highness' dominions of any article the growth, produce, or manufacture of those dominions.

ARTICLE VII.

His Highness the Sultan of Borneo engages to permit the ships of war of Her Britannic Majesty, and those of the East India Company, freely to enter into the ports, rivers and creeks situated within his dominions and to allow such ships to provide them-

FASAL YANG KA-AMPAT.

Maka tiāda būlih sa-bārang apa pūnya macham bārang-bārang di larāng-kan akan di bāwa masok atau di ka-luar-kan deripada tàlok rantau bāwa dūli yang-di-per-tūan Sultan Brunei; maka per-niāga-an antāra ka-rajā-an ka-rajā-an bāwa dūli "Queen" dan ka-rajā-an ka-rajā-an bāwa dūli yang-di-per-tūan akan jādi samata-samata biāsa dan chūma sakadar akan kena chukei yang akan di ator-kan fasal per-niāga-an ītu.

FASAL YANG KA-LIMA.

Maka tiāda lah chukei deripada sātu ringgit būlih di pinta dālam sātu "ton" deripada kapal-kapal Anggaris, yang sūdah di "rajister," yang masok dālam pa labuh-an bāwa dūli yang-di-per-tūan Sultan Brunei, maka chukei sātu ringgit yang di tantū-kan īni dālam sātu "ton" yang akan di pinta deripada samuā kapal-kapal Anggaris ītu jādi ganti samuā chukei yang lāin-lāin; dan lagi bāwa dūli yang-di-per-tūan ber-janjī iya ītu dagāng-an Anggaris akan ter-lepas deripada chukei sablah dālam, dan lagi deripada sa-bārang undang-undang yang akan kamadīan deripada apa-apa sabab māu di pakei dālam ka-rajā-an Sultan Brunei.

FASAL YANG KA-ANAM.

Maka bāwa dūli yang-di-per-tūan Sultan Brunei ada ber-janjī iya ītu tiāda lah akan kena chukei apabīla handak di antar-kan ka-lūar deripada ka-rajā-an bāwa dūli yang-di-per-tūan atau sa-bārang apa-apa yang di būat dālam ka-rajā-an nya ītu.

FASAL YANG KA-TUJOH.

Maka bāwa dūli yang-di-per-tūan Sultan Brunei ada ber-janjī akan mem-brī idzin kapal-kapal prang bāwa dūli "Queen," dan kapal-kapal "East India Kompani," yang būlih biāsa masok dālam pa labuh-an labuh-an, dan sungei-sungei, dan anak-anak sungei

selves at a fair and moderate price, with such supplies, stores, and provisions as they may from time to time stand in need of.

ARTICLE VIII.

If any vessel under the British flag should be wrecked on the coast of the dominions of His Highness the Sultan of Borneo, His Highness engages to give all the assistance in his power to recover for, and to deliver over to the owners thereof, all the property which can be saved from such vessels. His Highness further engages to extend to the officers and crew, and to all other persons on board such wrecked vessel, full protection both as to their persons and as to their property.

ARTICLE IX.

Her Majesty the Queen of the United Kingdom of Great Britain and Ireland and the Sultan of Borneo hereby engage to use every means in their power for the suppression of piracy within the seas, straits and rivers subject to their respective control or influence and His Highness the Sultan of Borneo engages not to grant either asylum or protection to any persons or vessels engaged in piratical pursuits; and in no case will he permit ships, slaves, or merchandise captured by pirates to be introduced into his dominions, or to be exposed therein for sale. And Her Britannic Majesty claims, and His Highness the Sultan of Borneo concedes to Her Majesty, the right of investing her officers and other duly constituted authorities with the power of entering at all times with her vessels of war, or other vessels duly empowered, the ports, rivers, and creeks within the dominions of His Highness the Sultan of Borneo, in order to capture all vessels engaged in piracy or

di-dālam ka-rajā-an nya ītu dan mem-brī-kan kapal-
kapal ītu akan men-dapat-kan per-bakal-an bagi
dērī nya sindīrī dengan harga yang pātut dan
mūrah deripada apa-apa bārang-bārang dan makān-
an dan per-bakāl-an yang ada ber-gūna kapada nya.

FASAL YANG KA-DILAPAN.

Kalau sa-bārang kapal yang me-makei bandērā
Anggaris ber-temu ka-rajā-an bāwa dūli Sultan
Brunei, maka bāwa dūli yang-di-per-tūan ber-janjī
akan mem-brī per-tolōng-an dengan sa-būlih-būlih
nya akan men-dapat-kan dan serah-kan kapada
yang ampunia kapal ītu sagāla bārang-bārang yang
būlih dāpat ter-lepas deripada kapal-kapal ītu. Maka
bāwa dūli yang-di-per-tūan ada lagi ber-janjī akan
mem-brī sa-punoh-punoh per-tolōng-an kapada
sakalīan "apsir" dan kalāsī, dan sakalīan ōrang
lain-lain yang ada dālam kapal yang ka-rosāk-kan
ītu, bāīk kapada tubuh nya atau kapada harta nya.

FASAL YANG KA-SIMBILAN.

Maka bāwa dūli "Queen" rājah yang mem-
rentah-kan ka-rajā-an negri "Great Britain" dan
"Ireland" dan Sultan Brunei ada lah ber-janjī
dengan sa-būlih-būlih nya handak meng-hilāng-kan
pe-rompak di-dālam lāūt-lāūt, dan selát-selát, dan
sungei-sungei yang tālok di-bāwa ka-dūa nya pūnya
parentah atau kuāsa, maka bāwa dūli yang-di-per-
tūan Sultan Brunei ada ber-janjī tiāda iya akan
mem-brī per-lindōng-an atau per-tulōng-an kapada
sa-bārang ōrang atau kapal-kapal (prahu-prahu)
yang di būat karja pe-rompak; dan lagi tiāda sa-kāli
kāli akan di brī nya idzin kapal-kapal, dan hamba-
hamba atau dagāng-an yang di rampas ulih pe-
rompak di bāwa masok ka-dālam negri nya, atau di
bīar-kan iya sakalīan di jūal. Maka bāwa dūli
"Queen" ada minta, dan bāwa dūli yang-di-per-
tūan Sultan Brunei ada sūka men-urot-kan per-
mintā-an bāwa dūli "Queen" akan meng-ada-kan
pagawei nya dan lain-lain ōrang besár yang dengan

slave dealing, and to seize and to reserve for the judgement of the proper authorities, all persons offending against the two contracting powers in these respects.

ARTICLE X.

It being desirable that British subjects should have some port where they may careen and refit their vessels, and where they may deposit such stores and merchandise as shall be necessary for the carrying on of their trade with the dominions of Borneo, His Highness the Sultan hereby confirms the cession already spontaneously made by him in 1845 of the island of Labuan, situated on the north-west coast of Borneo, together with the adjacent islets of Kuraman, Little Rusakan, Great Rusakan, Da-at and Malan Kasan, and all the straits, islets and seas situated half-way between the fore-mentioned islets and the mainland of Borneo. Likewise the distance of 10 geographical miles from the Island of Labuan to the westward and northward, and from the nearest point half way between the islet of Malan Kasan and the mainland of Borneo in a line running north till it intersects a line extended from west to east from a point ten miles to the northward of the northern extremity of the of the Island of Labuan, to be possessed in perpetuity and in full sovereignty by Her Britannic Majesty and her successors, and in order to avoid occasions of difference which might otherwise arise, His Highness the Sultan engages not to make any

pātut nya sūdah di pilih dengan kuāsa akan masok
pada segāla waktu dengan bāwa dūli "Queen"
pūnya kapal-kapal prang atau lain-lain kapal yang
dengan pātut nya sūdah dāpat kuāsa dālam pa
labuh-an, dan sungei-sungei, dan anak-anak sungei
yang di-dālam ka-rajā-an bāwa dūli yang-di-per-tūan
Sultan Brunei sabab handak men-angkap segāla
prahu-prahu yang ada būat karja me-rompak atau
jūal bilī hamba-hamba dan akan me-rampas dan
tahān-kan sabab me-nantī-kan hukum-an deripada
ōrang besár-besár yang ber-patut-an segāla ōrang-
ōrang yang ada me-lāwan ka-dūa-dūa bangsa pūnya
per-janjī-an dan kuāsa dālam perkāra īni.

FASAL YANG KA-SAPULOH.

Maka harus lah ada kapada rayat-rayat di-bāwa
bandērā Anggaris pa labuh-an tampat iya būlih ber-
lindong dan mem-bāik-i kapal-kapal nya dan di-
māna iya būlih men-aroh bārang-bārang dan dagāng-
an nya yang ter-gūna akan men-jalan-kan per-niāga-
an sabab dālam ka-rajā-an negri Brunei, maka bāwa
dūli yang di-per-tūan ada lah man-atap-kan yang
ter-lebih dahūlu sūdah sarah-kan nya dangan sūka
nya sindērī pada tahun 1845 akan pūlau Labuan
ītu, duduk nya di sablah tanggāra negri Brunei,
ber-sāma-sāma dengan pūlan yang kechil-kechil
yang ber-hampīr-an iya ītu Kurāman, dan Usikkan
damit, dan Usikkan besár, pūlau Dahat, dan
Malang Kasan, dan sakalīan salāt-salāt, dan pūlau
kechil-kechil dan lāut duduk nya sapāroh jālan
antāra pūlau yang ter-sēbut di-ātas īni dengan tanah
besár Brunei. Lagi pūn jāūh nya 10 "jeograpikal mil"
deri pūlau Labuan ka-sablah bārat dan ka-sablah
utāra, dan deripada tanjong yang hampir sakāli
sapāroh jālan antāra pūlan Malang Kasan dengan
tanah besár Brunei dālam suātu mistar mang-adap
ka-utāra sampei īya ber-temu suātu mistar malintang
deri dārat ka-tīmor deri suātu tanjong 10 "mil" ka-
sablah utāra di sablah utāra ūjong pūlau Labuan,
akan mem-punyāi sampei sa lāma-lāma nya dan

similar cession, either of an island or of any settlement on the main-land in any part of his dominions,
to any other nation, or to the subjects or citizens
thereof, without the consent of Her Britannic
Majesty.

ARTICLE XI.

Her Britannic Majesty, being greatly desirous
of effecting the total abolition of the trade in slaves,
His Highness the Sultan of Borneo, in compliance
with Her Majesty's wish, engages to suppress all
such traffic on the part of his subjects, and to pro-
hibit all persons receiving, within his dominions, or
subject to him, from countenancing or holding any
share in such trade ; and His Highness further
consents that all subjects of His Highness who may
be found to be engaged in the slave trade, may,
together with their vessels, be dealt with by the
cruisers of Her Britannic Majesty, as if such persons
and their vessels had been engaged in a piratical
undertaking.

ARTICLE XII.

This Treaty shall be ratified, and the ratifications
thereof shall be exchanged at Brunei, within twelve
months after this date.

This 27th day of May, 1847.

(L.S.) JAMES BROOKE.

(The Seal of the Sultan).

mem-egang kuāsa ·dan parentah ulih bāwa dūli
"Queen" dan pang-gantī nya pang-gantī nya, maka·
sopāya men-jāū-kan per-selisih-an yang akan ber-
bangkit dālam lain jūlan, maka bāwa dūli yang-di-
per-tūan ber-jangī tiāda iya akan sarah-kan (negri)
sa-rūpa ītu, bāīk sa-būah pūlau atau sa-bārang tampat ka-duduk nya tanah besár dālam sa-bārang
bahagī-an ka-rajā-an nya kapada sa-bārang lain
bangsa atau rayat atau ōrang-ōrang lain negri, kalau
tiāda dengan kridba-an bāwa dūli "Queen."

Fasal Yang Ka-sablas.

Maka bāwa dūli "Queen" ter-lālū lah sūka akan
meng-hilāng-kan sa-kāli-kāli fasal per-nīaga-an ber-
jūal bilī hamba, maka bāwa dūli yang-di-per-tūan
Sultan Brunei, sabab handak men-urot-kan maksud
bāwa dūli "Queen," maka iya ada ber-janjī akan
meng-hilāng-kan sakalīan per-nīāga-an yang bagītu
macham pada sablah pihak rayat nya, dan me-larāng-
kan sakalīan ōrang-ōrang yang tinggal dālam ka-
rajā-an nya atau yang tálok kapada nya deripada
mem-benár-kan atau mang-ambil apa-apa bahagī-an
dālam per-nīāga-an ītu; dan lagi bāwa dūli yang-di-
per tūan ada sūka yang sakalīan rayat-rayat bāwa·
dūli yang-di-per-tūan yang ka-dapāt-an ber-nīāga
ber-jūal bilī hamba-hamba būlih lah ber-sāma-sāma
dengan prahu-prahu nya di sarah-kan kapada kapal
prang bāwa dūli "Queen" saperti kalau ōrang-
ōrang bagītu serta prahu-prahu nya sūdah di-dapat-i
dālam mem-būat karja me-rompak.

Fasal Yang Ka-dua-blas.

Ada pūn "Taritī" ini akan di tetap-kan dan ka-
tetap-an ītu akan di tukār-kan di negri Brunei
dālam dūa blas būlan kamadīan deripada hejirat
ini.

27 hārī būlan "May," tāhun 1847.

Tampat chap,   Tampat chap,

SULTAN.   JAMES BROOKE.

ADDITIONAL ARTICLE.

His Highness the Sultan of Borneo agrees that in all cases when a British subject shall be accused of any crime committed in any part of His Highness' dominions, the person so accused shall be exclusively tried and adjudged by the English Consul-General, or other officers duly appointed for that purpose by Her Britannic Majesty; and in all cases where disputes or differences shall arise between British subjects, or between British subjects and the subjects of His Highness, or between British subjects and the subjects of any other foreign power within the dominions of the Sultan of Borneo, Her Britannic Majesty's Consul-General, or other duly appointed officers, shall have power to hear and decide the same without any interference, molestation or hindrance on the part of any authority of Borneo, either before, during, or after the litigation.

This 27th day of May, 1847,

(L.S.)　　JAMES BROOKE.

(The Seal of the Sultan.)

TREATY—MALAY.

TAMBAH-AN PER JANJI-AN.

Maka bāwa dūli yang-di-per-tūan Sultan Brunei
ada ber-janjī iya ītu dālam sagāla per-kāra apa-bīla
sa-ōrang rayat di-bāwa bandērā Anggaris ada kena
tudoh deri karna sa-bārang ka-salāh-an yang sūdah
di būat nya dālam sa-bārang tampat bāwa dūli
yang-di-per-tūan pūnya ka-rajā-an maka ōrang yang
kena tudoh ītu akan di pareksa dan di hukum-
kan ulih "Konsil Jenaral" Anggris sāja atau
lain-lain "apsir" yang di tantū-kan dengan sa-
pātut nya karna sabab ītu būlih bāwa dūli
"Queen;" maka sakalīan per-bechārā-an di-māna
per-bantah-an atau per-salisih-an akan ber-
bangkit antāra rayat-rayat di-bāwa bandērā Anggaris
dengan rayat-rayat bāwa dūli yang-di-per-tūan atau
antāra rayat-rayat di-bāwa bandērā Anggaris dengan
rayat-rayat bangsa asing yang di-dālam ka-rajā-an
Sultan Brunei maka bāwa dūli "Queen" pūnya
"Konsil Jenaral" atau lain "apsir" yang sūdah di
tautū-kan bechāra ītu dengan sa-patut nya būlih
dāpat kuāsa akan men-angar dan putūs-kan bechāra
ītu dengan tiāda būlih di kachau atau di ganggu atau
di lārang pada pihak sa-bārang kuāsa dālam negri
Brunei, bāik lebih dahūlu atau tengah-tengah atau
kamadīan deripada per-chiderā-an ītu adanya.

27 hāri būlan "May," tāhun 1847.

Tampat chap,   Tampat chap,

SULTAN.   JAMES BROOKE.

MALAY POEM.*

Al-hamdu li-lahi! pūji yang sāni,
Di turun-kan Allah tūan rabāni;
Berkat Muhamad Said ir rabāni,
Ia-lah makām mūmin nurūni.

Ayūhi! mūdah yang ber-hāti,
Meng-apa lūpa akan māti?
Malak al maut alil me-nanti,
Mang-ambil niāwa ber-gantī-gantī.

Ingat ingat tūan samuā,
Shair ku īni fikir-kan niāwa;
Sunggoh pūn maujud dan nirjāwa,
Akhir nya kalák ber-chari niāwa.

Sunggoh harta ter-lālu muliā,
Ia-lah kala māti tinggal lah dia;
Amal ibādad sāngat setia,
Bārang di-māna serta lah dia.

Harta nen chari sidikit bagei,
Sakadar chukop makan dan pakei;
Maut ītu sajah kau sampei,
Bārang ka-māna segrah lah sampei.

* Written on a will belonging to Datoh Maidin.

www.ingramcontent.com/pod-product-compliance
Lightning Source LLC
Chambersburg PA
CBHW031335070726
47496CB00017B/1127